The Monocle Guide to Good Business

Edited by *Andrew Tuck*
Foreword by *Tyler Brûlé*

Designed by *Monocle*
Proofreading by *Monocle*
Typeset in *Plantin & Helvetica*

Printed by *Offsetdruckerei Grammlich,
Pliezhausen*

Made in Germany

Published by *Gestalten*, Berlin 2014
ISBN 978-3-89955-537-0

© Die Gestalten Verlag GmbH & Co. KG,
Berlin 2014

For more information,
please visit *gestalten.com*

Bibliographic information published by the
Deutsche Nationalbibliothek. The Deutsche
Nationalbibliothek lists this publication in
the Deutsche Nationalbibliografie; detailed
bibliographic data is available online
at *dnb.d-nb.de*

This book was printed on
paper certified according to
the standard of FSC®.

Gestalten is a climate-neutral
company. We collaborate with the
non-profit carbon offset provider
myclimate (*myclimate.org*) to neutra-
lise the company's carbon footprint
produced through our worldwide
business activities by investing in
projects that reduce CO_2 emissions
(*gestalten.com/myclimate*).

The Monocle Guide to Good Business

From business schools to
apprenticeships, co-ops to
multinationals and cosy
offices to welcoming factories:
our handbook for budding
entrepreneurs, established
CEOs and everyone in between.

Contents

Since MONOCLE hit newsstands in 2007, well-run workplaces and the players responsible have been constant themes. At a time when the term "start-up" was suddenly short-hand for anyone with a business idea that could live digitally, we were more concerned with meeting family businesses in the likes of Bavaria and Tuscany that were showing how clever handiwork and a long-term view had made them leaders in their sectors.

When the measure of success was starting a business and seeing how quickly you could exit with a handsome return, we were sending our editors to interview the people who were concentrating on creating a better work environment by investing in good architecture, solid furniture and serving the best staff lunches. When admirable companies were those that could cut costs while improving margins and driving up that all-important ROI, we were sitting down to talk to entrepreneurs who were interested in building brands fit for the long haul and launching products that required proper apprentice programmes to manufacture them.

Along the way we noticed that our emphasis on a more human approach to running a business was becoming increasingly relevant. By the time the markets collapsed in 2008 we found our inboxes full of correspondence from readers who were using MONOCLE as a guidebook for setting up their own enterprises – or at least daydreaming about them. Time and again we heard from people who'd lost high-paying jobs that, on balance, they didn't actually like that much. There were lawyers who wanted to start a menswear business, bankers keen on brewing beer for a living and analysts who wanted to run the best florist in their hometown.

In many ways this book has been inspired by all those individuals who have had the sharp ideas and necessary courage to hang out their shingle. But it has also been created for anyone looking to refresh a string of shops they have inherited from granny, searching for a design firm to create a new identity or simply thinking about their next move.

We've always maintained that the best way to be inspired and stay on top of your game is to get out in the world and observe the people who are doing it best. *The Monocle Guide to Good Business* will hopefully help you chart a course to finding fresh ways to launch or run a respected, happy and agile workplace.

—Tyler Brûlé

GOOD BUSINESS

MONOCLE has always written about the world of work: entrepreneurship, running companies well (no matter what size the enterprise) and making stuff. But then these were all things that were important to us: we were living and doing them every day.

When we launched, MONOCLE magazine was a fresh-faced start-up with a bright idea. We were out to prove that there was a place in the changing media landscape for a business that believed in the power of print: from the words that made the page to the quality and warmth of the paper that we used. We also wanted to produce a magazine that would have a clear view of the world, offer handsome photography, be independent, have a global remit and use digital possibilities in a more innovative way than just an iPad version of our title.

But beyond that we were also out to run a successful company. We have had to make a lot of decisions as we have gone from a team of nine to 100 and expanded our range to include two seasonal newspapers, a round-the-clock radio station called Monocle 24, shops, e-commerce, cafés in Tokyo and London and a move into book publishing (you are holding one of its results). We have also had to think about developing a brand while staying true to our core beliefs. In short, we know quite a lot about the decisions that face people when running a company.

Meanwhile, in MONOCLE we have written extensively about the shifting world of work while giving people the advice and encouragement they need to start a business. And on Monocle 24 we have followed the business world on our weekly radio show, *The Entrepreneurs.*

All of this has happened at an interesting time. We have seen rapid growth in the use of shared spaces, the rise of a generation of people who only want to work for themselves and are immune to the lure of the corporate world, and a genuine shift in how businesses operate, with many old hierarchies sidelined forever.

This is why we have created *The Monocle Guide to Good Business.* It's a book for would-be business leaders, start-ups and established companies that feel it's time for some new ideas. It's a book to be used – write in the margins and turn over the corners of the pages. But don't expect management speak, nor miracles for untold riches. Our manifesto is a little different (and we hope delivered with some humour along the way). It's a quiet manifesto that respects what's gone before. It's not a book about staging a revolution. It's a book about doing things well (from how you run the show to the pens you buy) to make a company that will last. It's a book about doing a job you love. And even taking your dog to work.

A Monocle manifesto

University is a good thing

And an MBA course can give you some wise advice and helpful hints but all of this can be replaced by learning a skill from the shopfloor up. It is time to put greater emphasis on the merits of apprenticeships, of using your hands, having dirt under your finger nails and sweat on your brow. We need to see both academic and hands-on paths into work as equal.

Making things is important

After the global meltdown of 2008 there was a realisation (especially among those who lost their jobs) that western countries cannot only live off service industries. Nations need to protect their skills and their know-how. What did Icelanders do after the crash that nearly wiped out their country? They went back to fishing, making food products, design, technology and knitting. They reset their country with sleeves rolled up. This is a good thing.

People care about provenance

Where and how things are made. It's no good a business touting "Designed in Denmark" if it's then made in Vietnam. Be proud of where you are from.

Pay people a decent wage

And build that into the cost of your products. Don't outsource. Keep the chain as short as possible from design to manufacture. Then you won't be one of the businesses that has to go through "reshoring" production when your staff in, say, China point out that they want a salary increase.

People need other people to do their best work

The tech vision of us all as office-free nomads is a bad one. Good ideas and businesses are made through debate – of the face-to-face variety. And people are just much happier and more motivated when they work among like-minded types. That's why we are seeing the rapid take-off of the shared space phenomenon. It turns out all those lonely entrepreneurs trying to work from their bedrooms craved company all along. Let's stick together.

Remember human nature

The office needs to adapt and change but hot-desking and its like are too often foisted on staff by miserly management. It's not a sign of modernity or flexibility that you have nowhere to sit, just an indication of a company that doesn't understand human nature. Give people a good desk, a comfortable chair and a welcoming light. And then let them do their work.

But this is not to deny flexibility

Or our ability to work on the road. Be open to change.

New company, new rules

Working for yourself should be fun, rewarding and allow you to shape a company that matches your beliefs and life. Be cautious of falling in with how your rivals do things.

Travel

You want to win that contract in Niseko? Get the deal in Paris? Or how about the one in your neighbouring town? Well good luck trying to do that with a conference call. When you get into a room with people or take them for lunch, you change relationships and unearth new possibilities in a way that would never happen over email or a video link. And just as vital: you need to see who else is benchmarking quality in your field. Go see your competition in action. Also: trade fairs can be exhausting but the good ones should be in your diary.

Could you run your company from any city in the world?

If so, choose an HQ capital that also delivers the quality of life you want; balance urban efficiency with pleasure. But remember: a company should be part of the community it sits in. Come out from behind those walls.

Design good spaces for people to work in

Factories can have great natural light. Offices don't need to be bleak. Make spaces that people like to visit, linger in and be creative in. But don't add slides or bean bags. Treat your team like adults, not teenagers.

Spread the work

Management is important but over-elaborate power structures are hard to maintain. Don't be scared of a flatter management style. Sure, when things go wrong you need to be there but otherwise let people grow rapidly in their roles and even keep you a little tested.

It's your company

So of course you can wear shorts in the summer when no clients are around. But it's still a business essential that both men and women have a good jacket.

Respect tradition

Business cards work in all cultures: asking people to beam you their details does not.

Create companies to last

Think about employing future generations. Too many businesses are created by people looking for the exit strategy before the paint has even dried on their shop sign. We need to honour people who are in it for the long haul.

SETTING OUT

GET STARTED

Inspirational start-up stories and how to succeed

Preface

Where do you begin? Here. The first thing you need is some inspiration and the best place to get that is from other people who have taken those first steps and ditched their old lives for new ones as business owners. They know what it takes to run that perfect neighbourhood restaurant, start a fashion label from scratch or become a farmer (how much does a goat even cost?). But it's not just the need for start-up cash that they understand: they are also tuned into the importance of developing a brand, finding a market for their product and using retail to the best effect. So that's where we'll start: meeting a host of smart entrepreneurs with inspirational stories and businesses from small to actually quite big.

But you also need to have a roadmap that will take you from fledgling status to a finely formed empire. So here in chapter one we'll also guide you through 50 stages of entrepreneurship, from having a good idea to putting your feet up. Sure, you'll go off on a few diversions from any carefully plotted route but it's always good to have a map in your back pocket. It can help you get back on track if you ever end up really lost.

Contents

We cover everything you need to know to build a successful business, including initial research and investment, establishing your brand values, developing a good reputation and adapting to global markets.

FIRST STEPS GLOBAL

Preface: Be it your burning business ambition or a long-desired lifestyle change, inspiration can come in many forms. From herding goats to launching a magazine – via baristas and fashionistas – here's how some of the world's most forward-thinking entrepreneurs got their ventures off the ground.

01

How to create a neighbourhood restaurant

Company: Beard
Location: Tokyo
Founded: 2012
Staff: 2
Provenance: Vegetables come from Kochi prefecture and the farmers' market in Kamakura; fish is from the Mie area
Most popular wine: Scribe winery chardonnay (2011) and pinot noir (2012) from Sonoma
Most popular dish: Beef sirloin steak with French fries

Running a restaurant requires kitchen flair but it is ingenuity that can make the difference between a go-to favourite and an average stop. "You need basic skills in the field and self-confidence. On top of that, a sense of imagination," says Shin Harakawa (*pictured, top*), chef patron of Tokyo restaurant Beard.

Small, convivial and reliably good, Beard instantly struck a chord with diners; it's the neighbourhood restaurant that every city should have. Harakawa can usually be found in his Breton shirt cooking in the style he honed at a Michelin-starred restaurant in Sens, France and at Chez Panisse in Berkeley, California. His cosy bistro bears the influence of both but it's rooted in Japanese culture.

Starting Beard was a risk. Harakawa sunk all his savings plus a loan from his family into the new venture. Rather than picking an expensive location, he looked for a reasonably priced property that would allow him to spend on the interior and good ingredients. The Japanese-style house he chose wasn't in a particularly fashionable or convenient spot but it was the perfect setting for what he had in mind. Beard's success has proved him right.

That the restaurant can barely fit 13 customers is part of its relaxed charm. Harakawa chats to diners as he cooks and customers strike up conversations. Friends run into each other; new acquaintances are formed. The menu is refreshingly short and likely to feature excellent steak and chips, fresh fish and a seasonal salad. On Sundays, Beard opens for brunch – which is a Tokyo rarity – and serves ricotta pancakes, eggs and a weekly burger.

Harakawa describes his cooking as "simple food with quality ingredients". A Kamakura farmers' market supplies the vegetables; meat comes from a trusted wholesaler and sometimes direct from farmers and hunters. You get the sense that, if this stopped being fun, he would move on. And his advice to those who want to branch out on their own? "Truly enjoy what you do." — (M)

02

How to run a magazine

—

Company: The Surfer's Journal
Location: San Clemente, USA
Founded: 1992
Number of pages in every issue: 132
Number of surfboards displayed in the office: 16
Maximum number of minutes it takes each staff member to get to the office: 7

More book than magazine, *The Surfer's Journal* is a lovingly produced title that shows how a print-focused periodical can thrive in the digital era through a passionate concern for detail. The California-based publication covers the personalities, culture and history of surfing and was created as a result of reverse engineering.

Co-founders Debbee and Steve Pezman (*pictured, right*) had a background in surf magazines but when they set out on their own in 1992 they wanted to do things differently. They imagined heavy stock and a book-like feel – a reading experience. "We didn't plan to create something that was this expensive," says Debbee. "We just envisioned the product."

Each issue retails for more than $15 but for that price the 23,000 subscribers get a treat. The tone of the magazine, published six times a year, is set by its academic-looking cover: there is a single image and lots of empty space. "It's not loud, it doesn't make a lot of promises but it stands out in its quietness," says designer Jeff Girard.

Each issue has just six sponsors that contribute $51,000 apiece per year, lending their role an air of exclusivity. Housed in a small office close to the beach, *The Journal* boasts walls adorned with vintage surfboards and photography.

"Once we decided what we wanted the product to be, there was no question in our minds. We weren't going to compromise on product quality for a price point," says Debbee. "We decided

it was going to work at what we wanted it to be or we weren't going to be in that business."

But this perhaps belies the considerations attached to setting up a magazine. *The Journal*, for instance, required $250,000 of seed money. For a reader-supported publication like this, which asks readers to "pay ahead", there is a lot of pressure to deliver on quality. Print prices and print runs have to be borne in mind. Debbee's advice to aspiring editors-in-chief is, however, straightforward: "If you're starting up a magazine, print what you can afford to and then make sure you sell all of them."

She is convinced that there is still a market for print in what is perennially described as a digital age: "If there's a subject that almost seduces an audience with passion for something they are interested in, there is no medium like print," she says. "Make something that is worth holding in your hand." — (M)

How to reinvent a recipe

Company: Kohl
Location: Auna di Sotto
    sul Renon, Italy
Founded: 2004
Employees: 5
Annual production: 300,000 litres
Total flavours: 12

People often identify start-ups and their owners with sparkling new products or software that we hope will change our lives. Sometimes, however, a business doesn't need to reinvent the wheel to make it big but rather tinker with it to capture the attention of consumers.

Italy's South Tyrol, for instance, is already one of Europe's main sources for quality fruit: its valley floors produce more than 10 per cent of the continent's apple harvest and its hillsides are lined with grapes that yield crisp white and hearty red wines.

With his farm at higher climes, some 1,000 metres above sea level, locals thought Thomas Kohl was out of reach of either market. Yet after a stint studying winemaking at a local institute, Kohl opted to try his hand at high-altitude viticulture. After little success, he turned to planting apple trees in the 1990s. "At this altitude the fruit grows slowly and is smaller.

This concentrates the flavour – with hot days but cooler nights here we get less acidity," says Kohl (*pictured, bottom*).

After a few years of turning out garden-variety juice, Kohl came up with the idea of launching a line of gourmet juices in 2007. Where cattle once grazed, Kohl now makes single-varietal fruit juices from six apple types, including Elstar and Gravenstein varieties, the latter now shunned by big farms that look for easy-to-grow fruit to sell to supermarkets. Fruit is handpicked – with teams making numerous passes over several weeks to pick each fruit at its ripest – and then taken down the hill to be squeezed inside his converted barn.

"One of the challenges of our work is that it's a seasonal activity. We still have work to do the rest of the year in terms of promoting our juice," says Kohl. "I had to worry about the packaging and getting a graphic designer but had no idea of the costs involved."

Despite the fact it's demanding, Kohl doesn't consider his vocation an exclusive one. "I don't think one needs special skills as much as a passion for the product you are selling. If you have that, results will come sooner or later," he says. — (M)

04

How to start a farm

Company: Amaltea
Location: Roccaverano, Italy
Founded: 2006
Number of employees: 3
Production: approximately 2,000 cheeses made each week
Retail price per 250g: €6

The world of finance lures new recruits and gets them to spend long hours crunching numbers in front of computer screens. But they only ever put together products that appear on paper or in a presentation. Others opt to build a career around making something tangible and even tasty.

For the 400-odd inhabitants of Roccaverano, a medieval town in Italy's northwest, the turmoil of financial markets and Rome's topsy-turvy politics seems a world away. Life revolves around the town's piazza, which boasts a Renaissance church that's more than 500 years old and a lone bar. It's what prompted Daniela Saglietti and Giovanni Solerio (*pictured*), owners of Amaltea, to ditch their jobs in Turin to try their hand at farming. "It is a huge investment to get a farm up and running," says Solerio. "People think it's easier than it really is but you have to pour a lot in to get started." That said, the personal benefits

can outweigh the financial cost of some businesses. "The air is clean, there's no traffic and there's the view," says Saglietti, as she takes in the panorama of the foothills of the Langhe in northwestern Italy. There's little time to enjoy the scenery as she's interrupted by the sound of bleating goats.

The pair's livelihood is their livestock, which provides milk to make robiola cheese. Made from unpasteurised goat's milk the soft, snow-white Roccaverano variety is protected by DOP status: a labelling system similar to that used for champagne that guarantees a regional food's authenticity and method of preparation.

Twice a day, the 160-strong herd must be milked. The goats themselves are a hefty investment, costing more than €200 each. However, each goat can produce about 600 litres of milk per annum for up to eight years.

For all its romance, farming is as much an investment of time as money. Most days, Solerio spends three hours gently moving the herd so that it can graze on grass nurtured by sea breezes; leaves of wild chestnut and oak round off the goats' diet. But even after 14-hour days on the farm he has no regrets about swapping the city for the country. "We wanted a life that's more authentic, rooted in something real." — (M)

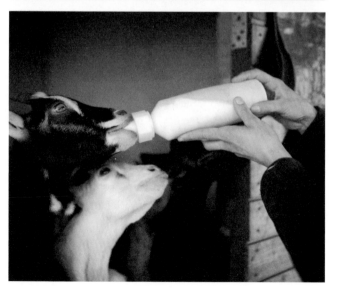

How to change your business plan

Company: Playtype
Location: Copenhagen
Founded: 2010
Typefaces for sale: more than 400
Clients include: the Danish police and Royal Danish Theatre
Most popular original font: Q

A traditional shopfront can be an excellent selling place, even for products that are not normally associated with ricks-and-mortar retail. That's especially true when you are working out how to get your product in front of people and make your mark.

This was the thinking that inspired the launch of Playtype, a concept store in Vesterbro, Copenhagen. The space initially opened as a pop-up to showcase the new online type foundry launched by the branding and design agency E-Types.

"The vision was to take typefaces to street level, creating a lifestyle brand and making typefaces sexy," says co-founder Rasmus Ibfelt, who started Playtype along with Jonas Hecksher (*pictured, top*) and three other partners.

What began as an attempt to get people excited about typography turned into a pioneering type foundry and concept store for the long term. "We needed a clever idea that could get people's attention," says Ibfelt. "So instead of using our budget on traditional advertising we used the money to buy a physical store."

The website Playtype created now offers more than 400 fonts for purchase, each one revealing at best a slice of design history and at least an interesting yarn. The Berlingske font, for one, consists of almost 500,000 characters and was designed for Denmark's newspaper of the same name.

The shop soon took on a life of its own. It has become a must-visit for typology types but also functions as a showcase for the work of its parent design agency. The interest of window-shoppers, tourists and design students is piqued by the eye-catching window displays. Take-homes include coffee mugs, laptop sleeves, posters, notebooks and clothing, which create a healthy new revenue stream. It is a simple idea done well.

"You need to do something unique. There's so much noise out there," says Ibfelt. "In a world where more and more things are decided because of data, business plans, marketing analysis or CFO visions, leave room for the unexpected. Be brave enough to start a new journey. Sometimes you have to reinvent yourself." — (M)

PLAYTYPE™
Online Type Foundry & Concept Store

06

How to start a cinema

Company: Ciné-Theatre
Location: Gstaad, Switzerland
Founded: 1955
Seats: 203
Screens: 1
Number of staff: 5

With the Alps' perfectly groomed pistes and après-ski options aplenty, culture and the visual arts don't always blossom on the slopes. It's for this reason that the family-run Ciné-Theatre in Gstaad, with its charming wooden kiosk and red-velvet seats, is a particularly romantic reminder that mountain living has a cosier side, too.

Owned by the Hagmann-Dietler family since the 1950s, the small cinema has become a vital part of the community. Manager Hansjörg Beck (*pictured, top right*) joined in 2006 after working for various film-distribution firms. "Our small venture has survived even though some hotels in Gstaad now have their own screening rooms – but we are the only purpose-built theatre," he says gesturing towards the more than 200-seat theatre.

In late 2010 the space got a much-needed technology revamp: the old loudspeakers, film projector and sound processor were replaced with top-notch professional digital equipment and a new Dolby 3D system was installed. "We have introduced a new box-office system and now it is possible to make reservations online," Beck says.

An innovative film programme has helped keep the independent venue ahead of its larger competitors. Rather than spoon-feeding its audience the latest Hollywood releases, the cinema curates a mix of domestic and international titles – which are, more often than not, screened in their native language. It shows some 110 titles a year and hosts up to four screenings a day in high season.

But few businesses are a one-man band. On hand to assist the management with the smooth running of Ciné-Theatre is a five-strong workforce, all from Gstaad. Projectionist Reto Neuenschwander (*pictured, right*) is a local celebrity. The former photographer has been working here for more than 25 years and everyone in Gstaad knows him by name.

Beck is optimistic about the future of culture in the Alps. "Every year we try to host official Swiss film premieres," he says. "This increases the culture credentials of the area and brings more art and film to Gstaad." This well-loved cinema goes to show that good ideas can grow in tough terrain. — (M)

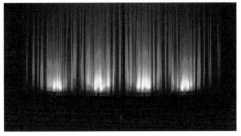

07

How to run a design shop

Company: March
Location: San Francisco
Founded: 2002
Staff: 8
Size of space: 140 sq m

Sam Hamilton (*pictured, above*) is the founder of design shop March in San Francisco. It's a world where image and attention to detail is key but she thinks that her job is about offering her customers more than just a place to buy nice stuff. "It's as much about the experience of being in the space as about selling the goods," she says, "so it really behoves me to have marvellous staff who love the product as much as I do."

Hamilton founded the crisply decorated space with a business partner in 2002, attracting a customer base of interior designers lured by the luxuries the pair sourced. When she decided to go it alone, her 11 years in marketing and design with Ralph Lauren in New York taught her a lot about the effort needed to keep her shop looking effortless. Tax, insurance and other bureaucracy are also an unavoidable, time-consuming part of keeping her affairs in order. "You need to be mentally prepared for the fact that it's not just about dressing a beautiful space. There's a whole world of behind-the-scenes stuff that's not so sexy and you have to own it all," she says.

Having taken the rough with the smooth, Hamilton is reaping the rewards of her hard work. Inside the shop a mix of globally and locally sourced offerings sit alongside special commissions. US-made cast-iron pans, mugs by a Tuscan potter and vintage dishes by Beatrice Wood all hint at Hamilton's commitment to well-made, thoughtfully designed products.

Another key to Hamilton's ethos is the idea that less is more. "I like to know your point of view when I walk through the door, not that you have 7,000 kinds of mugs," she says as country music twangs in the background. March has also branched out into kitchen design, though the company is keen to maintain its thoughtful approach and takes on only a handful of projects a year.

"When people come in it makes them really happy," says Hamilton. "Their eyes get carried in many different directions and it sparks thoughts about what they have in their home and the memories they had as a kid – it's exciting to them. Even if we're not ringing the register at that moment, we're all excited." — (M)

08

How to become a book publisher

Company: Nieves
Location: Zürich
Founded: 2001
Staff: 3
Titles released per year: 25

Although book publishing isn't the sure-fire money-spinner it once was, competition is pushing innovation and new business models within the industry. Benjamin Sommerhalder (*pictured, top right*) founded publishing house Nieves in 2001. The project, which began as a low-budget art and illustration series of zines, now releases 25 titles a year spanning zines, art and children's books. That's no mean feat in a market where e-books have challenged (and ultimately closed down) many publishers and bookshops.

Despite the publishing house-cum-bookshop's success, the Zürich-based business is low key. It's always had just three staff and doesn't plan to expand just for the sake of it. "The basic problem is that I am really bad at delegating things," says Sommerhalder, who set up the company aged just 23 after graduating in graphic design. "So it stays as it is and it works." Sommerhalder is unique in his willingness to let the artists he works with take creative control of their own work. They are free to choose the page size and count, plus the printing method of the publication. It isn't that he's uninterested; his calculatedly laissez-faire attitude has, unsurprisingly, made his authors very fond of their collaborations with Nieves. It also means that they are often very willing to return.

Alongside a single colleague and an intern, Sommerhalder oversees everything from the creative conception of the books to the everyday administration. The highest cost comes down to printing. "Because I am also trained as a graphic designer I do the graphic design together with the artist, so it's not a cost I have," he says. "I do the accounting myself – I don't need to have an accountant."

Despite the hard work that goes into each project and the day-to-day stresses of keeping the office in order, Sommerhalder's staunch commitment to self-publishing is a rewarding one. "In my case it is really about following your heart and being true to yourself," he says. "When I do that, when I really publish what I want to publish and am not distracted by too many other opinions, it is actually what people like the most – what works best for Nieves." — (M)

09

How to start a clothing factory

———

Company: Private White VC
Location: Manchester, UK
Number of staff: 80
Founded: 2010
Flagship store: Lambs Conduit
Street, London

———

When entrepreneur James Eden (*pictured, opposite page*) gave up a well-paid job in the City of London to buy an ailing clothing factory in a run-down part of his home-town of Manchester, he had his doubters. The region's illustrious past as the epicentre of Britain's textile industry was just that – history. But Eden's almost foolhardy devotion to the factory has led to the birth of a clothing brand, Private White VC. Single-handedly – and single-mindedly, for that matter – Eden is helping to put Manchester's textile industry back on the map.

Eden had personal ties to the factory, too. His great grandfather, Jack White, fought in the First World War and won a Victoria Cross for bravery. Like many of his peers, on returning home after the war, Private White VC himself went to work in his local textile factory, over the years working his way up from the factory floor to become owner. He worked there until his death in 1949. Jack White's great grandson, Eden, stepped in to salvage the factory when it was on its knees in 2008 before setting up his men's outerwear brand, named after his decorated ancestor. "The job Jamie has done since then is unbelievable," says Mike Stoll (*right*), who handed the factory on to Eden, "He's just too modest to say it." Nick Ashley, son of clothing designer Laura Ashley and now creative director of the brand, agrees: "James is a hero."

In many ways, a little of his great grandfather's bravery lives on in Eden, who gave up his comfortable job in finance. "My reality check soon bounced while working in the City," he reflects, patting the office dog, Brutus. "There was an opportunity here to get involved in something I cared about and was passionate about." Stoll, who still manages the factory, interjects: "Be clear, though: when he thought that, nobody else thought that. He's turned it into an opportunity."

The crumbling buildings around the factory in Cotten-ham Lane are a poignant reminder that the brand is inextricably tied to the area's past glory. Now – thanks to Eden – there is more than a glimmer of optimism for its future, too. — (M)

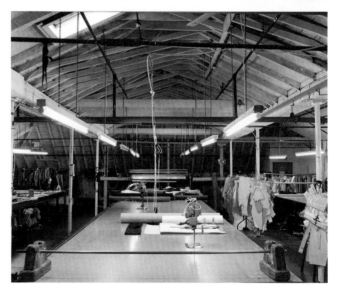

IO

How to start a furniture company

———

Company: Another Country
Location: London
Founded: 2010
Number of staff: 8
Furniture made in: UK, Portugal and Slovenia
Most popular item: Stool One

After a career spanning successful start-ups in the publishing and hospitality sectors, serial entrepreneur Paul de Zwart *(pictured)* founded furniture brand Another Country in 2010, with the simple aim of creating a brand and making furniture that's built to last. After launching its third series in early 2014, Another Country unveiled its first bricks-and-mortar shop in a space set over two floors on Crawford Street in leafy Marylebone, London.

"It was about having the experience of different types of start-ups," says De Zwart of his decision to diversify from the brand's online-only offering by opening the well-tended space as an embassy for the brand. "What really matters is the integrity, honesty and strength of the core idea; these core values are what take you through each phase of development."

Although De Zwart's business back story is an ambitious one, it means he has learned the importance of being conservative when going out on your own. He waited until the furniture brand was in a position to support a shop so that he didn't risk his stake in the venture or ever need to rely on outside backers for help.

"The first and most important lesson I've learned from experience in business is the need for caution and good management. Ignoring them breaks most businesses," he says. "Keep your costs to a minimum, look carefully at what you need and take a chunk off to be on the safe side."

As well as its impeccable inventory of simple, well-wrought furniture – from oak stools to benches, dining tables and day beds – Another Country also stocks exclusive and hard-to-find homeware that discerning shoppers won't find elsewhere in the UK.

There are perks to being in charge. "Being your own boss is inherently very fulfilling. You can see the fruits of your labour in a physical format," says De Zwart, surveying the shop. "If you're working for investors, shareholders or private companies then they define what success means. The more control you have, the more you can define what it means." — (M)

II

How to revive a family company

Company: Maruhiro
Location: Hasami, Japan
Founded: 1957
Number of staff: 14
Number of wholesale customers: more than 600
Most popular design: Blockmug

It's a common enough story in Japan: struggling family business calls on absent son to return home to reverse the company's fortunes. For Kyohei Baba (*pictured, left*) it meant giving up a career in fashion and returning to the small town of Hasami to work at the ceramics trading company started by his grandfather.

In Japan, the town of Hasami has been synonymous with pottery for hundreds of years. Not the fine porcelain of its famous neighbour, Arita, but the everyday crockery used in homes all over the country. Maruhiro, the Baba family business, puts ceramics from Hasami kilns into fashion stores and interiors shops.

Before Baba's arrival, Maruhiro was getting by but the future was uncertain. Baba made some key changes: he upped wholesale prices after noticing that the margins were much lower than those in the fashion industry. He has also sought new clients and now sells to shops directly. "We felt uncomfortable that our products were being sold in stores that we didn't know," he says. He pays close attention to what people are buying and has instigated a more organised system for recording sales and stock levels.

Baba has pushed the company in a more creative direction, launching his own ceramic brand called Hasami. With no funds to hire a designer and no ceramics training of his own, Baba took advice from local craftspeople who know exactly how to make a properly functioning tea pot and a plate with just the right curve. "We wanted to make things that people will love and use for a long time," he says. The first range of cups, pots and plates quickly found an audience and other products have followed.

Today, Kyohei Baba and his father, company president Mikiya Baba, have got the business back on track. Maruhiro sells to more than 600 different customers and sales are up each year. The Hasami brand is thriving, too. Despite this, Baba is modest about his success. "What is essential is people," he says. "They are everything: our staff, the local artisans who gave me advice and friends. We couldn't have done this without them." — (M)

I2

How to run a boutique hotel group

Company: Firmdale Hotels
Location: London
Founded: 1984
Employees: 1,300
Number of hotels: 9 and climbing

Tim Kemp is a quintessential Englishman: well dressed, well spoken and in possession of a slightly mischievous sense of humour. "It has always struck me that most of the people in the hotel business are in completely the wrong job," he says, half playfully. "They aren't welcoming and they seem to actively dislike people." He should know; he's been in the business since the 1980s.

Kemp opened his first boutique hotel in Dorset Square in London's Marylebone in 1984. Since then, he and his wife Kit *(pictured, right)* have grown the business into a mini empire consisting of nine hotels: eight in the most fashionable parts of London and one in lower Manhattan.

The success hasn't come as a surprise to Kemp, though. When he started out he offered a level of quality and service that was not available at the time: "When other people were getting their curtains from the Cash'n'Carry, I was getting mine from Harrods." He has always made a concerted effort to understand exactly what his guests want. "Most of the time, what they wanted was just what I wanted when I travelled: something interesting, comfortable, welcoming but also fun," he says.

The hotels' unique style has always been key to finding this balance. Kit is an award-winning interior designer and has overseen the look of every Firmdale hotel to date. "Most hotel designers seem to forget about the end user," she says. "Travelling somewhere new and staying in a new place should be an adventure." The Kemps' Ham Yard project in London's Soho is unmistakably her handiwork: the extensive use of textiles in the rooms and public areas is a hallmark of her style. Each of the 91 rooms has its own colour scheme and mix of fabrics.

The attention to detail has paid off. Firmdale's growth is underpinned by the constant reinvestment of profits, something Tim Kemp feels passionate about. "Hotels are normally owned by investment companies that take out profits," he says. "Whereas they put around 4 per cent of turnover back in, we reinvest between 12 and 14 per cent. We are always looking at the product and how to improve it." — (M)

 13

How to run a record shop

Company: Title
Locations: Sydney, Melbourne,
    Brisbane and Adelaide
Flagship store: Surry Hills, Sydney
Founded: 2006
Number of staff: 29
Number of outlets: 7
Weekly sales of Patti Smith's
    'Just Kids': Between 10 and 20

Australian media-retailer
Title piles its stock low and
sells it for what it's worth. The
brand's success has rewritten
how to revive the business of
dealing in the hardware of the
ailing music, book and film
trade. "Everyone said I was a
goose!" says owner Steve Kulak.
"But you have to disregard
other people's opinions and
follow your own passions."

Having spent the years
between 1980 and 1991 hitch-
hiking across the globe as an
aspiring writer – an experience
that saw him get shot in Africa,
deported from Moscow and
narrowly escape the Golden
Temple massacre in Amritsar –
Kulak is accustomed to risk. On
returning to his native Sydney
he chose to enter one of the
retail industry's most precarious
sectors: the mixed sale of books,
films and music. He started the
first Sydney Title store in 2006

with a simple formula: combing
a curated inventory of newly
pressed vinyl, hard-to-find
literature and cult films with
a smart retail space in an up-
and-coming suburb.

It proved an overwhelming
success. Kulak now has various
Title outlets across Australia's
east coast. He also oversees
a distribution company and
a publishing label.

Kulak sees his shops as social
destinations. He says that each
store manager knows 60 per
cent of their customers by name.
"These big pleasure palaces have
got a place," he says. "But when
you come to a Title store it is a
little more profound – you come
out with something deeper."

The company's policy of
stocking only items that "define
the cultural space" has been
equally important. It's a model
built on the belief that certain
titles, however unlikely to find
their way to the cash register,
are crucial for establishing the
brand's tone. "Do you know
how many copies of James
Joyce's *Ulysses* we've sold in
any of our shops? Probably
one," he says. "Is it in every
shop? Yes." This strategy is
typical of the fearless approach
that Kulak cultivated from his
years on the road. "It's like
travelling up the Congo: you
might get a spear in the arse
or you might not," he says.
"You can't step back for fear
of failing." — (M)

14

How to run a record label

Company: Brushfire Records
Location: Los Angeles
Founded: 2002
Number of employees: 4
Artists: 7
Jack Johnson's worldwide album sales: about 20 million

"Brushfire was created to put out records for our friends and we've tried to never veer too far from that simple credence," says Emmett Malloy (*pictured, top left*), co-founder of the LA-based record label. "Some days I do wish I had a few more helping hands and creative minds but I guess I don't want to outgrow our comfortable office."

It's easy to see what Malloy means: the former residence is more of a home than a workspace to the label's small team. "It's an early 20th-century craftsman house and they always possess so much character," he says. "I just tried to keep that old style intact." It's also a sentimentally short walk from Malloy's childhood home.

Malloy started the business with his longtime friend and internationally successful recording artist Jack Johnson in 2002. They didn't set out to launch a record label, though. Brushfire's beginnings lie in the surf-film soundtracks the pair produced as part of their previous venture, the Moonshine Conspiracy in Hawaii. During this period in the late 1990s, the pair were already inadvertently laying the foundations for their distinctly relaxed take on starting a record label from scratch and managing a growing list of artists.

Brushfire Records has played an important role in managing and developing bands such as the Bahamas and indie rockers Rogue Wave, alongside singer-songwriter Zach Gill, skateboarder-turned-songwriter Matt Costa and jazz-folk aficionado Zee Avi.

With about 20 million records sold, however, it's the mellow musical mood of the company's co-founder Jack Johnson that's given Brushfire the freedom to grow in a flagging industry and even to share their success with the musical community as a whole. This isn't a privilege Malloy takes lightly.

"I never feel that we didn't make a mark on this scene," says Malloy. "I know the scene is changing and that's OK, people will always want good records and good films so I just have to keep trying to make those with my friends and family." — (M)

How to run a coffee shop

Company: Omotesando Koffee
Location: Tokyo
Founded: 2011
Number of employees: 5
Weekly bean count: 25 to 30kg
Most popular order:
    cappuccino doppio

Early starts and long days mean coffee runs in the veins of the business-minded – and a global interest in better understanding its provenance means that selling it can be lucrative.

If you ever fancy trying your hand as a barista, this popular coffee haunt in Tokyo couldn't be simpler: a wooden house with a cube-shaped metal frame dropped inside, one barista and a vintage coffee machine. And yet the combination works to create something thoroughly unique and personal.

Eiichi Kunitomo (*pictured, top*) first opened Omotesando Koffee on a backstreet of Tokyo's Jingumae neighbourhood in 2011. The Fukui native's love of coffee has taken him from Osaka to southern Italy and finally to Tokyo, where he managed another popular café. Having made a name for himself as a barista, he decided it was time to branch out on his own. Kunitomo's concept was simple:

to serve delicious coffee from a stand where the barista and customer could talk to each other directly. He wasn't looking for a traditional coffee house and imagined his cube could be placed anywhere. Through local connections he heard about a wooden building that suited his criteria and had a leafy courtyard with room for a few benches outside. After teaming up with two Tokyo design outfits, Kunitomo launched his stand.

Kunitomo's rule of thumb has always been to promote simplicity and the menu reflects this, offering only coffee and homemade custard sweets. There's one person taking the orders and making them, too. The machine – a 20-year-old La Cimbali – is placed at a right angle to the counter so the barista can chat with the customers and they can glimpse the skill that goes into making their coffee.

Kunitomo's aim is not just to build a business but also to forge a Japanese coffee culture. As well as opening coffee stands for others and expanding his own, his back-to-basics model shows successful businesses needn't be complicated at all. "You don't need qualifications," he says. "You need the ability to make customers feel or enjoy something better. Skills are something you pick up along the way." — (M)

THINK BIG
GLOBAL

Preface: There are, of course, far more than 50 steps involved when it comes to reaching the peaks of business success. That being the case, consider the following tips as footholds as you make your own meandering and unique way to the summit.

OI
Inspiration
Know where to start

The first thing you need is an idea (or two, just in case the first one proves daft). You don't have to think of something that's unique – although this can be helpful in some instances. Often a fresh approach to an old format is the perfect place to start. A good coffee shop, a friendly lawyers' office, a modest but ambitious architecture firm, a cake shop with good buns and a nice window display: nothing new but things the public wants repeatedly.

02
Awareness
Look before you leap

Think what this means for your life – are you ready for the sweat and tears? Be clear about why you are doing this and be ready to make some sacrifices in the pursuit of happiness and satisfaction. Because while it may be momentarily glorious to tell your corporate boss that you have had enough of her and her temper, what lies ahead for any entrepreneur takes courage and involves numerous set backs.

03
Detail
Design a blueprint you can rely on

Create a plan. A really detailed one. You may not stick to it in the end but there are some essential questions you need answers to. What are your start-up costs going to be? Who will be your investors and how will they be repaid? What do you intend your profits to be in year one? Be modest, clear and honest – especially with yourself.

04
Research
Know what will work

Test that plan: check out your rivals and speak to people you trust. Have you been realistic in your pricing? How big is the market? Why is your opposition so successful? And make sure you don't just ask your close circle of friends: chances are they will either be over-enthusiastic or dispiritingly cautious.

05
Commitment
Stick to your idea

Don't dawdle. After you have spoken to everyone, don't get blown off course. Your head will spin if you ask too many people for advice. Let's say you want to start a small wine company with links from vineyard to retail. A survey of opinions will push you up and down market from Chile to Italy. But if you know your passion is for selling Spanish wines to Japan or Brazilian ones to Canada, stick with it.

06
Investment
Fund your business

Now raise the money. If you need investors, start with friends and family and show commitment by adding your own cash. Forget the Palo Alto venture-capital model (having a vague idea and getting a billionaire to pay for your vision) because beyond that bubble, investors want to see that you too are sharing the risk. You also want people who are in it for the long haul and will not jump at the first sign of trouble.

07
Ownership
Avoid legal action

Speak to a lawyer and register your invention. Make sure any shareholdings are clearly explained on paper, understand your liability and think ahead. Your company name may be very valuable in years to come – make sure it really is yours.

08
Modesty
Keep things simple

Kitchen tables are good for start-ups: it's perfectly normal for big businesses to have modest beginnings. Don't be tempted to take offices until you need to. Lots of companies require little more than a laptop and a phone to get started.

09
Collaboration
Be a part of something

When you are ready to vacate the kitchen, the shared workspaces that have appeared in cities from Paris to Buenos Aires allow people access to large offices and all the things that go with them. But they also give you a network of people to bounce ideas off and collaborate with. You pay a modest fee in return for a working environment that's inspiring, even if you are only using a desk for a few hours a week.

IO
Petiteness
Have only what you need

If you do need your own office or shop from the get-go, start small. Too many retail concepts, for example, fail because people just start off too big, paying rent for floorspace they don't need. Conversely, there are lots of shops no bigger than a few square metres that raise the bar in terms of inventiveness.

11
Equipment
Make work a pleasure

A desk, a chair, a laptop: get it right because it's likely you will be sitting here a lot. For the actual kit you need, turn to page 270. But there's also a pleasure factor to consider. Your working environment should make you feel good about the day ahead. A wobbly chair distracts, a desk that's too small frustrates and a laptop with a tricky demeanour soon infuriates. This is not about cash, just about choosing carefully.

12
Support
Have help on hand when your computer gives up

Make sure there is a plan for when your computer breaks down and the website crashes – you need an IT man or woman. Hours lost trying to retrieve your spreadsheets are wasted hours; get a support system in place unless you are a genius with tech issues. Failing that, hire a team member who knows the key you need to press to reset your day.

13
Appellation
Ensure immediate recognition

Choose a name for your company that will stand the test of time and work in all formats – and in various nations if you intend to go global. It also needs to be something that you can say on the phone and people will get first time. Having to explain or spell the name repeatedly will become very tiresome very quickly.

14
Elegance
Instigate clear and effective branding

Choose a font and a colour for your brand. You need to go to page 102 to get the full lowdown on this but keep it simple and elegant. If you find it all too much, remember that's why God invented Helvetica. And make sure everyone uses the same font on emails too because brands must be seamless and co-ordinated.

15
Correspondence
Deliver your message

Invest in stationery and business cards – they say an awful lot about you. While email is how 99 per cent of your correspondence will be conducted, have a good letterhead for those times when the need arises. Crisp, firm and precisely folded mail will underline that you are a brand that understands the details.

16
Values
Stay on track

Know your brand values – what do you stand for? Let's return to our wine company. What's at its heart: provenance, sustainability, craft, modernity and paying everyone in the supply chain a fair salary? You don't have to shout to the customers about these key elements of your brand (they just want a good wine) but you need to be able to go back to your values again and again and make sure they inform everything that you do.

17
Recruitment
Get the right balance

Pick your first staff carefully. OK, they can talk the talk and have the right skills but are they nice? Will they be there when the tough moments arise? Do they seem like the loyal sort? Gather people around you who can become a team.

18
Aesthetics
Create a co-ordinated look and feel

Don't blow the budget yet but have an aesthetic about everything you do. If your wine brand is about craft and provenance, bring those qualities to life in how you design your office or host wine tastings. There should not be a mismatch between how you present your company to the world and what it's actually all about back at HQ. Add integrity and honesty to that list of brand values.

19
Marketing
Let people know who you are

Choose a marketing plan – a simple one. How are you going to let people know that you have launched and that you have a new product? At every event and meeting get contacts so you can build up a database of useful names. Produce a newsletter. Print posters. Make tote bags. Just get your name in front of the right people.

20
Self-promotion
Take the direct approach

You don't need a PR just yet – you are the best person to tell your story. Public relations can work very well but nobody can relate your adventures better than you. A journalist will hear the passion in your voice and see the commitment you have made. Spend money on a coach who can help you with public speaking and presentation if you are nervous but wait until some proper money is coming in before getting in too deep with a big PR agency.

21
Party
Tell everyone you've arrived

Make some noise: have a party and get people to notice you exist. The launch party is a good idea for any business because you start that word-of-mouth chain that will bring people to your door and put a stop to the question, "Have they opened yet?" It's also a way of thanking your team. Serve one good white wine; perhaps a beer. Two hours. Done.

22
Networking
Spread the good news

Buy people lunch. It's amazing how much business will come from such contact. You can easily end up locked away during the early days and forget that you need to be out there spreading the word. Forge strong links with neighbouring businesses and meet your suppliers. Don't get drunk.

23
Reputation
Offer service with a smile

Respect word of mouth – the original social media – and the power of the personal recommendation. Lots of this happens online but a lot still occurs naturally as friends talk to each other: "Have you been to the new wine shop?" Do your best to keep people happy and always reply to emails, even from hard-to-please clients. It's funny how a simple and honest reply can often resolve everything. Go the extra distance.

24
Community
Have a local love-in

Base yourself in a community and be a part of it: get involved with neighbouring enterprises and start-ups. Local trading associations and business groups do good things but many new companies find ways of becoming part of their local scene without such formal backing. If you are running the local wine store you will get to know when people are drowning their sorrows and celebrating their birthdays. Join in.

25
Simplicity
Do it your way

Don't read too much literature – just do it. Business books can be useful but don't get caught up in complex theories. You just need inspiration and a guiding hand every now and then so pick what you read with caution.

26
Consistency
Work towards long-term gain

Brands are made through repetition so don't change course too easily. OK, so they don't get it at first but before you switch strategy make sure that you have given it a good go. It's hard to have any credibility if you are an upscale wine store one day and a cider store the next. Often it's not the product but the presentation that needs tweaking.

27
Submission
Get things off the ground

Let it take over your life in the early years. You may not have enough days off, you may not see your friends very often, you may earn less than you had hoped – but you will look back at these days as some of your finest. This is your life now.

28
Mentors
Seek a second opinion

Have a wise counsel: you need someone independent you can turn to for advice in stressful moments – some business coaches are helpful in this instance. When it looks tricky or you need to move to the next stage of your company's development it's good to have someone who can give you informed but very honest advice. We all need mentors.

29
Reinvestment
Stay topped up

Put money back into the business. Every single year. Even in the tougher times, your priority has to be making sure that you are staying relevant and well funded. The dividend can wait for the time being.

30
Web-ready
Carry out careful digital planning

Know when it is time for the website and the digital plans because these are not cheap options. It's hard for any business to exist without a website but only build what you really need. Web projects rarely come in on budget and the platforms they are built on date faster than the quirkiest fashion statement. Look at simple off-the-shelf products for stock control or e-commerce. You need less than they tell you.

31
Expansion
Aim for sustained success

Employ more people. It's a testing time when a business expands and clients can no longer have all of your attention. There are painful hurdles as you expand and you have to cede control on certain things. If you can, promote from within and reward loyalty. Outside hires can often go wrong if you are a small, tight organisation with a clear set of unshakeable values. Be cautious.

32
Exploration
Broaden your horizons

Go out into the world and take your show on the road. You want to be big in Mexico or Thailand? Well, go there. The world of video conferences and emails cannot let you see new ideas in action. Go meet the restaurateurs who are buying your wine. More business will always come from your adventures. Running a company is all about relationships. Let people see your skill and enthusiasm in the flesh.

Travelling the world to talk shop? It's worth doing your research first – offending your potential investors won't be great for business

33
Etiquette: taxis
When you're in Japan

Learn the appropriate business etiquette when you go abroad. Too many deals fail because people lack local knowledge and unintentionally end up insulting potential partners. In Japan, save the best seat for the boss. In taxis and private rides alike, the Japanese observe a strict hierarchical seating plan whereby the best seat in a taxi is behind the driver. If your customer is driving, the highest-ranked person must sit alongside to show respect.

34
Etiquette: surnames
When you're in France

The French sometimes give their surnames first when being formally introduced and it can be considered rude to call a colleague by his or her first name.

35
Etiquette: sobriety
When you're in Canada

In Canada, drinking alcohol is not usual practice during business lunches. Your best option is to stick to water – unless, of course, your gracious host suggests otherwise.

36
Etiquette: taste
When you're in China

In China, taste everything you're offered during the course of a meal – but never clear your plate as your host will assume you're still hungry and keep filling it. Between tastings, don't talk business; wait until the plates are cleared away.

37
Etiquette: acquiescence
When you're in India

Indians don't like to say no to a request. If they are unable to do something, you are unlikely to get a direct refusal. Similarly, use tact and subtlety if you need to explain why a business proposal is not possible.

38
Etiquette: informality
When you're in the USA

Americans like to be relaxed as those in charge are keen to relive the easygoing business practices of the 1960s. So, drop the formality – though it goes without saying that you should still keep a tight grip on your manners.

39
Etiquette: forenames
When you're in Denmark

In Denmark there are a few things to remember: Danes tend to use only their first names, women are greeted before the men and personal hellos and goodbyes are required for everyone present.

40
Etiquette: cheers
When you're in Sweden

Toasting in Sweden involves eye contact but tradition dictates that there is no clinking of glasses. Instead, an enthusiastic cry of "Skol!" and a nod to everyone around the table will do the trick.

41
Etiquette: preamble
When you're in the UK

In the UK, small talk is an essential prelude to business talk; the weather and the day's events are both acceptable topics. After skirting round the real reason you've met, everyone will be happy to attend to the matter in hand.

42
Etiquette: baggage
When you're in Brazil

Don't put your briefcase or bag on the ground. Aside from the fact it might get dirty – or, worse, stolen – most restaurants in Brazil provide hooks or stools to rest it on – and would prefer that you use them.

43
Pruning
Aspire to the greater good

Let people move on – don't keep staff who are bad at their jobs. It's one of the most painful things an entrepreneur has to do but you should not renew contracts or avoid difficult reviews if you have found yourself with staff who will never be able to help you.

44
Assistance
Make the best use of your day

Getting bigger? Employ an assistant. Today you booked flight tickets, tried to fix the photocopier, made some lunch and dealt with numerous questions from your team. There comes a point when you need an assistant who can give you time to do what you are good at.

45
Diversification
Break new ground

Start to stretch your brand – what else can your company and its name do? OK, so you have the wine shop but could you also have a wine hotel or run wine holidays? Or how about a catering business? Spread the brand with care but maximise its potential.

46
Retreats
Engender employee morale

Have company away days. You might try to get everyone to put aside an afternoon but it just never happens. Take them all away to the mountains or the countryside; somewhere nice and quiet. Two days for big ideas and big meals. Friendships are reaffirmed (no need for games or role play) and people get to think clearly about the way ahead. And make sure all management speak is banned; there should be no "blue-sky thinking".

47
Enlargement
Upsize at the right time

When no more desks can be squeezed in and there's enough money in the bank account, it's time to move on. Now your office can be a true demonstration of your brand's values. No need for flash but it should hint at the kind of confidence that says you are here to stay.

48
Reflection
Remember how you got here

Remind yourself how this venture all began on a regular basis; go back to those founding core values again and again, making sure you are staying true to your company's heritage. And be able to articulate your story (the real one, not a made-up one).

49
Celebration
Let people know they've done well

When you have a big win or when Christmas comes around, make sure you pop a few corks. In hardworking, growing companies it's vital that you know when to spread some cheer. These people are stars. Let them know it.

50
Rest
Take a break

Have a holiday. You deserve it. Sun on your skin, a doze in the afternoon, a long, long dinner. You'll forget it all for a few days and then you'll find your fogged mind clearing. On the final days you'll be revived and full of ideas for the years ahead. You'll even have the occasional smile as you think to yourself, "I am running my own company. I am my own boss. I *love* what I do."

NEXT STEPS

Learning, training, setting up and building a brand

Preface

What do you do now? Well, the first thing is to make sure you have the right training, which for many means attending a top fashion school or studying for an MBA. But for others, apprenticeships are a better way into business than the classroom. Because whatever your plans or ambitions, there comes a point where you need to roll up your sleeves and just get on with it (it's striking how many of the business leaders you will meet in this book started on the proverbial or literal shop floor as teenagers).

Then you should consider the kind of enterprise you want to run and how you can give it the potential for longevity and meaning. If you are serious about running a company (instead of fretting about an exit strategy from day one) then think about the family model that allows you to get aunts and cousins into the corporate mix and tends to encourage a belief in the long term, not just feeding dividends to shareholders every year. Or how about a modern take on the co-operative? Neither model should in any way restrict your ambitions or size.

Next you will need to sort out your brand, your logo and packaging. That's all here for you, too.

Contents

HIGHER VISION LONDON

Preface: With a striking headquarters and a key role at the heart of the UK's burgeoning creative industries, Central Saint Martins has reaffirmed its reputation as an artistic centre of excellence.

School: Central Saint Martins College of Art and Design
Location: London
Founded: 1989 as a result of a merger between Saint Martins School of Art (1854) and Central School of Arts & Crafts (1896)
Number of employees: 389
Number of premises: 2

———

Quote: *'Few design schools can boast the alumni power of Central Saint Martins'*

01

During term time, any given morning in London bears witness to students swarming like ants north of King's Cross, all heading to class at Central Saint Martins College of Art and Design. Men experiment with drop-crotch trousers tucked into leather riding or biker boots. Girls favour skirts and shirts topped with carefully constructed hair-do's. It's just as well these students care enough to dress beautifully because it's likely that in years to come they'll be at the forefront of their chosen creative fields.

Formed in 1989 following the merger of two older institutions – the Central School of Arts & Crafts and the Saint Martins School of Art – Central Saint Martins emerged from two schools founded at a time when craft and design education was recognised as vital to the industrial prowess of the UK. The UK has one of the largest creative sectors in Europe and leading this next generation of artistically minded businessmen and women is Central Saint Martins, one of six colleges that comprise the University of the Arts London – the largest creative educational establishment in Europe.

In 2011 the school moved into a new home at the Granary Building, part of Lewis Cubitt's 1852 Goods Yard complex. It's a soaring, cathedral-like space with the preserved brick façades of the industrial buildings. It's difficult not to be wowed and it's little surprise that the new campus has been showered with awards.

But of course it's not just the school building that attracts prospective graduates. Central Saint Martins' students are involved directly with their future industry throughout their studies. LVMH sponsored the lecture theatre and is one of several scholarship providers. The fashion department has teamed up for projects with Celine, J.Crew and Louis Vuitton to name a few; the graphics department with Hewlett-Packard, Tetra Pak and Kagome. "They come to us for ideas," says Anne Smith, dean of academic programmes and herself a former student. "When I studied here we did just one project with the industry. Today we turn brands away if they're only interested in brand association. The global industry looks to us to provide their designers of tomorrow." — (M)

Why you should come here:
Few design schools can boast the alumni power of Central Saint Martins. The school's graduates include fashion hotshots, Turner Prize-winning artists, film directors, musicians and even chefs. Attending gives students access to one of the best address books in the creative industry.

02

03

04

05   06

01
Classrooms seen
from the interior
main concourse
02
The concourse
is nicknamed
'The Street'
03
East Transit Shed
04
One of the
many workshops
05
Philip
Strawbridge,
BA menswear
06
Model workshop
07
Anne Smith,
dean, fashion
and textiles
08
The Granary
Building

07   08

BUSINESS CLASS MILAN

Preface: SDA Bocconi is the Italian business school that can tailor a course to meet the needs of any kind of student, whether a start-up novice or a boardroom executive in need of a refresher. The secret of good business is to never stop learning.

School: SDA Bocconi
Location: Milan
Founded: 1971 (Bocconi University was founded in 1902)
Number of employees: there are 1,970 between SDA Bocconi and Bocconi University
Number of premises: 1

———

Quote: *'We want students to have know-how they can use straight away on the job'*

01   02

03

04

Italy's reputation for producing family businesses that go on to be leading players in their industries is unmatched. But even family firms sometimes need help to navigate the global economy. That's where SDA Bocconi, a Milan management school, enters the picture. While the majority of higher-education institutions in Italy have failed to stay on a par with the successes of the country's business community, Bocconi offers one of Europe's best MBA courses.

"Our objective is return on investment," says Bruno Busacca, the school's dean. "We want students to have know-how they can use straight away on the job." The school also offers courses geared to working professionals who need to catch up on the latest business models. New ideas to win market share are in high demand.

"We create a tailor-made plan for busy executives so they receive one-to-one training on what interests them, be it big data or change management," says Busacca. SDA Bocconi doesn't only cater to academic students – managers from firms such as Fiat and Pirelli enrol in customised tutorials each year. To serve its students even better, Bocconi is upgrading – soon it will move into a €130m campus designed by Japanese architects Sanaa.

Outside the classroom, full-time MBA students – the majority foreigners – work on real-world projects with corporations. The school's food and beverage industries programme dispatches students to collaborate on product launches and marketing plans with staff at top firms such as Ferrero.

The hands-on approach is refreshing compared with other Italian schools' focus on theory; Bocconi accounting courses begin with students poring over the latest corporate balance sheets. Besides the appeal of living in Italy, many foreign students attend for the chance to be close to businesses operating in a sector the country is famous for abroad: luxury.

The curriculum allows them to see the boutiques and factories of major brands from Prada to Gucci and learn about their supply chain. Professor Stefania Saviolo, head of the Luxury and Fashion Knowledge Center, says matter-of-factly, "We try to give them a sense of how the industry works." — (M)

Why you should come here: Already occupying a central Milanese location, SDA Bocconi will have a new campus built by Tokyo's Sanaa architecture firm. The energy-saving design will feature a large park and sports centre with an Olympic-sized swimming pool.

06

05

07 08

EMPOWERING
LIVES
THROUGH
KNOWLEDGE
AND
IMAGINATION
SINCE 1971.

09

10

11

CHAOS THEORY
AARHUS

Preface: In the Danish city of Aarhus there's a business school with a difference. Kaospilot puts its students in the thick of things from day one, teaching them to think creatively in real-life situations about how innovative businesses can change the way we live.

School: Kaospilot
Location: Aarhus, Denmark
Founded: 1991
Number of employees: 20 in Aarhus, 10 in Bern
Number of premises: 2 (Aarhus and Bern, Switzerland)

——

Quote: *'There was no school in the world back then that could have taught us how to negotiate with the KGB. We asked ourselves what kind of education we could create to help us do what we were doing'*

01

"You won't find any textbook assignments or auditorium-style lectures here," boasts Christer Windeløv-Lidzélius, the principal of Kaospilot, as he strolls around the school's stunning glass campus in a former industrial area of Aarhus's port. Instead, students at this alternative business school learn by doing: taking on projects for big-name clients including Cisco, SAS, Carlsberg and Lego. "When students first arrive they are given two things: a key to the campus and a stack of business cards," says Windeløv-Lidzélius. "They start building their networks from day one."

Kaospilot is the brainchild of Uffe Elbæk, a prominent Danish politician and formerly Denmark's minister for culture. Established in 1991, the school's roots can be traced back to a Danish youth movement known as the Frontrunners, which organised a pro-democracy rock concert in Moscow at the height of the Cold War. "There was no school in the world back then that could have taught us how to negotiate with the KGB," says Elbæk with a grin. "We asked ourselves what kind of education we could create to help us do what we were doing."

Kaospilot now trains over 130 students from its home base in Aarhus and a sister school in Bern. At Kaospilot, however, learning isn't confined to the classroom, let alone the country.

Each year the entire school jets off to tackle a pressing social issue overseas, in cities from Bogotá to Cape Town. These international projects, coupled with a 2005 decision to switch the language of instruction to English, have contributed to the programme's soaring popularity abroad.

The school's unique educational model is reflected by the entrepreneurial nature of its students. "Dissatisfied with the Chinese occupation, a student built a national football team for Tibet," says David Storkholm, director of Kaospilot's creative-leadership programme and a former student himself. "And for his final exam they played in a match against Greenland."

Upon graduation, a host of opportunities in myriad sectors await the "Kaospilots". Eva Kruse, school alumna and CEO of the Danish Fashion Institute, says: "Being a Kaospilot is a lifelong identity. It led me to where I am today." — (M)

Why you should come here: Structured around a varied programme of creative thinking and group work, the Kaospilot style is perfect for those who want to go to business school but are concerned that a few years in the classroom might slow them down. It's a training ground for entrepreneurs in the real world, not just for academic students.

02

03

04   05

06

07

08   09

WE WILL BUILD IT
CHARLESTON

Preface: The American College of the Building Arts in South Carolina is preserving traditional skills by teaching them to the next generation of craftsmen. It's not just the students who benefit, though: the historic city is also being treated to some fine restoration work along the way.

School: American College of the Building Arts
Location: Charleston, USA
Founded: 1989
Number of students: 54
Number of premises: 2 (the main campus at the Old Jail on Magazine Street and craft specialisation facilities on James Island. In 2016, ACBA will move to new premises in a refurbished 1897 trolley-car barn)

——

Quote: *'We don't reject modernism. We just feel there is an equal place for tradition in the 21st century'*

01

Just beyond the College of Charleston is the city's historic Old Jail, a rambling fortress built in 1802. In the early 19th century the jail housed runaway slaves. A century-and-a-half later, the building is home to the unusual student and faculty body of the American College of the Building Arts (ACBA).

Originally established in 1989, the ACBA became licensed in 2004 as the US's only institute of higher education offering a four-year liberal arts degree in the traditional trades of pre-industrial-era Europe and the US. Using the jail building and more than 1,400 historic structures in Charleston itself as a laboratory, the school teaches its students building arts that have almost been lost, using stone, iron, timber, masonry and plaster.

While emphasis is placed on both preservation and new-build architecture, the ACBA clearly stresses old-world craft over 21st-century flash. "We don't reject modernism; we just feel there is an equal place for tradition in the 21st century," says professor of architecture and design, David Payne. "We are more about Andrea Palladio here than Rem Koolhaas."

At the ACBA, coursework is anchored around a traditional trade that students select when they enrol and that they master during their four years of study. Yet, whereas French *compagnons* are trained solely in technique, ACBA students receive an equally intensive academic education. Literature, mathematics and foreign-language courses comprise half of the students' schedules. But unlike at conventional colleges, academic subjects are integrated into the ACBA's overall mission to develop professional craftsmen.

While the Old Jail remains the ACBA's home base, its students work throughout Charleston. Out on James Island, for instance, is a satellite campus used as a workshop for the ACBA's carpentry, timber framing and architectural-metal programmes. Over on Meeting Street, meanwhile, students apply the final touches to an intricate plaster ceiling in a Georgian townhouse in the heart of Charleston's historic district. The students are employed, albeit without compensation, by a private contractor sourced through the ACBA's work-study programme. Like many ACBA endeavours, the Meeting Street project blurs the lines between education and enterprise. — (M)

Why you should come here: Few other schools immerse their students in the way the ACBA does. The Old Jail houses classrooms but also serves as an ongoing restoration project where the students and teachers can put their skills to work.

02

03

04

05   06

07   08

COOL SCHOOL BOLOGNA

Preface: The Carpigiani Gelato University on the outskirts of Bologna attracts students from all over the world, keen to learn the secrets of the perfect scoop. And with its eyes on more overseas expansion, the knowledge is being shared far and wide.

School: Carpigiani Gelato University
Location: Anzola dell'Emilia (on the outskirts of Bologna)
Founded: 2003
Number of employees: 35
Number of premises: 11 (Australia, Argentina, Brazil, China, Germany, Italy, Japan, Netherlands, UAE, UK and the US)

———

Quote: *'We see people coming to us, many in their mid-thirties, stuck and looking for a change'*

02

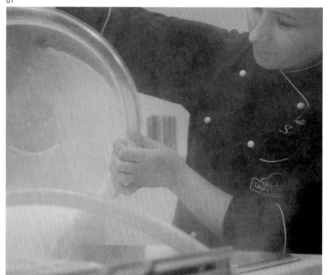
01

Rivalled only by pasta in popularity, gelato is a must-eat for visitors to Italy. The frozen treat's appeal is strong: on average, Italian ice cream parlours serve over €2bn of scoops annually to locals and tourists. In the hope of spreading Italian know-how abroad, one company has invested millions to teach gelato preparation techniques to foreigners.

Founded in 2003 on the outskirts of Bologna, the Carpigiani Gelato University offers courses year-round, many structured into week-long seminars, to those aspiring to the title of *gelataio*. Students huddle inside air-conditioned halls to hear lectures from instructors such as Luciano Ferrari. The Italian title of maestro is preferred to professor and instructors wear a chef's jacket to class.

Writing instructions on a whiteboard, Ferrari may run through ways to experiment with ingredients to make new flavours. In class, he stresses food presentation to those eager to open their own *gelateria* by taking a serving spade and carefully making wave-like impressions on the surface of gelato. During his talks in English to students, the term "ice cream" is one that is treated with contempt.

"When we refer to gelato we mean an artisan product that's creamy and made fresh daily with in-season fruit; ice cream is industrially produced," says Ferrari. "It has double the fat content, more air and ingredients to help it stay in supermarket fridges for days."

Nodding in approval is the school's Japanese co-ordinator, Kaori Ito. Her appointment is testament to the institute's desire to expand overseas – Carpigiani operates 11 schools in cities as far away as Shanghai and São Paulo. "We see people coming to us, many in their mid-thirties, stuck and looking for a change." Carpigiani's educational thrust complements the company's main activity: producing gelato-making machines, a business that makes over €100m a year with a huge percentage of the global market.

The initiative has been a runaway success, with over 7,000 graduates each year. In Bologna, foreign attendees easily outnumber locals, as students from Düsseldorf to Dubai look to learn the secrets of the chilled sweet. As one student, a former bank manager, says, "I used to work for a pay cheque, not for something I was passionate about. Now I'll see happy customers in front of me eating my gelato." — (M)

Why you should come here: The university focuses on teaching the practical and commercial skills needed to run a successful small business.

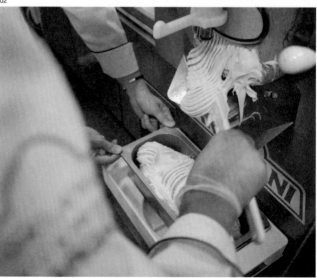
03

075

BUSINESS ANGLES
ALABAMA

Preface: Going back to the drawing board is usually frowned upon but McAlpine Tankersley never left it: the Alabama-based architecture firm shuns computers and design software in favour of the tried-and-tested pencil and paper.

Company: McAlpine Tankersley
Location: Montgomery, Alabama
Founded: 1983
Number of employees when founded: 3
Number of employees now: 12
Number of premises: 1

Quote: *'When someone new comes in, we pretty much throw them in the pool'*

On a balmy spring afternoon, architect Greg Tankersley makes the short walk from his home in Alabama to his design studio. Inside, a gauzy drapery separates a dozen tidy desk spaces. There's hardly a monitor in sight. Unusually in an era of construction defined by the alchemy of metal and glass, McAlpine Tankersley Architecture is dedicated to artisanal building.

That the company eschews computers has earned the practice a favourable and charmingly old-fashioned reputation among clients. "The physical act of drawing is something you pour yourself into," Tankersley says.

On hand is Brendan Boatwright, a Memphis-born architecture graduate who joined Tankersley's firm as an intern-architect after graduating from the University of Arkansas. While Boatwright learned the basics of architectural drafting in the first year of his university programme, here he has been required to master the task of hand-detailing the minutiae of complex renderings. Thanks to decades of experience with the firm, Tankersley proves a more than capable instructor. "If there's a detail we have to figure out, we'll figure it out together," Boatwright says.

With several sketches of a Tennessee farmhouse spread across his desk, Boatwright acknowledges a seemingly heretical practice in today's world: not a single architect in the firm uses design software such as Adobe or CAD. Instead it's the traditional tools of the trade: sharp Staedtler pencils, a compass for setting angles and a horsehair brush used to remove errant eraser flecks from precisely detailed blueprints. "I had been on the computer since the second year of architecture school," Boatwright says. "Here, I had to start over."

Indeed, McAlpine Tankersley is among the only top-tier design practices in the US to not be reliant on digital drafting tools. "To me, architecture has always been about an art – a computer loses that," says Tankersley. Meanwhile, what is central to Boatwright's progress is the attention he receives from Tankersley and his supervisors, whether sketching an elevation or detailing the construction of a window. It is intensive work and the design of a single residence can involve more than 100 schematic sketches.

The McAlpine Tankersley look is nuanced. Whether a small Cape Dutch house along the Florida coast or a modern stucco structure in Texas, there's a reverence for the lessons of architecture, from Lutyens to Voysey and southern architects such as A Hays Town. Projects use shingle, stone and wooden

clapboard and make reference to historic styles.

Tankersley's own apprenticeship involved a steady nerve. Just months after graduating with a degree from Auburn University he joined partner Bobby McAlpine in his then two-year-old practice. "The day I walked through the door, Bobby said, 'I've just designed a 5,000 sq ft [1,525 sq m] house and you're going to do the construction drawings for it,'" says Tankersley.

Ever since, the firm's approach to developing the technical skills of junior staff has remained very much unchanged. "When someone new comes in, we pretty much throw them in the pool," Tankersley says.

Boatwright spent five years as a student; earning a state architectural licence means the same again in terms of practical experience and half a dozen further examinations. At his desk he pores over plans of the farmhouse that will break ground in Tennessee.

The dedication to balance, composition and proportion is evident. When complimented on his drawings, Boatwright deflects the praise. "I still look at some of these and think, 'I can't believe I know how to do some of this stuff,'" he says. — (M)

LOUNGE

FAMILY ROOM & DINING

TRAIL BLAZERS FLORENCE

Preface: Set in a leafy Florentine courtyard, the studio of Italian tailor Liverano & Liverano is the perfect education for those ready to dedicate themselves to the company's time-honoured traditions.

Company: Liverano & Liverano
Location: Florence
Founded: 1948
Number of employees when founded: 2 (brothers Antonio and Luigi Liverano)
Number of employees now: 13 (owner Antonio Liverano, 9 tailors and 3 sales assistants)
Number of premises: 1
Bestselling product: bespoke suits

Quote: *'We need to invest in the youth and help them grow'*

"Young people today often brag that they've graduated from Istituto Marangoni [the prestigious Milan fashion school]," says tailor Antonio Liverano. "As for me, I received my fashion education on the streets of Firenze." At the age of 11 he moved to the city from Palagiano in southeast Italy to join his brother Luigi (11 years his senior) so they could pursue a tailoring career. After months of training at small ateliers, the siblings founded Liverano & Liverano.

Starting out in a workshop in Florence's Piazza Santa Maria Novella, today Liverano & Liverano occupies a large, light-filled space on Via dei Fossi – a charming cobbled street that has been a gathering point for tailors since Leonardo da Vinci's era. In the airy cutting studio, six junior tailors work in unison under the guidance of Signore Liverano. One of them is Hojun Choi.

In 2008, Choi moved from Seoul to Milan to study pattern design at L'Istituto Secoli after graduating in computer science from Sangmyung University. "Software and IT were my parents' choice," Choi says, explaining his unlikely career shift. "I always wanted to be involved in fashion." In 2009, his passion took him to Florence with the hope of landing a role at Liverano & Liverano. Getting on board wasn't an easy task. Choi

was turned down three times by discerning Japanese-born store manager Takahiro Osaki (Liverano's right-hand man) before he finally got to meet the master himself. "We were testing his dedication," Liverano remembers, amused.

Back then, Choi had one clear objective: "I just wanted to learn how to make beautiful suits," he says, reflecting the sincerity he has maintained while training. It's a slow, meticulous process at Liverano & Liverano. It takes up to two months and at least two fittings for new customers to have a bespoke suit measured and finished. Suits for returning clients can be ready after just one fitting as the studio keeps all paper patterns on file. The atelier's reputation for subtle, immaculate constructions is reflected in the price tag: bespoke suits here cost more than €4,500; their ready-to-wear counterparts, over €2,200.

Choi's apprenticeship has been similarly painstaking. He started with the basics. "First you need to learn how to hold a needle. Making a suit starts with sewing and it's a lot of hard work," says Liverano. "You need six years of dedication, sweat and tears to learn the craft." An ever-present mentor, Liverano's approach seems to be paying off. On the table are tools that a few years back Choi would not have known how to use. With a quiet accuracy and a steady hand the

apprentice goes through a suit fitting with a new client and then cautiously makes the necessary amendments.

After a few moments of contemplation, the master nods with approval. Choi's face lights up in response – one more test has been passed. "This is not work – it is culture. It requires love and respect," says the apprentice. The hardest thing to learn to date? "Everything," he says bluntly. "It's a job that goes between art and technique. It's a fascinating mix that engages you and every aspect of your life."

While Choi has a humble love for his trade and teacher, his boss has a bold confidence that comes from over six decades of expertise. He is the only master cutter here but he's determined to pass his insight on and foster new talent. "It was mostly older people that used to do this kind of work," he says. "Now we need to invest in the youth and help them grow. Only this way can we continue the tradition."

To prove his point he is planning to set up a three-year course under Liverano & Liverano that will be inspired by the same methods. "It will be a hands-on apprenticeship," he says. "We'll have just 30 students who are eager to learn. It's not about having the best techniques per se but being committed to the craft. It's about nourishing your passion." — (M)

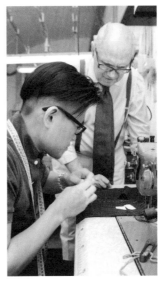

IT TAKES TWO
COPENHAGEN

Preface: After porcelain firm Royal Copenhagen's fine porcelain Flora Danica comes out of the kiln, a team of painters take over to create the brand's vivid floral designs. To hone those skills takes years – always under the watchful eye of a master craftsperson.

Company: Royal Copenhagen
Location: Glostrup, Copenhagen
Founded: 1775
Number of employees: over 700
Number of founders: 3
Number of premises: 11
Bestselling product: Blue Fluted Mega dinnerware

Quote: *'I will probably spend the rest of my life doing this'*

"I've never been good with computers or books but I've always been able to draw," says Royal Copenhagen Flora Danica apprentice, Jacqueline Tranemose Fredericia. "I saw an advert in my technical college newspaper inviting people to apply to study porcelain painting [a course in partnership with Royal Copenhagen] and I thought it sounded exciting. Actually, I thought, 'Yes, that's what I want to do for the rest of my life.'"

Flora Danica is the most exclusive product of Royal Copenhagen porcelain, a handmade dinner service with a tradition dating back more than two centuries. Fredericia must learn to paint some of Denmark's 3,200 indigenous plants that appear as part of the series during an initial, intensively supervised training period of four years. After that, all pupils have to undergo six years of on-the-job training.

In 2008, Royal Copenhagen moved virtually all production of its trademark Blue Fluted porcelain to its own factory in Thailand but the 15 Flora Danica artisans remained in Denmark. One models the flowers and 14 do the painting.

"I just don't think they will ever be able to make Flora Danica anywhere else," says Jacqueline's "master", Judith Sørensen. "You have to have the Danish light when you paint,

you have to be surrounded by the Danish plants to get them inside you. You must always be thinking, 'How would this flower be in nature? How would its curves be; how would it be in this light?'"

"Yes, and you have to express your feelings," adds Fredericia. After two years working together at close quarters, master and apprentice often finish each other's sentences. "Each day is different: the light and your mood are reflected in how you paint on any given day. And I always hear Judith's voice in my head when I am working."

The mutual respect and affection shared between the two women is clear: Sørensen acknowledges the compliment with a shy nod. "It's like handwriting, it's so individual," she says. "It's your soul, you could say. I can always tell who has painted a piece."

It is time and labour-intensive work, all undertaken at the company's base in the Copenhagen suburb of Glostrup. Painters copy original prints from the 18th-century Danish botanical guide *Flora Danica*, which was inspired by the work of Carl Linnaeus in Sweden. The artists use old-fashioned pen and ink before filling in using water-based colours and brushes made from soft cow and reindeer hair. They begin with a first layer of the lightest paints, then progress to a second darker

and a third darker still, before adding the gilding.

They must fire the piece after each stage and the gold must be polished. At the end, all the painters gather to quality-check one another's work. A plate can take between one and two days; a tureen up to two weeks.

When Sørensen first began working for Royal Copenhagen in the 1960s, its main markets were made up of the US, UK and Scandinavia. For Federicia's generation, Asia (predominantly Taiwan, Japan and South Korea) is a growing market, along with the Middle East and Russia. Sales are on the up and, fittingly given the company's royal roots, each year it supplies the Danish queen with about 50 Christmas gift plates.

When Sørensen says she plans to retire in the near future, panic flashes across her apprentice's face. "Oh, no, I can't work on my own yet. But I will probably spend the rest of my life doing this. It has become a second home. Judith and I are different but we enjoy each other's company."

When asked whether she can foresee a time when she might introduce her own innovations, Fredericia shakes her head vigorously: "No, no. My work shows my personality but for me, it will always be about honouring what Judith has taught me." — (M)

WINNING CAST LONDON

Preface: At a small workshop in London's Hatton Garden jewellery district, master goldsmith Gareth Harris oversees the production of fine metalwork while passing on artisanal skills to his apprentice, Stavros Constantinou.

Company: Smith & Harris
Location: London
Founded: 1981
Number of employees when founded: 2
Number of employees now: 3
Start-up cost: £2,000
Number of premises: 1
Bestselling product: Tumbler cup

———

Quote: *'Considering the people we deal with, trust is a huge part of the business'*

Master goldsmith Gareth Harris is rummaging for a twig in a box of solid gold, baling twine and cast-silver frogs – the inspiration for his latest project. The twig, which fell onto his head during a walk in London's Highgate Wood, has been transformed into a solid-silver reproduction that retains the fine grain of the original. Soon it will be crafted into a belt buckle and sold on Savile Row. "In our private work we can afford an element of play," says Harris. "Play is where you push yourself and discover where you want to be."

Harris has earned the right to experiment having been based in Hatton Garden, London's jewellery quarter, since 1981. There is a tradition of skilled metalworking in the district stretching back 1,000 years: armourers equipped the Knights Templar from nearby Fetter Lane and the machine gun was invented here. "Some of the tools we use are more than 400 years old," says Harris.

Another constant in the trade is apprenticeship, a tradition that stretches back for as long as the involvement of the Goldsmiths' Company guild, which has regulated the industry here since 1300. When we meet Harris's current apprentice, Stavros Constantinou, he is carefully bending a piece of silver. He turns to his master and asks him to check the results as the edge of the metal

has risen irregularly with the stresses of the process. Harris peers at the buckle. "I think we keep the imperfections," Harris says approvingly.

The firm has also worked with artists, creating work for them in silver and gold. These collaborations started with the Swiss-German artist Rolf Sachs and other commissions have followed. Constantinou has also been involved in technical work for the likes of Damien Hirst and Marc Quinn.

Constantinou arrived at the firm in 2004 following a degree in jewellery and silversmithing at London Metropolitan University. There he studied under Harris's co-founder, Dennis Smith, and first visited the workshop to finish his final-year piece: a church lantern (his uncle is a Greek orthodox priest). He impressed with his skill and character. "Considering the sort of people we deal with and the nature of our materials, trust is a huge part of the business," says Harris.

Constantinou's education contrasts markedly with Harris's more formal training: first a one-year pre-apprenticeship and then a five-year contract with Padgett & Braham, a gold and silver box maker. This was 1975 and a long way from the Victorian boom years. The industry was on the wane and only one of the other five apprentices Harris trained with

got jobs. But the decline led to the trade restructuring into its current form where, according to Harris, "We've gone back to a pre-Victorian model with lots of small workshops, all interrelated."

Harris encourages Constantinou to talk about his inspirations. Constantinou studied Mayan metalwork and enjoys making big pieces, looking to create an "innocence" in his work. Harris's own innovation is proved by a number of pieces he produces from his safe to illustrate his point: a series of "tumbler cups" so called for their ability to withstand the rigours of stagecoach travel. Harris has modernised the design by adding a lattice-work base.

This complex play of ideas, technologies and histories is working for the goldsmiths' trade in London. One-time competitors in Paris and Augsburg have seen their ancient structures fall away and yet the Goldsmiths' Company in London has invested £17.5m in the Goldsmiths' Centre, a training facility with subsidised workshops that opened in 2012.

On whether Constantinou is ready to strike out alone, Harris is candid. "There's no question. But it's a dreadfully expensive way of life here. It's a matter of managing your artistic temperament and the hard economic factors. Setting up on your own is always a leap of faith." — (M)

LOOKING AHEAD
PARIS

Preface: The demand for Maison Bonnet's beautiful handmade spectacles shows no sign of abating. That means that skills developed over the course of more than 80 years need to be passed on to the next generation – which is where apprentice Arnaud Falce comes in.

Company: Maison Bonnet
Location: Paris
Founded: 1930, though the Maison Bonnet brand came into being in 1950
Number of employees when founded: 6
Number of employees now: 10
Number of premises: 2
Family members involved: 4

———

Quote: *'An apprentice is essential: a custodian of a dying craft'*

In the dimly lit basement atelier of bespoke eyewear firm Maison Bonnet, Franck Bonnet deftly bends a tortoiseshell spectacle frame into shape over an open flame. His apprentice, Arnaud Falce, eagerly watches the procedure – just one of more than 36 steps involved in crafting a pair of handmade Maison Bonnet glasses.

Each pair requires up to six hours of manual labour for acetate pairs, eight hours for horn and up to 30 hours for tortoiseshell. Over the years the company's *haute lunetterie* approach has found fans in the form of clients that have included Le Corbusier, Yves Saint Laurent and Jacqueline Kennedy; all were undeterred by prices that today start at about €850 – and a waiting list of up to four months.

Founded in the 1930s by Alfred Bonnet, the spectacle maker is now run by the third and fourth generations of the family – Christian Bonnet and his two sons Franck and Steven – across two ateliers: one in the remote village of Sens, found to the southeast of Paris, and the other on Rue des Petits Champs in the capital, where Franck is based.

Maison Bonnet claims to be one of the last makers of tortoiseshell frames and Christian has been awarded the rank of *maître d'art*, an accolade granted by France's culture ministry and

held by an exclusive circle of just over 100 craftsmen.

It is these exacting standards of craftsmanship that made Falce decide it was the only place in the world he wanted to work when he graduated top of his optometry degree class. Knowing he was up against stiff global competition – the legendary firm fields apprenticeship requests from all over the world – he took a gung-ho approach. After bombarding Maison Bonnet with letters and phone calls, his persistency paid off.

"Christian agreed to meet me if I made and brought a pair of handmade glasses," says Falce. "My attempt in wood was a complete joke by Christian's standards but he said it was a good first try and took me on in his atelier in Sens."

Falce stayed there for a year until Franck spotted his potential and moved him to the Paris atelier – which is where, under Franck's tutelage, he has worked ever since. "My father's workshop is in a village in the middle of nowhere and the fact that Arnaud left his family to move there showed his dedication," says Franck. "That, combined with his technical expertise in optometry, means I can put him in front of clients to do the fittings, which include measuring the face in great detail."

Franck's own apprenticeship with his father Christian

began when he was 18 years old. This was an era when work was a tougher affair: mistakes were not tolerated and perfection was expected rather than commended. It's as a result of his own experience that Franck makes sure he is generous with praise to his new generation of apprentices and it's something that Falce appreciates. "He is very patient, just like a teacher," he says.

Franck, who is a paternal figure in the atelier, sees this careful tutelage as his duty. Since the onslaught of industrialisation in the 1950s, the art of making glasses by hand has slowly become endangered. As one of the last survivors, Maison Bonnet feels a strong sense of responsibility to pass on the knowledge to its apprentices.

The firm has not bought tortoiseshell since the 1970s (when it was made illegal to produce new batches) but still has enough stock left over to keep producing for some years. "Hardly anyone knows how to work with tortoiseshell anymore," says Franck. "It's so difficult and my father is terrified that the knowledge will cease to exist.

"An apprentice such as Arnaud is essential: he will be a custodian of a dying craft. He is also someone I have to hand over all my family secrets to. I must trust him completely." — (M)

01/04

Making the best of things
How to combine craft and graft
by Aisha Speirs

PREFACE: Craft and traditional skills are helping reinvigorate economies and shake up old business models across the globe by putting the means of production back into the hands of small-scale makers. Whether you're an ideas person looking to grow a world-class company or simply a skilled individual looking to make a little extra income, the craft movement is showing that a little know-how goes a very long way.

For a brief moment, I'm going to encourage you to put this book down and take a look around at the things that you treasure. Perhaps there's a worn and utterly incongruous ornament passed down through generations of your family, a tattered matchbox from a bar in the backstreets of a foreign city where you had a night you don't want to forget or even a scruffy stovetop espresso maker beloved for its ability to kick-start your day.

I suspect that you didn't log in to check a bank balance nor begin gazing fondly at a framed certificate of academic achievement. Most often, the things that mean something to us are tactile. They're objects with a smell, a texture and a weight. Much of their value may be sentimental but often they also embody a sense of craft – they've been given, found or made by someone else.

Craft plays an important role in the world of business. Just take a look at the success of New York-based website Etsy, launched in 2005. The online marketplace is now home to around one million artisans selling everything from artwork and furniture to jewellery, clothing and an assortment of handmade curios. It has garnered universal approval and is proof that consumers enjoy buying products from the hands that made them. It also shows that in kitchens, gardens and garages across the globe, people are devoting more of their time to craft.

In the UK, small businesses such as Wool and the Gang and By Hand London have picked up on the resurgence of home manufacturing. Both brands design clothing pieces sold as craft kits (Wool and the Gang produces an assortment of knitted pieces while By Hand offers dress patterns) that are bought by amateur knitters and sewers. Wool and the Gang has seen such success that it is now incorporating the talents of its knitting fans into the production cycle. The company sells products that have been made at home from customers' kits and then shares the profits on each piece with the product's maker. The firm has received £1.6m in seed funding from investors who see the potential of the business model.

Despite his piety and instructional tone, Victorian writer and godfather to the arts-and-crafts movement John Ruskin got it right when he said that "the highest reward for a man's toil is not what he gets for it but what he becomes by it". His belief that craft's value is greater than its price remains true to this day. In the 1980s, tucked away in the small and sleepy town of Greenwood, Mississippi, local Fred Carl Jr – then in the construction business – set about designing the perfect cooking range for his wife. Now the Viking Range is one of the most respected options on the market and for Carl's hometown, located in one of the poorest regions of one of the poorest states in the US, Carl's product has proven to be an economic lifeline.

While surrounding towns have struggled to keep their shops open and their populations intact, Greenwood has managed both. Employing a considerable number of local residents at Viking's factory, Carl plowed much of the company's profits into repairing Greenwood. That included the restoration of old buildings and shopfronts to lease out to small businesses and the building of a hotel and cooking school on Main Street to draw in visitors.

That said, having initially restored a building for Viking's office, Carl didn't set out to transform the whole town. However, having seen the effect of his work on one street, the project developed. The result? A successful business that has rejuvenated a town and its residents, all thanks to the success of a well-crafted product. Now home to charming restaurants, a welcoming independent bookstore and a dynamic architecture practice, Carl's investment in Greenwood has set the tone for the town as a place where things can be made.

Viking has set a fantastic example but it's not just big companies based in small towns that can have an impact. Small businesses choosing to make things in big cities have the ability to rejuvenate crafts that are threatened with extinction. For example, when New

York-based art director and designer Anna Karlin launched her eponymous furniture line she spent months sourcing craftsmen and artisans who could make the detailed brass, wood and glass pieces that she drew up. The result is a range of objects designed and manufactured entirely by specialists all over New York. Customers know where their pieces have been made and relish the fact that each one has a sense of place. Meanwhile, Karlin is able to keep track of the quality of each object without having to travel far from her busy studio. While it might have been cheaper to outsource the manufacturing of these pieces, Karlin benefits from having developed a network of makers who can quickly adapt to her various design needs.

The visibility of a company that makes things can inspire people in a way that a successful bank or law firm can't. While a visit to your financial planner or solicitor serves a purpose, it's rarely an exciting trip. But a visit to a company that makes your beloved sofa or a long-lasting pair of boots can touch a valuable nerve. A number of companies have cracked onto the benefits of sharing their manufacturing process with customers. Family-run silversmith Carrs in Sheffield, UK, Austrian shoemaker Ludwig Reiter and luggage company Globe-Trotter (which produces its vulcanised fireboard cases in Hertfordshire, UK) all regularly invite customers to visit their factories. By involving consumers in the craftsmanship that goes into making their quality products, these companies are not only making their reasonably high price tags easier to accept but also giving customers a sense of ownership over the brand, which in turn fosters loyalty and returning business.

Passing down these craft skills and supporting the schools and universities that teach them are as important to the business world as the schools that turn out graduates with MBAs. In the city of Bandung that lies on the western part of the Indonesian island of Java, entrepreneurship is thriving thanks to a combination of manufacturing and education. Central to Indonesia's clothing output, large factories and family-run cottage industries exist alongside some of the country's most prestigious design-and-technology schools. Surrounded by various scales of businesses making objects and clothing, students graduating from a university in Bandung are encouraged to stay in the city to set up shop, spurred on by the experience and success of the makers around them.

Having established itself as a city known for mass-producing goods that would eventually end up carrying the labels of international brands, Bandung is now home to hundreds of small-scale

fashion and design companies carving out a name for themselves and the city. The younger generations set to inherit their family's cottage industry are taking the skills they have grown up with and combining them with a greater knowledge of the marketplace to forge their own designs, brands and stores; the design graduates of the respected Bandung Institute of Technology are staying put. Capitalising on the production facilities and know-how around them, they're ensuring that the city's maker infrastructure is thriving for future generations by not only preserving Bandung's existing creative culture but also attracting more young designers to invest in the city.

The Indonesian government has recognised the impact that craft and manufacturing companies can have on the overall economy. In 2011, it founded the Ministry of Creative Economy, which was combined with the existing Ministry of Tourism. Supporting Indonesia's traditional craft industries – such as *batik* and woodwork – as well as younger tech start-ups is a valuable investment. In the Grand Indonesia shopping mall, home to some of Jakarta's most prestigious shops, is Alun-Alun, a store selling everything from Indonesian food to antiques, home goods and luxury fashion. Teeming with locals and international visitors, the shop is testament to the power of the country's craft business. The businesses in Indonesia that make things are valued for their direct contribution to GDP as well as being seen as an important driver of tourism.

Of course, not everyone is going to find success making things. Yet the moment that parents dread – when their offspring, treated to copious amounts of time and money in preparation for a stable and successful job, announce that they have chosen to pursue a career in woodwork or needlepoint – needn't be seen as so awful an outcome. Taking up an apprenticeship with a craftsman or enrolling in an artisanal course can promise as solid a career as any traditional university degree. The specialist skills of craftsmen such as Germany's *Zimmerer* (traditional carpenters known for their uniform of corduroy waistcoats) are in demand in countries all over the world. While a job in a bank might offer an assuring sign-on bonus, training as a chef or shoemaker is unlikely to leave you jobless if the economy takes a turn for the worse.

Countries that have preserved and supported their manufacturing sector (in Europe, this award goes to Germany) tend to weather tough times better than those that haven't. Plus, craftsmen heading to a studio to make something are doing far more for their mental health than office workers who stare at computer screens all day. But perhaps the best thing about a craft-based career is that it's really never too late to start. Take an evening class in leatherworking or cabinetry and maybe it will give you enough of a jolt to quit the nine-to-five and rely on putting your own two hands to work; or, if that is a leap too far, turn your hobby into a bit of extra cash. Get involved with companies that rely on small-scale home manufacturing such as Wool and the Gang, set up a stall at the next local craft fair or stay at home and join one million other artisans with an Etsy account. From full-scale manufacturing to specialist craftwork, there's business to be made with a hands-on approach. — (M)

Where to have a go at using your hands

1 **International Culinary Center, New York**
From perfecting the art of coffee making to practising charcuterie skills and bread baking, New York's International Culinary Center offers several "serious amateur" courses that will give your kitchen skills a substantial upgrade – and you won't have to quit your day job.

2 **Fungus Workshop, Hong Kong**
Love handcrafted leather pieces? Learn to make your own at this cosy studio in Hong Kong's Sheung Wan.

3 **Agrarian Kitchen, Tasmania**
If living off the land is a fantasy of yours, head to Australia where former food editor Rodney Dunn and his wife Séverine run farm-based cooking classes.

4 **Ceramics, Japan**
Spend a month in Japan to learn how to make your own ceramics pieces. For simple porcelain items for daily use, head to Arita; learn how to master the efficient, compact wood-fire kiln in Mashiko.

5 **New Legacy School of Woodworking, Bangor, Wales**
Located in picturesque north Wales, this school aims to fill the gap left by a decline in traditional apprenticeship models and offers modular courses that run all-year-round.

CLEAN LINES
GÜTERSLOH

Preface: Running a family business doesn't mean having to stay small. German white-goods producer Miele is still run by the same two families that founded it in 1899 but today it employs thousands. The key to success? Staying local and keeping its expertise concentrated.

Company: Miele
Location: Gütersloh, Germany
Founded: 1899
Number of employees: 17,251
Number of premises: 12
Bestselling product: vacuum cleaners, with around two million units produced each year

Quote: *'We are educated to think in terms of generations, not only in our products but also our employees'*

Carl Miele and Reinhard Zinkann set up a workshop to manufacture butter churns for northern German farms in 1899. They would have fallen off their milking stools to learn that over a century later their great-grandsons would still control the family business – one that now has over 17,000 employees, 12 manufacturing plants and a domestic product range that warrants over 400 catalogue pages.

A white-goods Goliath, Miele has never cut corners on quality or compromised on price by offshoring outside Europe. Ninety per cent of product manufacturing, including washing machines, fridges, vacuum cleaners and ovens, is still carried out in Germany – the company's headquarters are in Gütersloh, just a few kilometres from the original workshop in Herzebrock-Clarholz.

"At the time, our ancestors didn't know there were at least 40 other butter-churn manufacturers in the surrounding area," says Markus Miele, joint managing director and co-owner of Miele. Despite this, the founders persisted and just two years after they launched the company, the men invented the product that would be the making of the company: the Meteor washing machine.

Markus – and Reinhard Zinkann, the managing director who heads up sales – were never expected to join the firm. When both Markus and Zinkann were ready they were made aware of the handover process that was set in motion by the founders' sons – their grandfathers.

"We have written rules in the family that state you first have to attend an outside business for at least two years to prove leadership, knowledge and skills. Maybe our grandfathers also had it in mind that it would be better that other companies pay for our first mistakes," says Zinkann with a chuckle. "We are educated to think in terms of generations, not only in our products but also our

02

01   03

employees, ourselves and everything we do – it helps being independent."

Perhaps not the immediate image that comes to mind when asked to think of a family business devoted to craft, it's refreshing to see a multinational, multi-billion-euro company such as Miele hold fast to the ideals of the very craftsmen who founded the business in a small village nearby. — (M)

Family affair:
"Family companies have a very important advantage in that they can concentrate on the long-term strength of their business instead of having to take the often short-term interests of external financiers into consideration. They don't think merely in terms of quarterly reports but rather in generations. Further, they are also risking their own money and not that of external shareholders; this leads to maintaining a sense of proportion rather than taking a hectic or overconfident approach."
– *Markus Miele*

01
Markus Miele, joint managing director and co-owner
02
Exterior of the Gütersloh factory
03
Dishwashers en route to a distributor
04
Dr Rüdiger Hellenkamp in electronics
05
Drums being transported to assembly
06
Hand-assembling washing machine frontages

04   05

06

07

08

09

Carl Miele
1869 - 1938

Reinhard Zinkann
1869 - 1939

12

10

13

07
Miele fire
brigade
08
Testing the
electronics
09
Handling parts
for washing
machines
10
Drums ready
for assembly

11
Jochen Menke,
a guide at
the factory
12
Busts of the
founders
13
Vintage Miele
vacuum cleaner
14
Miele's own
freight train

11

14

SECOND NATURE
JELS

Preface: For Dinesen, wooden-plank manufacturing is a family concern that spans five generations. Its use of the highest-quality materials allied to a commitment to craftsmanship and passion for wood and nature have kept the family business going strong.

Company: Dinesen
Location: Jels, Denmark
Founded: 1898
Number of employees: 85
Number of premises: 5

Quote: *'It's important to have an honesty in what we communicate. As long as the values are consistent then I am happy'*

Imagine you are the fifth generation of a family firm with a hard-won global reputation for supplying hand-finished wooden planks of the most fastidious quality, used to floor the dining room at Noma, London's Saatchi Gallery, the private homes of notable architects and sundry royal palaces. Not only that but you also share your first name with three of the five heads of your family.

One imagines you would either be inclined to preserve your company in amber out of sheer terror or embark upon a revolution to impose your will. But, wisely, Hans Peter Dinesen is charting a middle course in his role as art director of the company in question: Dinesen, which is based in the small rural community of Jels in southern Jutland, Denmark.

"Over the past few decades my mother [Heidi] and father [Thomas] created a strong clarity for our brand in our promotional material based on these large, wide planks with a minimalist, Nordic aesthetic," says Hans Peter, referring to the mighty oak and Douglas fir planks, up to 15 metres long and 50cm wide, on which the company built its reputation.

"That clarity isn't limiting: it means that we can diversify with the same clarity. Instead of restricting ourselves to one aesthetic I want to emphasise the possibilities of nature, the beauty of imperfection."

That sense lies deep in Hans Peter's DNA. "In our family we have always spoken about trees. My first paid job here was weeding the yard when I was 13. It was always me who my school friends would come to when they needed wood to build a camp."

Dinesen has grown steadily since Thomas and Heidi took over in 1989 – it has also successfuly recorded a profit every year since the economic crisis of 2008. Hans Peter claims to feel no pressure when it comes to the responsibility of taking charge, instead "only privilege that I can carry on the

01

02

03   04

legacy of telling people about the infinite variety in nature".

"The most important thing has always been that our customers are satisfied," says his father. "It's important to have an honesty in what we communicate. As long as the values are consistent then I am happy." — (M)

Family affair:
"Over the past couple of years, I've had great opportunities as an art director for my family's firm. While redesigning and retelling our history I stumbled upon a lot of interesting work and ideas from my ancestors. Merging my ancestors' ideas with my father's visions into a new visual identity was an eye-opening experience. Working alongside my father and the company he built with my mother gives me great joy. I feel a responsibility to maintain our healthy values but also to look in new directions and constantly educate myself about the world around me."
– *Hans Peter Dinesen*

05

09

01
Hans Peter (left) and his father Thomas inspecting oak planks
02
Dinesen headquarters in Jels, Jutland
03
Oak cross section used to print PR material
04
Architectural model made from Dinesen's high-quality wooden planks

05
Exterior of the Dinesen administration offices
06
Work bench on the hand-finishing line
07
Hans Peter gets to work on new PR material
08
At the timber yard
09
Lake behind the factory

07

06   08

CLEAN SWEEP
VILA DO CONDE

Preface: Soap manufacturer Ach Brito may be a relatively small global player but with its loyal customer base and a new generation ready to take up the reins, the future smells sweeter than ever.

Company: Ach Brito
Location: Vila do Conde, Portugal
Founded: 1918
Number of employees: 50
Number of premises: 2
Family members involved: fourth-generation Aquiles Brito
Bestselling product: Citron Verbena Claus Porto bath soap

———

Quote: *'It's important to start the next generation on the lowest rung of the ladder'*

For Aquiles Brito (*bottom, on right*), the sweet smell of success is a daily occurrence. As the owner of family-run Portuguese soap maker Ach Brito, his typical workday sees him surrounded with the aromas of almond, honeysuckle and wild orchid, a few of the scents offered in his brand's line of toiletries that well-groomed locals have used for generations.

"We've been through the Great Depression, World Wars and the [Carnation] Revolution with customers," says Brito, dipping his nose into a mixer to sniff the lemony notes wafting out of the machine. "It's an intimate relationship – after all, our products end up in people's bathrooms."

Founded in 1918 by Brito's great-grandfather, the company's range includes bathing and laundry soaps, a popular lavender fragrance first sold in the 1920s and even a speciality soap made with pine tar for people who suffer from eczema. Tradition is taken seriously at the company, with several mechanical machines from the 1940s favoured over fancier automated production.

"There are no computer viruses to worry about," says Brito, pointing to a sorting machine with its engine hissing and thumping as it guides rectangular-cut bars along at a pedestrian pace for packaging. "We aren't after 24/7 production. Most soaps are still wrapped by staff. It goes from their hands to the customers' hands."

This approach has been a safe bet for the company's bottom line – revenues top €5m a year with the brand expanding overseas in recent years with its premium collection of Claus Porto bars made from natural ingredients, individually wrapped and sealed with wax.

Operating in a sector dominated by multinational conglomerates, Ach Brito's philosophy (and future) is grounded in its family set-up. "To prepare the next generation you need to be careful – they can be used to having too much money," says Brito. "It's

02

01   03

important to start them on the lowest rung of the ladder – they need to work at the warehouse and then move up."

With two sons it would seem that the future of Brito's company is in good hands but the fourth-generation soapmaker doesn't have expectations. "I don't want to put any pressure on them to run the business; they have to decide. It's a company that was founded in 1918 and as the owner you feel an obligation to carry on this tradition. The family name is the company and consumers treat your products differently because behind it is a story and a family." — (M)

Family affair:
"Staying in the same family's hands has been a success for us. But while it's important to acknowledge our heritage as a strength, looking back on the past is not the way a business continues to be successful. Success is built on hard work, which requires us to constantly look for ways to improve."
– *Aquiles Brito*

04 05

06 07

08

09

01
José Fernandes (left) and Aquiles Brito
02
Freshly made soap cut on assembly line
03
Paste is mixed with natural dyes and aromatic oils

04
Soap goes through a refiner, is heated to 70c then moves through a vacuum chamber
05
Wooden drying racks
06
Soap balls

07
Ach Brito factory
08
Staff wrap the bars by hand
09
Ach Brito's old-fashioned wrapping

FEAT OF CLAY
HATTING

Preface: Thanks to a unique combination of father-son skills and its presence at headline-making Danish restaurant Noma, ceramics firm KH Würtz has evolved as an international success.

Company: KH Würtz
Location: Hatting, Denmark
Founded: 1981; restarted in 2000
Number of employees when founded: 1
Number of employees now: 6
Number of premises: 1
Family members involved: 2
Start-up cost: €53,500
Bestselling product: dinner plates

Quote: *'I grew up with my father's aesthetic; it's part of my DNA'*

At Copenhagen's Noma and other highly ranked Scandinavian restaurants, the avant-garde cuisine isn't all that's new and Nordic – so is the rough-hewn crockery. Each piece is uniquely handcrafted by father and son Aage and Kasper Würtz.

As a teenager in the 1970s, Aage apprenticed at one of many potteries then thriving in Jutland on the Danish mainland, before becoming foreman of a ceramic lamp studio. In 1981 he started his own tableware workshop but as aesthetics shifted to minimalist white, factory-made porcelain, Aage took a career detour teaching at a primary school. In 2000, as handcrafted ceramics returned to favour, he was back at the potter's wheel.

At this time his son Kasper was studying Danish literature at Aarhus University but found himself drawn to ceramics. He soon left the academic world to join his father, learning throwing and firing techniques on the job. In the KH Würtz division of labour, Aage's forte is wheel-turning, producing assured shapes with just the right curves. Kasper has made advances of his own in the glazing process, giving Würtz-ware its characteristic hues and speckling. Critically, he's also added marketing and merchandising to the resurgent family business.

"I grew up with my father's aesthetic; it's part of my DNA," says Kasper. "Working together in a small studio, we can rely on a family shorthand to know what we mean. In addition, we don't have the usual workplace constraints about when or how to criticise each other's work. That, we sometimes do too easily. My son and daughter will be free to choose whatever future they like but we would be pleased to welcome them into the family business one day."

In 2004, Noma's owner-chef René Redzepi received a KH Würtz dish as a gift and asked to see more. Kasper promptly loaded 25 samples into his van, drove to Copenhagen and spread out the goods for Redzepi in the car park outside Noma. A large order resulted and Würtz-ware

01
Aage and Kasper Würtz
02
Former dairy farm adjacent to the workshop
03
Trimming the base of a bowl with a loop
04
Glazing process

05
Kasper at work
06
Applying the Würtz signature
07
Bowls are fired for eight to 10 hours
08
Firing kiln
09
Finished bowls

02

01   03

soon became part of the restaurant's brand identity.

Other restaurants around the world began placing orders and father and son found themselves at the forefront of an emerging tableware protocol, with an emphasis on rustic crockery that suits modern tastes.

Kasper says he and his father "aim to approximate the organic and the natural" in a process that involves mastery at the wheel and a deliberate courting of randomness when glazing. "It takes all our efforts but we do it because the results are beautiful," he says. "That's why we're glad to be working with chefs. Like us they're intuitive and favour an organic aesthetic." — (M)

Family affair:
"At the outset I envisioned problems but I find it fantastic working with my son. I taught him to make the best dishes possible and now we challenge each other without competing. The efforts we make to advance our work are done for each other."
– *Aage Würtz*

04 05

06

07

08 09

MORE IN STORE
SHAFTESBURY

Preface: The traditional village shop is not just a place to pick up groceries – it can also be the social heart of a community. That's the case with Semley Village Stores, a co-operative providing essential services and inspiring its locals with an inclusive approach.

Company: Semley Village Stores
Location: Shaftesbury, UK
Founded: 2012
Number of employees when founded: 1
Number of employees now: 31 (1 paid and 30 volunteers)
Number of premises: 1
Bestselling product: Mrs Mack's organic poppy-seed dressing

Quote: *'There are lots of people in the village who bake for the shop'*

There was a time when every English village had a post office, a pub, a church and a general store. But supermarkets and high rents have conspired against local businesses – so many have closed as customers climb into their cars to buy groceries elsewhere. The community of Semley in the Wiltshire countryside suffered similarly until villagers decided it was time to revive their local shop.

"We called a public meeting to begin with to see if there was any interest and about 50 people turned up," says committee member Pene Cairns. "Of course, there were a lot of sceptics but we ploughed on. We raised some money and one from the group bought the premises. There was a lot to learn."

Around a year later Semley Village Stores opened its doors, selling local produce, bread and basics such as baked beans and tomato ketchup. With the help of a nearby interior designer, Cairns has created a warm, cosy take on the classic English shop – wooden boxes of fresh vegetables and baskets of fruit sit in the window and locals can buy stamps, drop off dry cleaning and drink coffee in the shop's café. "It's created a centre for the community," says Cairns. "People see each other when they didn't before – unless they happened to attend church, of course."

"It's very much appreciated by the village," says Lal Poynter, the manager and the shop's only salaried employee, as she explains a critical part of Semley's supply chain: locals are paid for supplying cakes and other produce for the shop. "We try and have local suppliers – as near as possible. There's lots of people in the village who bake for the shop. We're not a deli. We're not strictly organic either. We're a neighbourhood shop selling good food."

The shop is also tech-savvy. Customers can order online, sign up to volunteer, check the community noticeboard for upcoming events or simply donate some money to the

01

02 03

04

01
Volunteers Maureen Masters (left) and Mary Anne Mackaness
02
Honey and walnut sourdough
03
Bacon and mushroom tarts
04
Shoppers stocking up
05
View of the store from the street
06
The shop has space for a sit-down
07
View of Saint Leonard's Church from the shop

shop's coffers. They can also peruse the strict rules for membership that clearly state that "Semley Shop Limited exists in order to carry out business for the benefit of the community [not] for anyone's private benefit".

Semley is a project that's part of a wider move away from supermarket dependency and is changing the shape of village life. "Our philosophy is you don't travel," says Cairns. "If you've run out of sugar you don't get into your car, you walk to your village shop." — (M)

Why it works:
Semley is staffed by volunteers – and stocked with them in mind. If its members ask for a service or a product, more often than not they get it. Its co-operative structure is changing the buying habits of the village while fostering loyalty and community spirit.

05

06

07

SOCIAL NETWORK TOKYO, VANCOUVER

Preface: Creating a successful business doesn't have to mean going solo. It's lonely at the top so why not take a few – thousand – like-minded friends along? These co-ops in Japan and Canada have thrived by making a virtue of their members' passion.

01 03

Company: Pal System Consumers' Cooperative Union
Location: Tokyo
Founded: 1977
Number of employees: 3,357
Number of premises: 8 warehouses and 62 shipping centres
Deliveries per week: 800,000
Co-op members when founded: 38,000
Co-op members now: 1.38 million
Bestselling product: Konsen milk from dairy farms in Hokkaido

Not many grocery outlets give tours of pig farms but Pal System Consumers' Cooperative Union isn't just any retailer. Since 1977 the Tokyo-based co-op has tried to change the way consumers in Japan shop for food and how farmers produce it – without a single store.

With 1.38 million members across eastern and central Japan, Pal System has shown that a grocery delivery service can be an alternative to the supermarket. The co-op has grown from 15 groups of consumers in the Tokyo metropolitan area into one of the largest of Japan's 590 co-operatives, with sales of around ¥190bn a year.

Pal System has never posted a financial loss. How does it thrive in a market saturated with speciality grocers and convenience-store chains? "We reveal how products are made and who makes them," says Pal System spokesman Shinji Ueda.

The co-op charges customers up to ¥2,000 to come into the fold. Every two weeks a catalogue is delivered featuring rice and vegetables grown on organic farms, additive-free meats and eco-friendly detergents.

The real boon for members are the field trips; the co-op organises 12 a year, to pig farms in Akita prefecture and paddy fields in Niigata. "It allows us to hear what consumers want and forces us to explain the methods we use," says Kazuyuki Kusama, who tends 18 hectares of paddy fields in northern Japan.

That attentiveness stretches beyond any remit that most retailers would recognise. When the Fukushima nuclear disaster contaminated farms that sell to Pal System, the co-op took a stand against nuclear energy. It provided an example of how co-operatives, free from the need to please investors, can become advocates for consumers. — (M)

Why it works:
Pal System has fostered fierce loyalty with a transparent process that gives customers an appreciation of how their food is grown. Farm tours narrow the gap between city and rural dwellers, making farmers more responsive to consumers and increasing their awareness of the market.

04

05

01
Trucks bear the Pal mascot, Konsen-kun
02
Eggs are from hens fed on rice mixed with feed
03
Pal's bestselling Konsen milk is pasteurised at low temperatures
04
Grocery items for delivery are sorted by hand
05
Preparing deliveries at the distribution centre

Company: Mountain Equipment Co-op
Location: Vancouver
Founded: 1971
Number of employees when founded: the co-op originally operated with volunteers and 1 paid employee
Number of employees now: 1,716
Number of premises: 17 stores and a campus outpost, distribution centre and head office
Co-op members: 4.1 million

According to company lore, Mountain Equipment Co-op was conceived while four Vancouver friends were waiting out a storm in their tent during a climb on Mount Baker in Washington State.

A year later, in 1971, they founded MEC with the goal of making quality outdoor gear available to Canadian climbers at a minimal mark-up. The idea was to create a democratically run consumer co-op – one reason why shares could be purchased for only CA$5. MEC is Canada's leading retailer of outdoor recreational gear with 17 stores nationally. Its logo is an iconic feature on any backpacking Canadian's kit.

Although governed by co-op principles, CEO David Labistour points out that MEC's relevance and success has been determined by how well it has competed as a retailer in the North American market. "Our approach [is that] every operational aspect has to be structured as well if not better than our competitors," he says in MEC's Vancouver head office, which used to be a car-parts warehouse.

The scale of the organisation – as many as 80,000 members have voted in board elections – means its profile has become more complex. MEC has diversified into paying for trail maintenance and investing in the preservation of wild places.

The co-operative structure has also fostered a spirit of loyalty among its employees. Matt Armstrong, sales representative from MEC's Vancouver store, has worked for the co-op for over a decade, "We call them the 'velvet handcuffs': it's tough to leave here," he says. "You're selling gear that you love alongside inspirational colleagues." — (M)

Why it works:
With 10 per cent of Canada's population as members and millions of dollars in turnover, MEC has size on its side. The staff, often experienced specialists themselves, engender trust in customers but the organisation's real strength is product development: having a close relationship with buyers means the co-op knows exactly what to put on its shelves.

01 02

01
MEC CEO David Labistour
02
MEC employee Jackie Degoeij
03
Advice is on hand in the co-op's shoe department
04
Inside the cavernous Vancouver store
05
Staff are trusted experts on the equipment sold because they use it themselves
06
The MEC flag, with its iconic logo, flies over downtown Vancouver

03

05

04 06

WRAP
IT UP
JAPAN

Preface: The next stage in your company launch? Create your brand. Here you can read tips on everything from choosing a name to designing a logo – and for an understanding of the importance of packaging, there is no better place to start than Japan.

As country branding goes, is there a better national flag than Japan's? At once graphically crisp and symbolically resonant, it is a triumph of simplicity and instantly recognisable. That the Japanese are so good at branding should not be a surprise: boiling a country or a company down to a single logo is rooted in Japanese culture. Families have been devising their own crests – or *mon* – for centuries. The imperial family has one of the oldest and surely the finest – a stylised chrysanthemum – but the tradition of the aptly designed crest lives on in modern Japan.

Look around and *mon* are everywhere: restaurants, shops and brands often have their own – some new, others years old. Mitsubishi, the name of which literally means "three water chestnuts" (and also "three diamond shapes"), has a logo with three red diamonds that is visually minimal but rich in meaning. Maisen, a popular chain of *tonkatsu* pork-cutlet shops and restaurants, has a classic brown and yellow *mon*

from 1965 that has visiting designers in paroxysms of delight. It can be admired on its own terms as a distinctive logo but it also has a deeper reading since its circles are designed to represent a gurgling spring.

The graphic identity that Japan produced for the Tokyo Olympics in 1964 was brilliant in many respects but one of the greatest contributions was the series of simplified pictograms designed by art director Masaru Katsumi that are now part of the visual vocabulary of the Games. At a single glance, athletes and spectators could identify a range of 20 sports without the need for translation into multiple languages. When asked, Katsumi said that he had simply applied the Japanese practice of designing a crest to the project.

Japan is a country that pays attention to detail; no gift is too humble to be worthy of elaborate wrapping and no purchase too cheap to justify some decent packaging. Has any other nation turned the lunch box into an art form?

01

The Japanese bento is a perfect combination of nutritional and aesthetic balance, perfectly presented in a small, neatly divided container. In convenience stores, even *onigiri* – a rice ball that usually costs no more than ¥130 – is given a wrapper so intricate that it carefully separates the seaweed from the rice to keep it from going soggy on the shelf.

With presentation holding such importance in Japanese gift giving, the converse is also true: a poorly wrapped gift is hardly worth giving. It can seem curious to the outsider: the elaborate confection of *washi* paper and ribbon with only a couple of chocolates inside or the exquisite gift set of canned food from a smart Tokyo supermarket. The point is the gesture and the way it looks and feels.

It helps that, with the exception of fast fashion retailers, wrapping is still standard practice in Japanese shops.

Packaging is a key element for Japanese retail brands but it doesn't start and end with a strong logo and a carrier bag.

Look around Tokyo and brands are wrapping their products in a rich variety of textures, papers and boxes. It is all of a piece with the attentive service and beautiful merchandising.

Rebranding can refresh a weary brand but it can sometimes be superfluous. Why would Top's, makers of retro chocolate cakes, want a new logo when their existing one sits perfectly with the products they've been selling since 1964? When Japan Airlines was being nursed back to economic health recently, one of the best strategic moves was to revive the old corporate logo: the elegant red crane that had been dispensed with in 1989.

From the *kaiseki* to the *kimono*, Japan clearly knows about presentation. Whether it knows how to market itself is a whole other matter. Modesty is another Japanese characteristic and one that sometimes gets in the way of the hard sell. No such problems here: read on for our confident advice on successful branding. — (M)

02

03

04

05

❶

The game of the name
Choosing the right one

Devising a good name is the most fundamental act of branding. Plenty of research needs to be done, especially if you are going for a foreign language or made-up words (a cross-reference in several dozen languages is a must to avoid branding bloopers). Your name should not be solely for one target user: you need a balance between the obvious and the obscure. A family or first name often does the trick.

01
United Arrows
carrier bag
02
Boxed shirt from
Beams menswear
03
Winged Wheel
shopping bags
04
Top's chocolate
cake packaging
05
Marks & Web
bath products

01

03

04   05

❷
Set in tone
Designing a logo

Whether a simple typeface
or an elaborate emblem, your
company has to have a logo.
A strong logo can become the
stamp of your brand and set
the character and tone of your
company. Don't be afraid of
cute – anthropomorphic logos
stick in the mind and make
people smile. For instance, some
of our favourite logos from Italy
are centered around a charming
or intriguing visual talisman:
Agip's six-legged dog or
Bialetti's mustachioed man.

06
Shochu from
Yamatozakura in
Kagoshima
07
Tsutaya book
cover and
carrier bag
08
Wrapping
service at Tokyu
Hands

06   07

❸

Whose hue?
Balancing colours

There is no rule on colour palette and unfortunately our eyes have been made to suffer as a result: many companies have become successful using a bold, brash (and nasty) colour scheme. You should try and think in terms of noise volume: some things need to be quieter than others but on certain occasions you need to turn it up. In the skies, Lufthansa's colour scheme is one of the most successful and always manages to exude good taste. In the 1960s, graphic designer Otl Aicher developed his own yellow (officially known as Ral 1028) for the airline. The warm glow of Lufthansa's exclusive colour emanates friendly service and comfort as well as complementing the more efficient greys or navy blue that are used onboard and online.

09

09
Gift wrapping
is the norm in
Japan
10
A carrying
handle is fitted
11
Wrapping
options at
Tokyu Hands

08

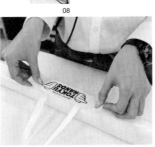

10

11

01
Rusk from
Tsuruya
02
Bento box

03
Takeaway
coffee cups from
(left to right)
Cream of the
Crop Coffee,
Omotesando
Koffee and Be A
Good Neighbor
Coffee Kiosk

Top five designers
Who to commission

Akaoni Design
This studio in Yamagata is led by Motoki Koitabashi. Whether it's a jar of Onuma honey or an illustrated vegetable pamphlet, there's a modern *mingei* (folk) flavour.
akaomi.org

Tomohiro Kato
Talented designer with a feel for Japanese packaging materials. Beautiful, simple work includes cups and bags for Omotesando Koffee (*see page 36*).
ed-ing-post.com

Hidemi Nakaniwa
Refreshingly quiet design. Delicately folded paper and wooden boxes feature in packaging he has designed for organic green tea and Japanese sparklers.
nakaniwadesign.jp

Yurio Seki
Seki has struck gold with earthy designs that combine Japanese craft with a hint of Scandinavia, picked up from time spent studying textiles in Sweden.
salvia.jp

Taku Satoh
One of the biggest names in Japanese graphic design. Consistently strong, clean packaging designs for everyone from Issey Miyake to Cleansui water filters.
tsdo.jp

01

❹
Personality type
Developing an identity

When thinking about what makes your company's brand, try to expand the thought process beyond simply the logo, colour palette, business card and letterhead. Your business needs to have a clear identity. Don't worry – this does not have to be as rigid and formulaic as you might imagine. An expansive and detailed brand identity for a very small business might not be necessary and might even go against the grain of what the company is about. Certain key facets of your brand's identity should have coherence. Choose a reliable and adaptable typeface and stick to it. Identities – and this goes for people as much as it does companies – need personality to thrive and go places.

02

03

04
Incense sticks in
cardboard tube
from Lisn
05
Cosmetics
from Three
06
Ise udon
07
Wrapped
box at Isetan
department store

04   05

❺
Out of order
Making things clear

The entry point to your brand needs to set the right tone. Whether it's a shop front or a homepage, the first-impressions philosophy is exactly the same; only the tools and platforms differ. In the same way that a website can be overloaded with information, a shop or office space can send out confused messages. The material choice is key, from business cards to the lighting level in the reception. Branding should be an interactive experience, after all.

06

07

08

❻
Show time
Integrating your brand

You've created the perfect logo, you have a confident, well-defined brand identity that includes a strong colour palette – now flaunt it! Traditional Japanese and Italian retailers have retained (often unintentionally) strong brands that their international rivals would kill for. This is in part down to saturating their material with tasteful by-products. If you're selling biscuits, be sure to tell people where they were made and where you can buy them. No self-respecting Parisian bakery would fail to include their logo and address on the packaging and this print-heavy approach could work on your brand. Shop uniforms work in the same way: neat, high-quality and comfortable outfits can put people at ease on both sides of the counter.

08
Gift box from Arts & Science
09
Tin of ginger sweets and box of bean paste 'monaka' from Higashiya
10
Hato Sabure dove biscuits

09

10

BRIGHT
IDEAS
GLOBAL

Preface: Branding in action shows
how a good font or logo embeds in
the mind. Simplicity usually wins
out over trickery – but you can have
a bit of fun while you're at it.

01

02

03

04

05

06

06

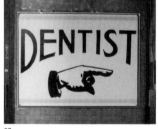

07

08

01
Escuela Taqueria
Mexican restau-
rant, LA
02
Bar in Tokyo's
Omotesando
neighbourhood
03
De Bijenkorf
department
store, Eindhoven
04
White Squirrel
coffee shop,
Toronto
05
Curry Up, Tokyo
06
Deli and bakery,
Cairns, Australia

07
Dentist sign in
Toronto
08
Opticians, Turin
09
Entrance to
Vondelbrug
(Vondelpark),
Amsterdam
10
Tea shop,
Stockholm
11
No-smoking
sign, Lugano,
Switzerland
12
Vitagliano
Fratelli
menswear shop,
Palermo, Italy

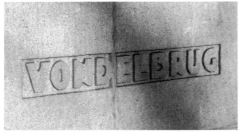

09   10

11   12

13   14   15

16   17

18   19

20
Arthouse Le
Paris, Zürich
21
Yamato
Transport, Tokyo
22
Acme Oyster
House, New
Orleans
23
BioRex cinema,
Helsinki

24
Stefan Paul Zahnärzte
dentist, Zürich
25
City of Rio de Janeiro
sign, Ipanema Beach
26
Aso Bit City model
shop, Tokyo
27
Larmatic alarm sign,
Stockholm

28
Kawiarnia
Tatrzanska
restaurant,
Tarnów, Poland
29
Laundry shop
sign, Stockholm
30
Uncle Torys,
a character from
Suntory whiskey,
Japan

31
Bodmer book-
shop, Zürich
32
The Original
Farmers Market,
LA
33
Borsalino hat
shop, Rapallo,
Italy

30

31

32

34 35

33

36 37

38 39

40

Preface

How do you run a company, a disparate and complex empire or a luxury brand that's at the top of its game? Well there's one way to find out: ask the people who do that every day. Over the following pages we ask great business leaders to tell us how they see their work and how they have risen to the challenges that have shaped their companies. Their answers are revealing: it soon becomes clear that they have all come up with their own very personal business strategies and management techniques. They are not followers. And not one of them relies on business speak; they all talk with an honesty and clarity that we can learn from.

But there are also some more surprising lessons worth remembering, like how being the boss means you can bring your dog to work and why even the most humble CEO should own at least one good jacket.

This is a chapter about lessons – some important ones and some that should make you smile and be rather happy about your place in the world of work. After all, this should be fun.

Contents

3

NEED TO KNOW

All the knowledge you require to succeed

GOOD COMPANY GLOBAL

Preface: Running a new business will constantly provide fresh experiences – and many new surprises, too. But a few simple lessons on how to keep companies happy and healthy should help prepare any new entrepreneur for the challenges ahead.

I

Go for a run
Fitness

It's tough at the top, even if there are only two of you in the business. The hours, the thinking, the takeaways – they take their toll and you need something that will help clear your clogged-up mind. As such, harness the power of a pre-work run. There's something liberating about zipping up a running jacket and tying up your Nikes to head off for a lap of the park (London), palace (Tokyo) or lake (Zürich). OK, maybe not the whole lake.

2

Trust your instincts
Strategy

You plot and scheme, you run over the business plan again and again, but sometimes you have to listen to something else: your heart. The difference between being a plodder and a grower is knowing when to throw the dice on a well-considered gamble. It's taking that second shop when friends say hold on or doubling an order because you just know it will sell. It can't be taught or bought but knowing when to let heart rule head is the thing that successful business folk have in their DNA.

3

Think smart
Wardrobe

A pitfall for fresh young entrepreneurs is an unwise tendency to only dress down. Jeans, trainers and a T-shirt are all well and good but have a pressed shirt ready. More importantly, men and women should have a transformative jacket hanging in the office for those last-minute meetings. Something navy or grey that fits – which can also be packed into a Rimowa and bounced back into action with a determined shake.

4

Make palpable contacts
Business cards

Business cards have been around forever and for good reason: they work. There was a grim moment a few years ago when people tried tricky things with phones to bounce on contact details. But a jacket pocket filled with a handsome batch of numbers after an industry event makes you feel connected. Clients who find yours will feel the same way. Just a small piece of card can lead to all sorts of adventures. And, yes, handy on dates, too.

5

Roll your sleeves up
Team leading

When you start off, do everything from ordering the stationery to helping unload the truck. Make the company grow around you and imprint your business DNA on it all; from fonts to furniture, you need to shape what this enterprise looks like. As your team grows they will admire a boss who expects everyone to work as hard as each other. Lead from the front and you will always know when colleagues are getting it right.

Things to do today:

Make sure all money is now in the account.

Meet the architect – what's his plan for the new space?

Buy the paint and collect the desk.

Oops! Hire a van to do all of the above.

Have lunch with the investor (mum) and graphic-design team (brother) and decide on font and logo.

Make a list of all neighbouring businesses we could partner with.

Get jacket cleaned for the launch.

Run.

Eat well.

6

Say thank you
Etiquette

In the modern office where your every move can be "liked" on social media, you'll find a generation of people who feel they should get a big thumbs-up (and not just an emoticon one) simply for coming to work. But that makes sincere and deserved thank-yous even more valuable. An email is fine, a written note and a bottle of wine is even better. It's funny how many companies lose good staff because they fail to show appreciation. Go on. Be nice.

7

Pick the right space
Location

Before you sign the lease on your first office, pause for one moment. You may be here for a couple of years – do you feel safe? Is there enough natural light? Can you look out of a window? While budgets are undoubtedly constrained you'll need a place where you (and your team) want to linger. Simple things can help create a space that people like working in, including a comfortable chair and a desk that doesn't wobble.

8

Get a dog
Workplace

Running your own company lets you make up the rules as you go along without fear of upsetting the people in human resources. You are in charge. So bring your dog to work to let her entertain you (and hopefully your colleagues), lead you on mind-clearing walks or just curl up by your feet when afternoon stretches into night. A raft of data shows that office dogs make people relaxed and more productive. Who's a good girl, then?

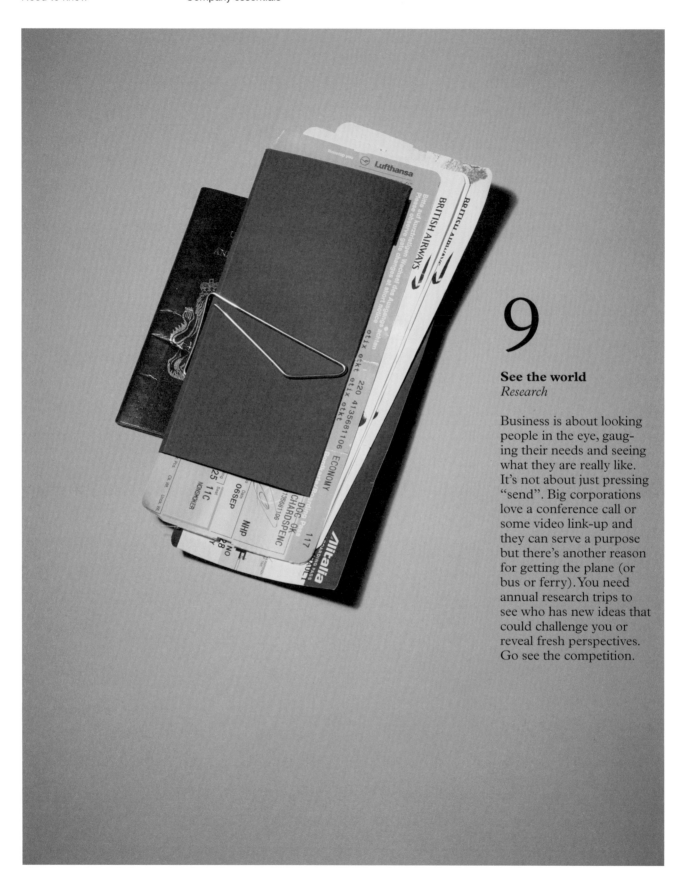

9

See the world
Research

Business is about looking people in the eye, gauging their needs and seeing what they are really like. It's not about just pressing "send". Big corporations love a conference call or some video link-up and they can serve a purpose but there's another reason for getting the plane (or bus or ferry). You need annual research trips to see who has new ideas that could challenge you or reveal fresh perspectives. Go see the competition.

10

Lunch with your team
Meal times

The team that eats together stays together. A sandwich at your desk leads to a chunk of pastrami wedged behind the shift key, greasy fingerprints on the just-finished proposal and the determined odour of brie at work. Stop. Tell your crew to stop. Head to the corner café or share sandwich-making duties in the office. Ideas will spark and friendships will become fixed.

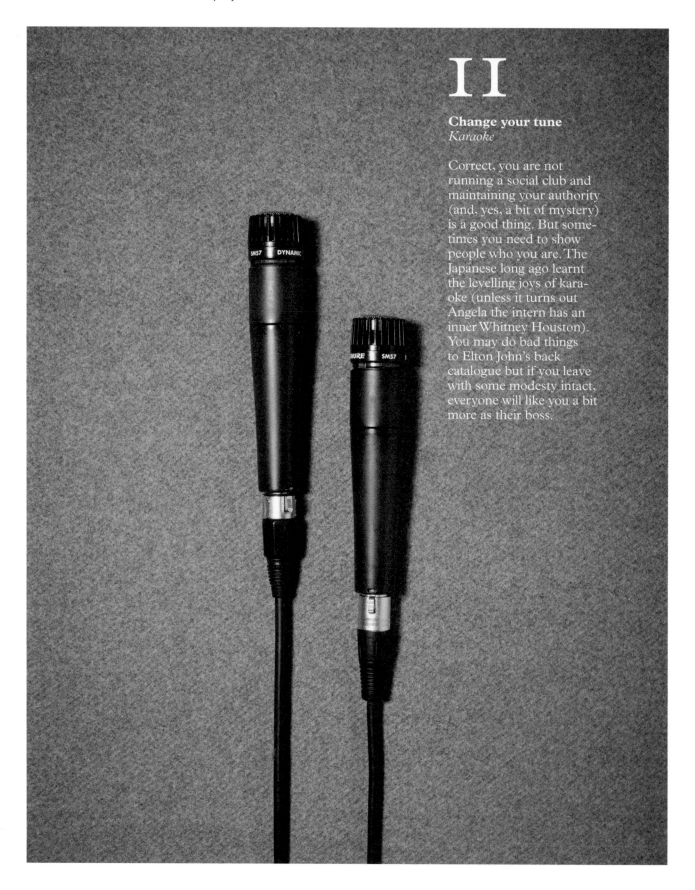

II

Change your tune
Karaoke

Correct, you are not running a social club and maintaining your authority (and, yes, a bit of mystery) is a good thing. But sometimes you need to show people who you are. The Japanese long ago learnt the levelling joys of karaoke (unless it turns out Angela the intern has an inner Whitney Houston). You may do bad things to Elton John's back catalogue but if you leave with some modesty intact, everyone will like you a bit more as their boss.

12

Do it your way
Relaxation

Running your own business is all-consuming and the triumphs and setbacks can reach every part of your life. Perhaps we can't all follow the example of wonderful Italian stores and stick a sign in the real, or proverbial, shop window come August saying that we will not be around for a month but you need the equivalent. Time on a sun lounger, glass in hand, is not just fun (and running a company should be fun) but also restorative.

02/04

Ditch the MBA for Sartre

Why the great thinkers mean good business

by Sophie Grove

PREFACE: The ubiquitous master's in business administration has a lot to answer for when it comes to dull management and unimaginative business models. But there is a world – in fact, a whole history – of philosophical tracts filled with important insight and energising thoughts for those who dare to look beyond the business shelves and take a seminar with some more cerebral teachers.

Writers, satirists and filmmakers of the 20th century ploughed much of their creative energy into imagining the destructive effect industry might have on the workplace. The dystopian epics of Fritz Lang's *Metropolis* or Charlie Chaplin's slapstick larks in his final silent film *Modern Times* were wry attacks on the machine age and the tyranny of the production line.

Few in the 21st century have sought to tackle one of the most insidious modern oppressions of working life: that of shallow corporate managerial thinking. So much of the business world has adopted a studied, technocratic approach to management. Its effect on the culture of the workplace has been profound: just look at the language. Our top-tier executives have embraced a vocabulary of jargon: boardroom decisions are made with talk of "leverage", "delivery", "moving forward" and "squaring the circle". They communicate with flow charts, action plans and PowerPoint to soul-sapping lengths. Often this language simply evades the issue. You can "sunset" a project rather than shut it down.

All this forgets that business – the crafting, decision-making and innovation that make a venture succeed – should be creative. And that to manage is to inspire. Much of the business world has lost its verve; it is devoid of both art and nuance.

This is, in part, down to the MBA mindset. The coveted master's of business administration taught from Harvard to Hong Kong is designed to shape the CEOs, financiers and entrepreneurs of the future. It is a syllabus of monetary strategy, analytics and case studies with a dash of ethical theory thrown in to guard against the culture of greed that many cite as one of the causes of 2008's fiscal meltdown. It is also much emulated and reinterpreted by the badly designed yet bestselling managerial tomes you see suited hopefuls clutching on the underground at rush hour or buying in haste at airports.

So much of the moil of the workplace could be given new vim and meaning if managers set aside their self-help manuals on the secret of leadership and picked up something creative, thought provoking and humane. There should be more art to business and to the education that precedes it. Through art, business minds can learn how to really inspire. This is not about vigorous sketching or improvisational drama groups where would-be CEOs twirl and express but rather the study of liberal arts.

Some progressive establishments are already onto this (*see our section on training grounds from page 66*). A certain enlightened group of educators have incorporated the study of philosophy, psychology, literature and history into their business syllabus; some more than others. "I believe that [Jean-Paul] Sartre can be considered as the philosopher of entrepreneurship," says Loïck Roche, director and dean at Grenoble École de Management, who holds two PhDs: one in psychology from Paris V University and one in philosophy. "One of Sartre's key ideas is that the Being manifests itself through its willingness," he explains. "Man is nothing else than what he does. This is the first principle of existentialism, Sartre's philosophy. In short, everyone is free to succeed in life."

Roche is an expert in management, wellbeing and performance at work and believes some of the big thinkers from the past are critical to our understanding of good business. Managerial textbooks may be designed to motivate but Roche thinks France's most contemplative philosopher puts it better. "[Another] idea lies in the relationship to the Other. The Other is necessarily a problem because my freedom confronts his. In order not to plunge the Other in absurdity, with loss of meaning – as demonstrated by Sartre in [his novels] *Nausea* and *The Wall* – the only way out is to engage oneself to create something that will not destroy the Other's freedom."

Confused? Don't be. Roche's approach is just a cerebral way of encouraging businessmen and women to understand the very essence of doing. It shows them that they are free to create and

Good reads for the business philosopher

1 The Enchiridion, *Epictetus*
Roll with the punches. That's the essence of this ancient Greek philosopher's practical precepts. We can control opinion, pursuit and desire but we can't marshal health, property and reputation. Don't be put off by obstacles: plough on.

2 Conjectures and Refutations, *Karl Popper*
In this 1963 text the Vienna-born philosopher muses on the importance of trial and error. "All our knowledge grows only through the correcting of our mistakes," Popper says. Entrepreneurs take note: you will learn from your setbacks.

3 The Pleasures and Sorrows of Work, *Alain de Botton*
In his approachable prose, De Botton explores what makes jobs either fulfilling or soul-destroying, whether you are a rocket scientist, accountant or biscuit maker.

4 The Work of Art in the Age of Mechanical Reproduction, *Walter Benjamin*
Benjamin's 1936 essay discusses the meaning of art in an age of ubiquity. Though of its time, this is a good read for any entrepreneur contemplating originality and manufacturing in the modern era.

5 The teachings of Heraclitus of Ephesus
This ancient Anatolian philosopher's maxim, "Character is fate", is often proven true in business.

innovate. Take action – start something and become, in the process, relevant and vital.

Roche is also a proponent of something called Slow Management, a school of thought (rooted, in its modern sense, in the endeavours of HP founders, Bill Hewlett and Dave Packard) that believes giving workers meaning and recognition at work is key to productivity and growth.

For this he prescribes the French-Algerian journalist, novelist, playwright and reluctant philosopher Albert Camus and his 1942 paper on the story of Sisyphus, condemned by the Greek gods to push a stone up a hill for eternity. "If there were to be only one management book on leaders' shelves it would need to be *The Myth of Sisyphus*," says Roche. "The essential is there. Above all, men and women in businesses need meaning and recognition. Even if their work is repetitive, even if they are condemned to doing the same thing every day as Sisyphus had to. People, as explained by Camus, must be inspired by their managers."

To study the precepts of motivation and the need for career goals by reading some of history's great texts may sound idiosyncratic or even frivolous – but it works in a way that encourages nuance, creativity and real understanding. This story is a reminder that men and women need to be able to foresee a desirable future at work no matter what they do. When work becomes futile, productivity and morale drops; it applies from the boardroom to the factory floor.

Roche believes in stoking the minds of business folk to develop a rigorous "intellectual muscle structure" in his students that encourages dexterity: the ability to think critically. "One of the key skills that must be acquired by students is the capacity to think differently, the capacity to have courage. As Nietzsche would recommend: to learn to go against our personal convictions when it is necessary."

It's unlikely all deans of management will take Roche's expansive, radical and very Gallic view. Yet other universities and companies are starting to find ways of integrating liberal arts with business, and vice versa. Bentley University in Massachusetts has created an MBA that fuses faculty in business and the arts and sciences. Other institutions, such as the Aspen Institute, have been working to broaden the graduate business syllabus for some years – it set up the Aspen Institute Business & Society Program to do just that.

"We've recently launched work on the undergraduate front, which is explicitly framed around more fully integrated liberal arts and business," says Claire Preisser, the Aspen Institute's senior programme manager. Is this about creating a more mindful CEO? "I think there is a question of what we mean by the 'right' type of CEO or entrepreneur. For us this would mean someone who leads with values, who takes a long-term view, who embraces a nuanced view of the firm that goes well beyond maximising shareholder value."

Granted, you shouldn't expect to see suited City-bound hopefuls on the Tube clutching copies of *The Myth of Sisyphus* any time soon. But, that said, the worlds of business, art and science are undoubtedly becoming ever more entwined.

This has been helped by some icons of success: Budapest-born business magnate George Soros and former Time Warner CEO Gerald Levin – the man who arguably created HBO – both majored in philosophy. Soros studied the discipline at the London School of Economics under the Austrian-British Karl Popper while Levin examined the links between Jewish and Christian theology as a philosophy major at Pennsylvania's Haverford College.

More recently, several significant figures in the technology world, such as Canadian entrepreneur and Flickr co-founder Stewart Butterfield (who has bachelor's and master's degrees in philosophy from the universities of Victoria and Cambridge), have shown that an expansive education is not lost on the world of business. And now the entrepreneur-technologist-cum-philosopher Dr Damon Horowitz has become Google's in-house philosopher and director of engineering. Horowitz is perhaps the most vocal and high-profile authority on the intersection between the arts and business and has a foot in both. He lectures in cognitive science as well as computer science at Stanford, NYU and the University of Pennsylvania – and teaches philosophy to inmates at San Quentin state prison.

The world is in need of the "right" type of CEO or entrepreneur equipped with moral courage and new approaches to business. The practice of so-called "humane capitalism" as seen in factories such as that of Italian businessman Brunello Cucinelli – who has created a venture that venerates and inspires his factory staff (*see page 218*) – proves that these academic principles can transform business models. Cucinelli has a theatre and "philosopher's garden" on his factory site and likes to quote Socrates by saying, "A day will come when philosophers will be needed to rule the world."

His colleagues in the textile industry may not agree. But either way, his venture is living proof that the study of philosophy – where the principles of ethics begin and end – can bring profits as well as art, creativity and integrity to the workplace. — (M)

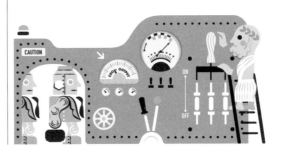

LIFE OF LEATHER
PARIS

Preface: How do you marry heritage spanning generations with rapid growth? The answer, according to Pierre-Alexis and Axel Dumas – artistic director and CEO at global fashion house Hermès – is to embrace the culture of 'slow luxury'.

Company: Hermès
Location: Paris
Founded: 1837
Number of employees: 11,000
Family members involved: 10
Number of premises: 25 subsidiaries and 315 exclusive stores worldwide

—

Quote: *'Some employees have worked here for generations; I knew their parents and they knew mine'*

Hermès is one of the most recognised fashion houses in the world. But as it's a family-run business with a focus on craft, those in charge prefer to manage by looking inwards rather than chasing markets.

"This is not a company, it's a house – and one that has protected me since I was young," says Pierre-Alexis Dumas (*pictured, on right*), artistic director of Hermès and the sixth generation of family owners. His office feels more like a chic studio apartment than the nerve centre of one of the most recognisable brands in fashion.

"We're just farming the land here. It was farmed before us and will be farmed after us," says Pierre-Alexis. "You can add your layer to the terroir but there's no real sense of ownership." He seems acutely aware of being one of the few great fashion houses remaining in family hands. "Sometimes I'm not sure if we manage the company or if Hermès manages us," says Axel Dumas (*pictured*), Pierre-Alexis's cousin and Hermès's CEO.

The Dumas cousins grew up together, immersed in the ateliers from an early age and spending summer holidays with the families of Dumas, Guerrand and Puech – several of whom also hold senior roles at Hermès, the company that their forefather Thierry Hermès founded as a harness maker back in 1837.

Nowadays the company is a very different place. Although one of France's great heritage brands, Hermès' real growth has been recent and meteoric. In 1978, it was a house of 400 employees – today's staff stands at 11,000.

It's not just the workforce that has grown. Having started out as a leather specialist, Hermès now has 16 product lines, from silk to fragrances and watches. How do the Dumas cousins achieve harmony across the *métiers*? "The answer is you work a lot," says Pierre-Alexis. "I'm not looking at what other people are doing because I don't have time. We have more than 175 years of history, so we develop according to internal creativity and intuition, not external trends or marketing gimmicks." The commitment to staff also remains unchanged with investment in training and the running of the Club des Anciens for retired Hermès artisans.

"The Hermès family is not just people with the surname Dumas, Puech or Guerrand," says Axel. "Some employees have worked here for generations; I knew their parents and they knew mine." Despite Hermès being a booming international business, the Dumas cousins still manage with a sense of familiarity unusual in a company of this size. "Everyone has a different relationship to the brand but they're all valid." With this in mind, the Dumas cousins have set up a committee of key employees across the *métiers* to cross-fertilise thinking and help guide development.

Although Pierre-Alexis's emphasis is on encouraging the artisans into new interpretations of the Hermès brand, he has a healthy respect for the "money men". "Facts and figures are important – they set your limits," he says. "My job is to work closely with Axel and the financial team but to understand the special needs of our artisans and help them bring new visions to life." Being able to shift speeds when working with different teams is key for both cousins.

This "slow luxury" approach distinguishes Hermès in a world of rapacious brand expansion. These contrasting approaches to luxury came into conflict when Bernard Arnault, chairman of LVMH, announced he had accumulated an initial 17 per cent of the Hermès stock, which prompted outrage. "People don't really know what luxury means anymore," says Pierre-Alexis. "I'm very concerned by the disconnection from craft that we see happening today."

The company works with 33 ateliers and 4,400 craftspeople across France and manufacturing has always been a key part of its branding, rather than something done behind the scenes. The company actively communicates the workmanship involved to an increasingly savvy consumer. "The danger is that everyone has caught on to this now and are making a mock-up of craft," warns Axel. "It's easy to talk in this way but difficult to execute."

The cousins seem comfortable with balancing heritage, family and growth, however. "I'm not a guardian of the brand," says Pierre-Alexis. "My job is to keep Hermès evolving." Rather than the family history being inhibiting, it appears to be a solid scaffold for the future.

"We're managing for the next generation," says Axel. "It's not just about our individual success or quarterly results but about the legacy." — (M)

The rules

1 What time do you like to be at your desk?
Axel Dumas: At 08.50. I never miss dropping my son off at school and he starts at 08.30.

2 What's your management style?
AD: I try to delegate as much as possible while focusing on making sure that everybody is aligned to our strategy. I talk a lot – hopefully to ensure that our values stay vibrant.

3 Are tough decisions best taken by one person?
AD: When someone stands to lose something or when a choice is difficult, I feel it is better to do it oneself rather than have someone else fall on the sword.

4 Do you read management books?
AD: Yes and no. I dutifully buy management books, store them next to my bedside table and eventually take them on holiday with novels or essays. I do read the *Harvard Business Review*.

5 Where's the best place to prepare for leadership: an MBA school or on the job?
Pierre-Alexis Dumas: Always look for mentors. Mine were Stanley Marcus, Jean-Louis Dumas, Joseph Ettedgui and many more.

6 How do you manage a team?
PAD: Hands on.

7 What technology do you carry on a trip?
PAD: A pen, pencil, good paper, an eraser and my Leica.

8 Do you want to be liked or respected?
PAD: I see myself as a dream-catcher.

9 What does your support team look like?
PAD: The dream team.

10 What would your key management advice be?
PAD: Always surround yourself with people greater than you.

THE LONG VIEW
STOCKHOLM

Preface: From fostering a legacy of female managers to weathering significant cutbacks, here's how Eva Hamilton, head of Swedish public-service broadcaster SVT, established herself as one of the country's pre-eminent CEOs.

Company: SVT
Location: Stockholm
Founded: 1956
Number of employees when founded: 70
Number of employees now: 2,100
Number of premises: 28
Most watched show globally: Nobel Prize awards ceremony

Quote: *I get my ideas in conversations, not by sitting alone under a tree and thinking'*

"I'm good at making people feel noticed, I'm good at giving people enthusiasm about their work and I'm good at seeing the big picture instead of getting worked up about the small stuff."

Before there's even a chance to ask the question, Eva Hamilton has summed up her best qualities as a manager. The CEO of Sweden's public-service broadcaster SVT since 2006, Hamilton is known for her speed and straightforwardness and seems to be a person who has put a lot of effort into getting to know herself – good sides and bad. Years of management courses and training on the job have taught her to embrace certain qualities and suppress others. Her spontaneity belongs in the latter category.

"My whole life has been a struggle to keep this spontaneity in check," she says. "As a manager at this level you can't be spontaneous. There are managers under me who are responsible for different things and I can't just undermine them by going straight to people and telling them what I think they should do."

On the other hand it can often lead to great results, such as unexpected meetings with the news editor, which Hamilton has been known to hold in the news anchor's make-up chair.

"I happened to see her so I asked her to sit with me and we talked about the programme, which had been worrying me. It turned out to be the most important meeting of the day."

Hamilton is no stranger to the newsroom floor and is not one of those managers who stay in their office behind closed doors. She likes to be among her staff. As she walks through the TV centre's seemingly endless corridors, people stop to chat and some even receive a warm hug or a motherly stroke on the cheek.

"I'm very dependent on interaction. I get my ideas in conversations, not by sitting alone under a tree and thinking," she says. "As the highest manager, you can either choose to constantly keep a poker face and say, 'I know which path we should choose, just trust me.' Or reveal to your management team that in this particular case I have no damn clue, and look for the answers together. Even though ultimately, I still take the decision."

Hamilton's career at SVT spans more than 20 years. She started as a print journalist but got a job as a reporter at the channel's news show, *Rapport*. Reporting led to news anchoring and a position as the network's Brussels correspondent. But on coming home to Sweden, she felt a need for change. She had been offered a management position elsewhere but SVT's CEO at the time, Sam Nilsson, persuaded her to stay, saying, "If you want to be a manager, why not be one here?" Hamilton advanced step by step until her appointment as CEO.

Hamilton's toughest decisions to date have been caused by an SVT cost-cutting programme. Four hundred people had to be laid off and several production units were shut down. "In a situation like that, you must be able to communicate all the way through the company why this has to be done. No empty phrases. Because even if you're not losing your job a colleague is and that leads to sorrow and guilt," says Hamilton.

Although Sweden is internationally viewed as a country of equal opportunities, female CEOs are a rarity. Women are especially absent in heavy industries such as steel and paper. In media, the situation is different. Radical female journalists started advocating equal career opportunities strongly in the 1980s, using their newspapers and television shows as powerful megaphones. Consequently, women increasingly occupied positions that paved the way for future careers – editors, correspondents and anchors.

"Over the years, more and more women have moved up in the organisation, and today SVT has a rich, experienced supply of female managers at level two, just under the top," Hamilton says.

"The steel, engineering and paper industries began changing only eight to 10 years ago, and have almost no women on that level. A woman in that environment becomes a lonely abnormality observed as an exception. That's a difficult situation."

Being at the top hasn't been without its challenges. But while having a family is often considered an obstacle for women wishing to climb the career ladder, Hamilton, who has raised four kids, claims otherwise. "If you're lucky enough to have healthy kids it's fully possible. Healthy kids and a good man." — (M)

The rules

1 What time do you like to be at your desk?
09.00. But before that I've already been talking for 45 minutes on the phone in my car.

2 Where's the best place to prepare for leadership: an MBA school or on the job?
On the job, absolutely. But these days you won't be considered for a top-level job without the adequate education.

3 What's your management style?
I'm the opposite of a lone wolf; I work best in a team. I need to have contact with the organisation and my management team, who I have great confidence in.

4 Are tough decisions best taken by one person?
They have to be taken by the CEO. I must be able to stand behind them with my whole being because they will meet a lot of resistance. But I never take a tough decision without having spoken with my management team first.

5 Do you want to be liked or respected?
Both! But if I have to choose, respected. If you're guided by a desire to be loved, you'll become a very bad manager.

6 What does your support team look like?
My closest team consists of 12 people. We have a weekly meeting and in addition to that, I meet each and every one of them every two weeks.

7 What technology do you carry on a trip?
My iPad and my smartphone.

8 Do you read management books?
I used to but these days I think that I know best.

9 Run in the morning? Wine with lunch? Socialise with your team after work?
No wine with lunch or with the team after work; rather at home with dinner. And I don't run in the morning but I train with a personal trainer once a week.

10 What would your key management advice be?
Never underestimate your co-workers' needs to be seen and noticed. It's more important to praise than criticise because criticism is something people are very good at giving to themselves.

THE BEAN COUNTER
TRIESTE

Preface: As gatekeeper of Illycaffè, one of the world's most famous coffee brands, president and CEO Andrea Illy faces some intense competition. Here's how he has kept the company not just above water but thriving.

Company: Illycaffè
Location: Trieste
Founded: 1933
Number of employees: 990
Number of premises: 8
Family members involved: 6
Bestselling product: Illycaffè has just 1 blend of coffee made from 9 types of Arabica

Quote: *'The numbers don't interest me – it's the quality'*

When the topic of family-run companies comes up in conversation in Italy someone invariably quotes the well-known proverb stating that the first generation creates, the second preserves and the third destroys. It's an adage Andrea Illy is familiar with and one the CEO has successfully debunked as head of Illycaffè, the coffee firm founded by his Hungarian grandfather in Trieste in 1933.

In charge of one of Italy's most respected brands, Illy admits that people in his position face a special set of challenges compared to the average Fortune 500 boss. This is still very much a family operation. Andrea works alongside his brother, Riccardo, who is vice-president, and his sister Anna, who has the role of liaising with the company's network of coffee growers from Araponga, Brazil to Yirgacheffe, Ethiopia. Their mother, Anna Rossi Illy, still serves as honorary president.

"As manager of a family business you embody the brand, which in our case happens to be our last name," says Illy, sitting in his wood-panelled corner office where a portrait of his late father, Ernesto Illy, hangs on the wall in front of him. "You are the custodian of a heritage, a know-how that you are trying to preserve for the next generation."

While the weight of responsibility is, at times, particularly great for a family owner, Illy has learned not to micromanage every detail. "The model has its limitations. We try to be a family-run business but without being patriarchal."

In place of an autocratic management style typically seen at family firms, Illy opted to give greater power to his executive team. "We made a monumental change and, for the first time, brought in someone from outside the family to take on the role of general manager – which used to be me – since I work the same number of hours as when I started 20 years ago but the company has grown tenfold and is 100 times more complex."

Illy's approach means that he places great trust in people who don't share his surname to run an enterprise that employs 990 people and has annual sales of more than €360m. "Executing things isn't simple – your colleagues need to be motivated and feel they share in the project you're envisioning."

It comes as no surprise that Illy's first job when he started was as quality-control supervisor. He developed protocols to ensure that high standards were met from bean to cup, which led to the awarding of ISO certifications. Among the company's rigorous controls is a sorting machine that uses a laser to analyse 200 beans a second in order to discard defective ones. "The numbers don't interest me – it's the quality," says Illy.

Touring the factory floor, Illy passes a wall inscribed with the ideal parameters for brewing espresso: 7g of coffee brewed for 30 seconds at 90C under 9 ATMs of pressure. The calculation comes from the book he co-authored, a year after becoming CEO. Appropriately titled *Espresso Coffee: The Science of Quality*, the tome covers everything from the DNA of the bean to the effects of caffeine.

Besides executive courses and learning on the job, the bookish Illy scans the management section of bookshops for new releases. Although in favour of MBA programmes to prep would-be managers, Illy believes his scientific background (he holds a degree in chemistry) has given him a leg up when it comes to seeing the big picture in business. "In chemistry it's a systemic approach: A + B + C. The breakdown of steps to figure out how things interrelate." In order to find the best-quality coffee in the mid-1990s, Illycaffè diversified the sources of the company's beans, buying them directly from the growers.

Illy has also been instrumental in developing the profile of the coffee industry through education. Since 2002, the company has run the Università del Caffè in Trieste, teaching producers and consumers technical coffee-making skills as well as managerial and marketing know-how. Meanwhile, with the University of Udine and Trieste, the Trieste Coffee District and the Consortium for Molecular Biomedicine, Illy and the Ernesto Illy Foundation have developed an international master's degree in coffee science and economics, teaching everything from agronomy to business management. For Illy, this is not just about his company but about raising global standards.

Still, Illy confesses some aspects of his work are not easily taught in the classroom. "Running a family business is not like a public company with shareholders. It is not a profit machine: you are a stakeholder building something for the long run." — (M)

The rules

1 What time do you like to be at your desk?
Generally, I'm in the office by 09.00. If my family is in Trieste, I leave by 20.00.

2 Where's the best place to prepare for leadership: an MBA school or on the job?
Both. The manager with only practical experience won't work. An MBA gives you a boost and gives you a framework.

3 What's your management style?
I'd call it visionary. I develop a plan and then my team carries it out.

4 Are tough decisions best taken by one person?
Generally, I think decisions should be discussed together by the team.

5 Do you want to be liked or respected?
Respected but it shouldn't be reverence. I think it's important that there's trust.

6 What does your support team look like?
I have a general manager with whom I have a close working relationship. He acts as co-ordinator and deals with the heads of department.

7 What technology do you carry on a trip?
A MacBook Air and a Samsung smartphone.

8 Do you read management books?
Yes. I browse bookstores whenever I am travelling for work.

9 Run in the morning? Wine with lunch? Socialise with your team after work?
I run 6km three times a week before work. No wine at lunch. If we have guests, I'll serve Brunello from sister company Mastrojanni, but then drink two espressos.

10 What would your key management advice be?
We live in an unsustainable society. The business community needs to come up with new strategies.

HOME COMFORTS
VALENCIA

Preface: Rosa Lladró is the president of Lladró, the Spanish porcelain company begun by her father and uncles in the 1950s. Having ducked a manufacturing downturn in Spain, she explains how to combine family and financial success.

Company: Lladró
Location: Tabernes Blanques, Valencia
Founded: 1953
Number of employees when founded: 15
Number of employees now: approximately 1,000
Number of premises: 1
Bestselling product: Arabian purebred horse figurine

Quote: *'We're a global business but also a small creative workshop'*

"I see my role as a balancing act," says Rosa Lladró, the second-generation owner of the eponymous Spanish porcelain house. "I have a responsibility to the family, to my staff, to Valencia and to the fairytales that made our business." Surely that's a lot of responsibility for the youthful president? Rosa pauses, smiles and replies in precise but heavily accented English: "Yes. But I was brought up to expect this."

Rosa and her younger sister Ángeles Lladró (the company's vice president) were immersed in the company ethos from an early age, growing up in the porcelain workshop that her father Juan and his younger brothers José and Vicente, founded in 1953. "You can't draw a line between where the family ends and the firm begins. The business has always functioned through a committee; I have always valued open discussion and debate."

This emphasis on family values extends to Rosa's relationship with her staff and the factory's central courtyard features an open-air swimming pool, basketball court, giant chessboard and alfresco restaurant. "Our business is reliant on human skill. We don't use machines because although they seem to help at first, they produce limitations in the long run and by then the skills are lost." Although innovating through collaborations with young designers such as Barcelona's Jaime Hayon, the manufacturing process remains almost unchanged from the one used in the 1950s.

"We're a global business but we're also a small creative workshop. I don't try to second-guess the market. I'm not hung up on market research, it's more about imagining the next step in the story and allowing our artisans to go there."

Running the firm by consulting and listening is key for Rosa, who involves family members and workshop artisans in important decision making. "Maybe this makes me a soft touch in some ways but it's a great safety net against rash decisions, especially in uncertain times."

Uncertain times is something of an understatement. As one of Valencia's leading firms, Lladró has certainly not been immune to the region's dramatic decline. Walking through the Mediterranean city, it's hard to imagine that it was outstripping national growth figures until the middle of the 2000s. Building sites are studded with abandoned cranes and youth unemployment has soared. Reliant on manufacturing, property and construction, Valencia was left exposed when big business collapsed in 2008, with almost 200,000 jobs disappearing in 2010 alone.

"We're one of the lucky ones," says Rosa, "but I've had to make some very difficult decisions." Even before the global recession, Lladró's key markets in Europe, Japan and the US seemed to have reached maturity, with sales falling in 2003 and the company ending the year in fiscal debt for the first time. "I had to lay off staff who had been with the company for many years and, as a family operation, that's painful. We also had to develop a much more serious strategy in new markets."

This change in tactics marked a rebirth for the company, with the developing luxury markets of China and India becoming a focus: it sells through 40 locations in China alone. Walking around the museum at the company's main site, called Lladró City of Porcelain, you can see that the garland-bedecked Marie Antoinettes, ethereal ballerinas and frolicking cherubs that built this unashamedly chintzy empire have been joined by figures of Hindu gods and Chinese dragons. The company's most opulent offering – a 100-piece depiction of an Egyptian queen boating on the Nile – retails for €130,000 and was developed to decorate newly wealthy homes from Mumbai to Shanghai.

As radical as these product changes may be, Rosa is clear about where she sees the company's future. "Being in Valencia is key. We're a family workshop and you can't break that up. It would be like breaking a figurine into pieces. Everything is close here; in 20 minutes you're at the beach, in an hour you're in the mountains. It influences how we run the business; there's something in the blood."

Family duty is obviously a guiding light for Rosa. Would she have aspired to manage a firm if she hadn't been born into the Lladró dynasty?

"I don't think I'm a natural manager," she answers. "Perhaps an artist would have made more sense. But I'm passionate about preserving our work for future generations. We're the kind of company that the modern world seems keen to erase." — (M)

The rules

1 What time do you like to be at your desk?
Whatever it takes to get the job done.

2 Where's the best place to prepare for leadership: an MBA school or on the job?
Every job you take makes you see business from another angle. Practical skills are better than abstract thinking.

3 What's your management style?
I try to be consistent and be the same person in the office that I would be at home with my family. The same on Sundays as I am on Mondays.

4 Are tough decisions best taken by one person?
I believe in discussion until everybody agrees. It's the only way that you can run a family firm because no one likes a dictator in the family.

5 Do you want to be liked or respected?
I would like to be respected. But if I do something that conflicts with my morals just to be respected, then that's not OK for me.

6 What does your support team look like?
My father teaches me something new every day, as does my sister. We work closely with our board of directors, who I think must be the smartest and most honest in Spain.

7 What technology do you carry on a trip?
I always have my iPhone and iPad, for everything from social media to my morning news.

8 Do you read management books?
No. I like to read the financial press instead.

9 Run in the morning? Wine with lunch? Socialise with your team after work?
I run in the evening and then have a glass of wine to unwind.

10 What would your key management advice be?
You have to listen and be open minded. Learning how to combine perspectives can be the most important management tool.

FRESH START NUREMBERG

Preface: Christian Struck was set the imposing task of rebooting a multinational's entire brand. But when that company is a national institution such as German electronics specialist Grundig, the challenge becomes even greater.

Company: Grundig
Location: Nuremberg
Founded: 1945
Number of employees: 1,750
Number of premises: 9

Quote: *'History doesn't make great products. You always need a vision for the future'*

Take a walk through the industrial eastern suburbs of Nuremberg, the home of Grundig's German headquarters, and it is clear how proud this Bavarian city is of its most successful son. Max Grundig's legacy is immortalised in the Max-Grundig-Platz, the towering Grundig Akademie and the Grundig Stadium where the local football team plays.

Grundig's HQ, just off the main thoroughfare of Beuthener Strasse, is a former factory – office workers now sit where video recorders were once made – and this is where to find Christian Struck, the company's director of brand management. In the canteen at lunchtime, Struck nods to everyone and cheerfully says "*Mahlzeit*" ("*Bon appétit*"). "I think I am a people person," he says as he tucks into a bowl of ice cream. "When I'm trying to work out our long-term strategy – that's when I have to close the door and be alone."

Struck's role demands plenty of thinking time. He heads a team of 18 people tasked with a comprehensive company rebranding. In 2012, Grundig started making white goods – refrigerators, dishwashers, washing machines and other household appliances. For a company synonymous with TVs and radios, this new move ushered in a huge shift in strategy. "We now see ourselves as a home-electronics brand with a product for every room," says Struck. He has been working on a new corporate identity and also guiding an external design agency based in Munich through the development of a range of new products. "It was clear we needed to move the brand in a new direction. It had to be younger and more dynamic," he says.

For Struck, the brand's core values are the same today as they were when Max Grundig set up the company in the aftermath of the Second World War. Its founder quickly became one of the faces of West Germany's *Wirtschaftswunder* (economic miracle). "Grundig is a brand for the upper-middle market," says Struck. "Our products still have to be reachable. They are not the cheapest but they are affordable and worth the money because you know what is behind them: longevity, quality, German precision and trustworthiness."

Despite this, Struck is keenly aware that the past alone won't propel his vision for the brand. "You cannot rely on history," he says. "History doesn't make great products. You always need a vision for the future."

The company overhaul has also been a question of survival. When Struck came on board in 2007 Grundig was struggling, having lost ground to Asian competitors. Around the same time, Grundig was bought by Koc Holding – one of the largest investment companies in Turkey and owner of electronics giant Arcelik – which vowed to restore its fortunes. "This gave us the opportunity to renew some of our products and to move into the white-goods market," says Struck.

Struck's life now reflects the new international face of Grundig. He spends one week of every month in Istanbul, where he has a team of three people. "One of the main issues has been the language difference," says Struck of his time in the Turkish commercial capital. "We are all talking in our second language so there is more room for misinterpretation. That means we have to communicate more – write more emails and pick up the phone. You have to be open."

Openness is something Struck considers essential. "Good managers are always approachable and they have to be able to listen," he says. For him, openness also applies to the creative process for everything from new advertising campaigns to brochures and business-to-business communications. Struck tries to foster and encourage the creativity of his team rather than simply instruct. "I work with some very talented people," he says. "I suppose my job is to lay down the parameters of the discussion and then let them have the freedom to come up with ideas. I never want to limit their thinking."

Struck's remit may be radical but his plan is to progress slowly and carefully, presenting Grundig's new look to markets incrementally. The brand has taken huge strides forward under Struck's stewardship but there are still many challenges ahead. In spite of that, the pressure of managing a team based in two countries and the global image of the historic German institution doesn't seem to wear him down. In fact, his mood improves as the day goes on. "I really love my job," he says. "No two days are the same." — (M)

The rules

1 **What time do you like to be at your desk?**
I often work late into the evenings so I normally come in at 09.00. In Istanbul, it's more like 08.00.

2 **Where's the best place to prepare for leadership: an MBA school or on the job?**
On the job. When I was at university, management courses weren't that popular. Also businesses are so complex – you have to adapt.

3 **What's your management style?**
Open, approachable and empathetic.

4 **Are tough decisions best taken by one person?**
They should be decided by logic. Whether this means by one person or a group of people, it doesn't matter that much – although some things need one person's guidance.

5 **Do you want to be liked or respected?**
It is nice to be liked but respect is the most important thing. I try to be as respectful as possible with my colleagues, too.

6 **What does your support team look like?**
I don't have a secretary or a personal assistant.

7 **What technology do you carry on a trip?**
I take my iPhone and I'm afraid I'm an iPad addict.

8 **Do you read management books?**
Yes, although I find them very repetitive sometimes so I often skip whole chapters.

9 **Run in the morning? Wine with lunch? Socialise with your team after work?**
Jogging is boring – I get on my bike at the weekend. I can't drink wine before 18.00. And I'd like to socialise with my team more but I'm often the last to leave the office.

10 **What would your key management advice be?**
Be engaged and open. Also, be willing to take advice if it is offered to you.

QUICK ON THE DRAW
TOKYO

Preface: The CEO of Japan's largest chain of entertainment shops is peculiarly sketchy on management – he never gives orders, positively encourages failure and doesn't even have his own office – yet he's particularly successful, too.

Company: Tsutaya
Location: Tokyo
Year founded: 1983
Number of employees when founded: 2
Number of employees now: 3,000
Start-up cost: ¥1m
Bestselling products: books and magazines

——

Quote: '*I never tell anyone what to do. I wouldn't want to be told what to do*'

Muneaki Masuda isn't in his seat for more than a few seconds before he fishes a pencil out of a case and starts sketching on a large sheet of paper. He writes "music", "books" and "movies", then "lifestyle", and draws lines connecting them. "This is what I'm going to talk about," he says.

For Masuda, jotting down what's on his mind is instinctive. He sketches during meetings and while giving speeches. He's even been known to take notes while behind the wheel of his car. It's as if Masuda – the founder and president of Culture Convenience Club (CCC), operator of Tsutaya, Japan's largest video, game, book and music retail/rental chain – wants to log every fleeting thought. He says it's not just a quirky habit.

"If I have an idea for a project and I want to share it with others, what's the best way to do that?" He hands the paper to his staff. They turn his notes into a PowerPoint presentation, index it and store it in a database. "All of my employees have their own database," he says.

With a controlling ownership stake in CCC, Masuda wields considerable influence over the company's future strategic decisions. But his management style is hands-off when compared to the paternalism that characterises many of Japan's biggest companies. "I never give orders or tell anyone what to do," he

says. "I wouldn't want to be told what to do."

Masuda, 63, opened the first Tsutaya store in Osaka in 1983 when he was 32. He stocked the shelves mainly with US films that weren't available in Japan and had no Japanese subtitles. What some saw as his business naivety was in fact a shrewd push into an unexplored market.

Tsutaya now has more than 1,400 shops nationwide, mostly run by franchisees. The company also has a formidable presence online and a vast database of customer-buying patterns. By any measure, Masuda's idea has been wildly successful. If he were to sell up, he would be hundreds of millions of euros richer. But Masuda doesn't seem ready to exit anytime soon: he has yet to name a successor. And for major strategic decisions, Masuda has the last word. "I leave parts of the business to some people but they can't look after it all," he says.

The opening of a megastore in Hakodate city, northern Japan, was part of a rollout of 100 new outlets. But one of CCC's boldest projects is three Tsutaya buildings on a leafy 12,000 sq m plot in Tokyo's Daikanyama, a neighbourhood of embassies and independent fashion labels. Masuda pulls out his old sketches of the Daikanyama project and they reveal that he's agonised over the smallest details: how the staff will offer

recommendations, what customers will use to search the archives of thousands of magazine titles and what food the café will serve.

The project also spawned a new venture: running libraries. The company opened its first library in collaboration with Takeo, a small city on the southern island of Kyushu. A café was also added to the library, as well as Tsutaya retail sections – books, magazines and rental DVDs and CDs. The aim, CCC says, is to improve the library's services while saving money for the city – running the library costs 10 per cent less than the €1.1m the city spends on the public library annually – and the results have been impressive. The library attracted a year's worth of visits in the first three months – some 260,000. Since then, CCC has signed two more library deals with other cities in Japan.

When Masuda needs to think deeply about something, he heads off to a café. At CCC's Tokyo headquarters, he doesn't have an office or even a desk. Usually he just flits between meeting rooms or holds discussions in his car on the way to an appointment. Having spent a decade as a salaryman before starting his firm, Masuda knows what he doesn't want. "I had incompetent, ignorant bosses. Working for someone like that you lose hope. Everything that I felt was wrong with that company I vowed not to do if I had my own," he says.

One thing he wanted to make a part of CCC's corporate culture was the willingness to experiment – and fail. "One of my staff just sent me an email to say that his project had flopped," says Masuda. "I knew that it would fail but I let him do it his way. What did I say to him? That was a good experience. Now I expect great things from you."

Several years ago he decided to take firmer control, organising a €680m management buyout before delisting CCC's shares from the Tokyo bourse. "Customers have to come first," he says. "That is what Tsutaya has been about from the beginning." — (M)

The rules

1 What time do you like to be at your desk?
I have no desk. I have no office, either. My workplace is wherever information is available. I hold meetings while on the move, in my car.

2 Where's the best place to prepare for leadership: an MBA school or on the job?
You can't groom a leader in a classroom or in a meeting room. The only way is through on-the-ground experience.

3 What's your management style?
I don't give directions or issue orders. I don't like to work that way. Only you know what makes you happy. I don't think anyone wants to be ordered around. That's why freedom – to decide on your own, to fail – is so important.

4 Are tough decisions best taken by one person?
The role of management is to make decisions. I tend to decide things on the spot. Putting off important decisions is a problem.

5 Do you want to be liked or respected?
A person in this line of work has to be likeable.

6 What does your support team look like?
I tend to prefer staff who are individualistic.

7 What technology do you carry on a trip?
An iPad Air, iPhone, laptop. But a sketchpad and pencil are more important for jotting things down.

8 Do you read management books?
I write books. I don't read them. [Masuda has written five books.]

9 Run in the morning? Wine with lunch? Socialise with your team after work?
I hold meetings at lunchtime. I run in the evenings. Nights are my most important business hours. My real work starts after I leave the company offices. It's when I meet business partners. I also socialise with employees at barbecue parties or at my vacation home in Karuizawa.

10 What would your key management advice be?
Don't listen to what customers tell you. Instead think about how to work in their interests.

TEAM CAPTAIN
MELBOURNE

Preface: Sir Rod Eddington takes leadership inspiration from the sports field – whether he's leading flag-carrier airlines, helping steer a media empire or part of the top tier of a financial giant.

Company: JP Morgan
Location: Melbourne (regional HQ)
Founded: 1799 in the US
Number of employees: 260,000
Number of premises: 160
Key services: asset management; commercial and investment banking

Quote: *'The thing about sport is that you learn to make the most of what you've got but accept your limitations'*

As the non-executive chairman of JP Morgan Australia and New Zealand, Sir Rod Eddington enjoys one of Melbourne's most opulent office spaces. From the 32nd-floor boardroom there is a view that spreads from Australia's most recognisable sporting structure, the Melbourne Cricket Ground, to Flinders Street Station, the iconic railway terminal. It is a vantage point that seems almost designed for Eddington's two great extracurricular passions: transport and athleticism.

Eddington's CV includes stints as the CEO of British Airways, a non-executive director at News Corporation and the chairman of Infrastructure Australia. He has also spent time as the CEO of Cathay Pacific, president of the Australia Japan Business Co-operation Committee and the chairman of Lion, Australia's largest brewer. How can one man manage such a diverse portfolio of roles?

"You've got to compartmentalise," he says. "I've always been curious so I enjoy both the familiarity of things I understand well and being involved in things that are new."

His grounded upbringing in rural Western Australia has never left him. "You learn to beware of hubris quickly in the bush," he says. "You learn it in class, at home and on the sports field."

The latter point has been particularly important to his management style. When he wasn't training with the air-force reserves during his engineering degree he played cricket for the University of Western Australia and was later the president of Vincent's Club, Oxford's most prestigious sporting society.

"The thing about sport is that you learn to make the most of what you've got but accept your limitations," he says. "It's a perfect preparation for business." These days Eddington rarely takes to the field but continues to draw inspiration as a spectator. "I am a huge fan of [Australian Rules football team] Fremantle Dockers' captain Matthew Pavlich," he says. "He keeps his dignity through both success and failure."

The same could be said about Eddington, who is no stranger to crisis. In 2008 he was a non-executive director at the Australian asset manager Allco Finance Group when it collapsed with a billion dollars of debt. It was also he who successfully steered British Airways through the weeks following September 11, a time when the airline found itself losing as much as £2m a day. He managed to increase the airline's annual operating profits to £540m by the time he left in 2005, a feat that earned him his knighthood. "Me and my direct team met every

morning for the better part of a month," he says of the September 11 crisis. "In difficult times you have to over-communicate."

Similar strategies were also adopted during his role in News Corporation's handling of the phone-hacking scandal. "That was an example of where a board had to do everything it could to find out what happened and put it right," he says. Eddington's position as a director at Australia's largest news organisation allowed him to observe and learn from one of the country's most powerful – and controversial – business exports: Rupert Murdoch. "Really successful business leaders are passionate about the industry they are in," he says. "I've never met anyone that is more passionate about the media business than Rupert."

Eddington has never shied from policy debate. He accompanied Tony Abbott to Japan during his free-trade-agreement negotiations and had a close relationship with former prime minister Kevin Rudd. In 2008 he also released an extensive report on improving transport in the state of Victoria, which advocated a tunnel between Melbourne's east and west. "The tyranny of distance conspires against us in Australia. I think that when you're an island continent if you don't have transport links then you live in isolation. We need to be better connected," he says.

While officials welcome his advice, he is quick to point out that a good manager always pick his moments carefully. "It doesn't matter who you are, you can wear out your welcome," he says. "But I like to think that if I ask to speak to a senior person in business or politics, they will take the call because they know that I respect their time."

He takes a moment to gaze over the train tracks. Despite running flag carriers for the UK and Hong Kong, it seems his strongest loyalty still lies with his home country. "I've lived in a lot of places," he says. "But they don't come much better than this joint." — (M)

The rules

1 What time do you like to be at your desk?
These days, about 08.00. When I was a chief executive it was usually 07.30.

2 Where's the best place to prepare for leadership: an MBA school or on the job?
On-the-job training really matters but whether you do an MBA or not, it's important you get exposure to the most recent academic thinking.

3 What's your management style?
Inclusive. For the really important decisions you need to have the input of the whole business.

4 Are tough decisions best taken by one person?
Sometimes you have to take them by yourself but often – particularly if time permits – there is a chance to get others to test you.

5 Do you want to be liked or respected?
To be successful you have to be respected but it is difficult to be respected if you're disliked.

6 What does your support team look like?
Small. When I was at BA I had a PA and a driver because I was often whizzing around.

7 What technology do you carry on a trip?
A BlackBerry, another mobile phone and often an iPad.

8 Do you read management books?
I take good ideas wherever I can find them.

9 Run in the morning? Wine with lunch? Socialise with your team after work?
I walk some mornings. I enjoy being at functions with people I work with but the days are gone when I can have wine with lunch.

10 What would your key management advice be?
Never stop learning.

A LONG SHELF LIFE
LONDON

Preface: The managing director and saviour of furniture manufacturer Vitsoe, Mark Adams, tells how he brought the eminent brand back from the brink, the importance of character and why money men are best avoided.

Company: Vitsoe
Location: London
Founded: 1959
Number of employees when founded: Niels Vitsoe and Otto Zapf working with Dieter Rams
Number of employees now: 59
Number of premises: 7
Bestselling product: 606 Universal Shelving System

Quote: *'We wanted to symbolise that we're all in this together'*

"No, managers and management are not referred to here," says Vitsoe managing director Mark Adams, sitting in his office in London's Camden Town surrounded by a wall that's full of the 606 Universal Shelving System by Dieter Rams, a design that the company has manufactured since 1960. "We have leaders and we have mentors. Leadership is conferred by people deciding to follow."

Like Rams' designs, Adams' approach to his position is democratic, no-nonsense and single-minded. It was this special determination and vision as managing director that brought Vitsoe back from the brink.

Roughly 35 years after Niels Vitsoe established the company with partner Otto Zapf in Germany, the once triumphant marque of modern design was flailing – even if it did distribute Rams' shelving – and run by an octogenarian with no succession plan. In 1993, around the time of Niels Vitsoe's 80th birthday, Adams, who owned the licence to distribute Vitsoe products in the UK, got a call from the bank saying the company was three weeks away from closure. As its largest customer, Adams was asked by the Vitsoe family to help. And so he did: remortgaging his house, closing the German arm of the business and shifting operations to the UK. "We lost everything," says Adams. "And we rebuilt it from zero."

Vitsoe is now a buoyant business. It has standalone stores in London, LA, New York, Munich, Copenhagen and Tokyo. Its recovery has taken a long time but that is the result of a team effort that Adams puts down to his staff. "First and foremost, [we look for] character. Skills come second," he says. "People can learn the skills but you can't change the character." The final recruitment stage involves applicants spending a trial day at Vitsoe, with old-timers sitting down at the end of the day for "as long as necessary" to assess candidates. Here, Adams sees his role as editor in chief instead of managing director. "Whenever we have lowered the bar, usually because we're desperate to recruit, it has nearly always been a mistake."

This meticulous recruitment style has helped forge a friendly atmosphere at the Vitsoe HQ. Its buzzer is answered by whichever member of staff happens to be nearest, not by a receptionist; coffees are taken around a communal table. It's truly a happy family, albeit a large one, with far too many siblings now jostling for space.

And it was this factor that forced Adams into offering Vitsoe arguably its third lease of life. Loyal customers and suppliers were offered a chance to buy company bonds. Vitsoe needed to raise a fair sum in order to build a new home.

The invitation came in the form of a charmingly familial and beautifully designed document, in which Adams set out his plan and included his telephone number in case there were any queries. He succeeded and went ahead with plans to complete a new production building in the West Midlands.

What led to this decision to turn to the Vitsoe community instead of venture capitalists to secure the company's future? "Because it is, almost without exception, the beginning of the end when you start bringing in people whose interest is just financial," he says. There is more to it than that: he has sought to create a different type of company, defined by shared interests and collaboration.

"We wanted to symbolise that we're in this together," says Adams of the three-sided knot on the bond document. "Bring in the venture capitalists and you are not all in it together."

Respecting his two forebears – Dieter Rams and Niels Vitsoe – is Adams' primary mission to this day. With good reason, he says: "When the chief executive of Barclays knows nothing about why the Quakers [who founded the bank] set the bank up, when Cadbury can be sold in six weeks flat and 200 years of values can get chucked away; that is what happens when you start with the assumption that 'they can come in and take 20 per cent and it will all be the same'. So we ain't gonna risk it."

Given that the company almost collapsed because its patriarch hadn't planned for the future, Adams is determined to make sure Vitsoe is braced for it. The company secured the global rights to Dieter Rams' original furniture designs and has since released the 620 Chair Programme and 621 Side Table.

Yet Adams' hope is for Vitsoe to go beyond Rams one day – perhaps even go beyond furniture. He is open to what he calls a "living experiment". "The world is going so fast," he says. "What we are doing now is allowing our minds to be completely open for where this company could be." — (M)

The rules

1 What time do you like to be at your desk?
Around 07.00.

2 Where's the best place to prepare for leadership: an MBA school or on the job?
I am deeply sceptical of the whole MBA world.

3 What's your management style?
It's more about leading – articulating a vision and persuading others to follow.

4 Are tough decisions best taken by one person?
Ultimately, yes. But one person has to be relentless in gathering the opinions of others, far and wide, before taking that decision.

5 Do you want to be liked or respected?
You cannot stand for something and be liked by everybody.

6 What does your support team look like?
A company of great people. I don't do PAs.

7 What technology do you carry on a trip?
An iPhone and iPad and, for the past 28 years, a Braun ET 66 [designed by Dieter Rams].

8 Do you read management books?
I would say *The Selfish Gene* [by Richard Dawkins] is a good one.

9 Run in the morning? Wine with lunch? Socialise with your team after work?
The bike is my run. Wine at lunch? I would say virtually never. The last time was probably 18 months ago with somebody I thought I should keep company.

10 What would your key management advice be?
It's about looking out for others rather than yourself. It's about modesty, self-effacement, altruism. It's about less ego. That's my advice – doing it quietly.

THE ICE MAN HELSINKI

Preface: Finland's icebreakers are crucial for keeping the Baltic Sea navigable and its ports open. Captain Tommy Berg is at the helm of Arctia Shipping's 'MSV Fennica'. He says keeping the ship on the right course is ultimately a team effort.

Company: Arctia Shipping
Location: Helsinki
Founded: 2010
Number of employees when founded: 388
Number of employees now: 279
Number of ships: 7
Start-up costs: a new icebreaker costs from €130m to €150m

Quote: *'It's important people feel like they're working towards a common goal'*

Many teams are close-knit. Most, though, do not share a home – and most managers do not eat breakfast, lunch and dinner with their employees. For Tommy Berg, captain of the Finnish icebreaker MSV *Fennica*, these working conditions are both an advantage and a challenge. While living with his team for weeks on end allows him to focus entirely on the job, it also requires a diplomatic management strategy. "We live half our lives here on the ship and half at home," Berg says as he sits in his wood-lined cabin on the second deck of the *Fennica*. "I believe that the time spent here at work should be fulfilling."

The *Fennica* belongs to the state-owned Arctia Shipping, which has a fleet of seven icebreakers. Commercial vessels rely on the icebreakers: they ensure that ships are able to reach the harbours in winter. Outside the icebreaking season the ship can be chartered to work elsewhere. During Berg's years in the job, trips have taken him to Africa, Greenland, Mexico and Brazil. The *Fennica* is equipped with a dynamic positioning system that enables the ship to stand still out at sea and be used as a construction platform. It has also been rented by Shell to secure the company's oil and gas exploration on Alaska's northern coast.

Berg, who lives with his family in a small village on Finland's west coast, is one of two captains on the *Fennica* and usually works three or six-week shifts. The crew consists of 23 people and is split into three divisions: catering, which looks after cleaning and cooking; the deck, including deck officers and crew; and the engine crew. "I often use the phrase 'fair play'," he says. "And that's a two-way street. If I'm fair to you, I expect the same back and vice versa. Working in an environment like this, you need to put a lot of thought into how we're going to make things work. In my experience, orders that are just delivered from a higher authority aren't the best way."

Co-ordinating this team is crucial. Before any important decision – when working in challenging shallow waters or pulling up exceptionally heavy anchors, for example – Berg consults his network of experts or the captains of the *Fennica*'s sister ship, *Nordica*. "A ship like this is so complicated that there's no way for you to have all the expertise required to make these [technical] decisions. Most are made in discussions with others," he says.

Normally Berg starts the day by checking in on the different departments and then works from his office – these days, being a captain entails lots of paperwork. "I'm not a big fan of sitting alone in the office," he says. "Even if I'm not needed, I like to pop in on the bridge."

Occasionally, Berg has to double as the ship's medical doctor – he and some other senior crew members have the basic skills to stitch a wound and give injections. He also plays the role of psychologist. The long periods spent together and away from friends and family put unusual pressure on the crew. "Being out for weeks is tough. Usually the problems are about not getting along with someone," he says. "The most important task for a captain is to create an atmosphere where people feel like they're working together towards a common goal. So I've told everyone that they're welcome to talk to me; my door is always open. OK, sometimes it might be closed and that means I need some time for myself."

Berg has a two-room cabin, consisting of a study-cum-meeting room and a bedroom. During their free time, Berg and the crew use the ship's gym, watch DVDs or do crafts. "Many guys like to make fishing nets, while the women usually knit," he says. And being a Finnish ship, the *Fennica* naturally has a sauna – it's popular and it's always warm.

Berg worked his way from a 20-year-old deck officer to captain, an experience he finds invaluable today. At the bridge he seems at home, enthusiastically explaining the functions of different buttons and drawing diagrams to show how ships stuck in ice are rescued by the team. Softly spoken but with a natural authority, he seems a perfect fit for the job.

"What motivates people is giving them challenging tasks and responsibility and then letting them see it through to the end," he says. "That can still be difficult for me – letting deck officers take care of their work by themselves – but I remember how annoying it was to have a captain breathing down my neck when I was in that position." — (M)

The rules

1 What time do you like to be on deck?
At 06.30. I'd prefer to sleep later but I want to start the day at the same time as the crew. That way, you know right away what's happening.

2 What's the best way to prepare for leadership: getting a degree or out on the job?
The best way is to start from the factory floor and work your way up.

3 Are tough decisions best taken by one person?
No. I work with my team.

4 Do you want to be liked or respected?
Liked. It's important that everything works and that the ship does what it should – but here we also need to be able to live together.

5 What does your support team look like?
The heads of departments onboard and the captains of the sister ship.

6 What technology do you take on a trip?
Just my MacBook and my iPhone.

7 Run in the morning?
Yes. I like to run on the gym treadmill, especially during stressful periods. It helps to clear my head.

8 Wine with lunch?
No. If anyone is caught drinking they are immediately sent packing and picked up by a helicopter.

9 Socialise after work?
Not really. I kind of socialise with them all day long.

10 What would your key management advice be?
Try to let people participate in the decision-making process. That leads to the best results.

BUSINESS MATTERS
GLOBAL

Preface: Dressing for the workplace is about balancing personality and practicality. The constantly evolving environments where we work provide ample opportunity to be creative but keep in mind the importance of first impressions when it comes to new clients – clean and simple often works best.

I

Perhaps you want to change career so that you can dress how you like every day and that may mean a T-shirt and some good jeans. But polished shoes and a suit with a hint of character should not be rejected out of hand. Making the effort to look the part can be interpreted by investors and clients as a sign of respect and an indicator of bigger commitments to presentation and style. Sometimes just the buttoning of a shirt collar and the caress of a tie can make you feel primed for the day ahead.

Look the part
Work attire

2

You don't need to "power dress" to make your mark in the boardroom or on a visit to the factory floor. The options for looking right are numerous when you are running the show. Balance comfort and sharpness but have a bit of fun, too (a good heel can be part of your armour).

3

There's a middle path (for both men and women)
that increasingly carries the day. An unstructured
jacket that can still impress when slightly crumpled,
a chino made from a crisp cotton and a knitted tie that
can be comfortably worn in most work environments
are the way ahead.

PHOTOGRAPHER: *Seishi Shirakawa*, FASHION DIRECTOR: *Akio Hasegawa*
HAIR AND MAKE-UP: *Kenichi Yaguchi*, MODELS: *Idye Harada from INDIGO & Youki from AMAZONE*

Preface

People are ever more mobile. They can decide where they want to work. And many of those same people get to a point where they realise they need to find a base that offers a satisfying balance between business efficiency – somewhere that lets you travel with ease, has a good network for supporting trade and an office space that's painless to rent – and the elements that you need for an enjoyable quality of life.

That means a village, town or city that can give you things to do when the office day is done and also offers a bit of an escape nearby (skiing on Saturday morning, anyone?). You don't have to base yourself in a big city to get your work done. Be it a small city or rural refuge, there are plenty of people who have discovered that they can have the networks and support they need in spots that not long ago would have been considered way off the grid.

These are the entrepreneurs with a philanthropic streak who see running a business as a way to fix a town or a city. However you see your role in this mix you'll find lots of places to add to your travel itinerary in your hunt for the perfect territory from which to run your empire.

Contents

4

BUSINESS CITIES (AND VILLAGES)

The changing business landscape and where to base yourself

BRISBANE
AUSTRALIA

Preface: Situated on Australia's east coast, Brisbane offers a manageable and inviting location for businesses while being well located for connecting with clients in Asia or the US.

Population: 2.2 million
Key trades: energy and resource sectors
Time to register a business: 1 hour
Annual hours of sunshine: 2,900
International flights: 24

———

Quote: '*Being isolated, you get this petri dish effect where you're naïve to what's going on in the rest of the world*'

Brisbane is Australia's third-most populous city – an upstart oasis in the midst of a conservative state. With Asia and LA just an overnight haul away, it's in a prime position for growth. The city council has developed an economically focused digital strategy to shape Brisbane as a start-up hub along the lines of Boulder, Colorado. It sees strength in not being the primary city but instead being of a manageable size and having a great quality of life.

Ben Johnston is the shaggy-haired co-founder and director of Brisbane design studio Josephmark. Since his firm broke onto the world stage with a design for a cult music website he has become accustomed to regular flights to Los Angeles for work. Yet as he wanders around the electricity substation his company calls home, he insists his hometown's remote location is a boon.

"Being isolated, you get this petri dish effect where you're naïve to what's going on in the rest of the world and you start

benchmarking things," Johnston says. "It wasn't until we started working with North American companies that we realised the expectations we set for ourselves are very high on a global level."

Brisbane's creative economy has also gained traction. Takeshi Takada and Colin Renshaw cofounded visual-effects studio Alt.vfx in 2011 and have received global attention for work with Qantas, Pepsi and Diageo. The Alt.vfx office is the kind of dream workspace that could only exist in a climate such as Brisbane's: a sprawling warren sandwiched between two former church buildings with a meeting room that doubles as an atrium, an open-air kitchen and rooftop desks for when the office is packed.

Brisbane's civic identity is also shaping a unique entrepreneurial culture. Whereas an exodus of twenty-somethings to Sydney and Melbourne was once inevitable, more and more Brisbanites are now staying at home in subtropical comfort. From bespoke menswear outlets such as Andrew Byrne's The Cloakroom to bustling micro-developments such as Winn Lane, the city also has a new strut in retail. "Brisbane is a forgiving market and a great place to start a business," says Byrne. "People are always interested in something that's new. There isn't a cut-throat edge."

Jessica Huddart, Josephmark's creative director, explains that the firm's international trajectory will never see them leave Brisbane behind. It has invested in two small bars in the city and she organises collaborations between local creatives that exhibit at Brisbane's Powerhouse Museum. "We're a very community-minded company," she says. — (M)

01
Alt.vfx staff outside their office
02
Workspace at Alt.vfx
03
Clint Harvey shows off the letterpress machinery in the print-history department of Design College Australia

04

05

06

04
View of
Brisbane River
from South Bank
05
City Hall on
King George
Square

07

06
Evan Shay,
venue
manager of
Alfred &
Constance
07
Public seating at
Brisbane Library

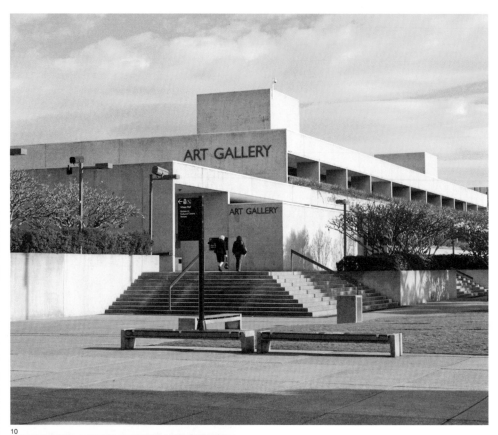

08
Atavist Books in
Fortitude Valley
09
Andrew Byrne,
proprietor of
The Cloakroom
10
Queensland
Art Gallery,
South Bank
11
Bar at Alfred &
Constance
12
Josephmark
director
Ben Johnston
13
Brisbane River
and central
business district

15

13

16

14

17

On the ground

1 With Brisbane being the de facto international airport for many nearby South Pacific nations, there are market opportunities aplenty in paradise.

2 This is a sports-mad city and you'll find your meetings tough going if there's any sniff that you don't know the difference between rugby league and union.

3 Brisbane City Council has blanketed most of the inner city with free wi-fi.

4 Don't just soak up the energy of the West End creative scene – contribute to it. Australians are much more welcoming when you're the one throwing a party.

5 This is a city that likes things a little looser in the every day. Dress as though surfing is always a possibility.

ZÜRICH
SWITZERLAND

Preface: Showing a dynamism not often associated with Switzerland, the city of Zürich is attracting a new breed of start-ups with its sturdy business infrastructure and an impressive quality of life.

Population: 1.2 million
Key trades: financial and service sectors
Time to register a company: between 1 and 3 weeks
Annual hours of sunshine: 1,500
International flights: 166

Quote: *'If you have a good idea it's easy to find funding and get your business off the ground'*

Zürich, the lakeside city famous for banking and confectionery, has experienced something of a metamorphosis. It has always been a popular hub due to the ease of doing business, low tax rates and security but change is in the air. A vibrant start-up culture is putting paid to the conception that all things Swiss are a bit dull.

While the world struggled after the 2008 financial crisis, Switzerland was busy attracting bright minds and innovative entrepreneurs. ETH, one of the world's leading universities for technology and natural sciences, played a major role in this.

"University research projects often develop into interesting businesses and Walt Disney set up its research lab close to the campus to profit from a creative workforce," says Michel Bachmann, co-founder of Impact Hub Zürich, a company supporting entrepreneurs.

The city's government takes a keen interest in promoting an innovative environment and supports young businesses. "If you have a good idea it's easy to find funding and get your business off the ground," says Benno Seiler, deputy director of urban planning in Zürich.

The city's can-do spirit coupled with great services and connectivity also appeals to global ventures. Google and IBM are just a couple of the behemoth multinationals that have pitched their tents here. "Zürich has one of the best infrastructures for business: the banks, the post, the trains, the trams and the proximity to the airport make this the ideal place to set up your headquarters," says Chandra Kurt, a Zürich-based wine consultant.

Zürich consistently ranks as one of the world's most liveable places, not least because of its proximity to nature. Besides the choice of museums, galleries, theatres and open-air dining options, the city's charm is most apparent in its off-the-beaten-track venues. Everything is accessible on foot or by bike.

The canton of Zürich generates 20 per cent of the national GDP and its growth poses challenges – mostly due to space. "Zürich has changed greatly," says Daniel Freitag, co-founder of Freitag bags. "There is hardly any affordable space available for those who need more than just a desk. Still, as long as entrepreneurs have a good team and are well connected, Zürich is a great place to start a business."

In the years ahead, Zürich must find creative solutions to sustain the good life. If the city can maintain its mix of under-stated chic, bustling business and effortless efficiency, this lakeside hub will continue to feel like the place to be. — (M)

01

02

01
Wohnbedarf furniture store
02
Christian Hunziker, co-owner of menswear store Pelikamo

03
Andrea
Wiegelmann
of Swiss
publishing
firm Niggli
04
The city's
efficient tram
network
05
Zürich is known
for its *Badi*:
open-air bathing
areas usually
with a bar
attached to
them, found
along Lake
Zürich and the
Limmat River

03   04

05

06
Barbara
Messmer of
Wohnbedarf
furniture store
07
Zürich's
proximity to the
mountains is a
major plus point

06

08
Boats can be
hired for a cruise
on the lake
09
The Viadukt
development
houses shops
and cafés

07

08   09

On the ground

1. An excellent education and apprenticeship system has created a highly qualified and multilingual workforce.

2. In terms of starting capital, for a private company think upwards of 20,000 Swiss francs; for a PLC it's closer to 100,000.

3. Local staff costs are high but tax rates remain relatively low.

4. Sustainability is highly valued in Switzerland – this is where forward-looking theories of eco-sufficiency are created and executed.

5. The city is safe and nature is on your doorstep – you'll find world-class ski slopes just one-and-a-half hours away.

10
Clouds restaurant
11
Michael Ringier, CEO of Swiss publisher Ringier AG
12
Hospitality at the Käsers Schloss whisky and farm shop
13
Swiss department store Jelmoli
14
One of Zürich's many green spaces

12

11

13

14

MADRID
SPAIN

Preface: Development in Spain is occurring on a smaller scale than the pre-crisis years, with a young group of entrepreneurs revitalising the hospitality and retail sectors in Madrid.

Population: 6.5 million
Key trades: IT and telecommunications, media and publishing, finance, insurance
Time to register a business: at least 3 weeks
Annual hours of sunshine: 2,900
International flights: 146

Quote: *'There has been an explosion of creativity from young Spanish people since the crisis'*

Spain has had some tough moments in recent years as the economy shrank and unemployment climbed. But for start-ups – especially ones that want to be based somewhere with an eclectic social scene – Madrid has lots to offer.

If the pre-crisis years were characterised by grandiose infrastructure projects, development is now on a smaller, grass-roots scale. The sound of construction echoes from countless new shops, bars and restaurants springing up across the inner city. After losing their jobs and exhausting their efforts in a dismal job market, many young, educated *Madrileños* have opted to open their own small businesses.

Buoyed by lowering rents and often backed with finance from supportive family members, many of these entrepreneurs have flocked to the hospitality sector. Antonio de Santiago opened his bar and restaurant Circo de las Tapas when he was 29. With a background in advertising he is new to the industry but, judging by the consistent crowds, his risk seems to have paid off. De Santiago inspected 60 available venues before settling on the formerly run-down street and, since opening, has witnessed the area flourish, with at least seven similar new businesses opening nearby. "There has been an explosion of creativity from young Spanish people since the crisis. Small theatre spaces, modern restaurants and clothing stores are regenerating entire neighbourhoods," he says.

The city council also encouraged the capital's new, spirited entrepreneurial culture by creating Madrid Emprende: a municipal network of small-business incubators. Designed and built with public money, they are managed by private companies and business schools.

Part of the government's challenge has been to take a step back. The centres have been allowed to evolve organically, with a focus on shared workspaces and providing needs-based services such as marketing advice and access points for local government services.

There have also been changes in retail. Rocío Muñoz and her online retail venture La Real Fábrica is throwing a lifeline to a series of iconic Spanish brands. She has a growing customer base in the UK and Japan, enticed by her carefully selected range of Spanish goods from traditional crafts to food and cosmetic labels.

David Castro's young artisan beer label, Cervezas La Cibeles, is being exported to Japan, the US, Sweden and Norway and the small brewery now sells more than 150,000 litres a year. "We're the backbone of the economic recovery in Spain," he says. — (M)

01

02

04

03

05

06

07
Entrance to Sol
Metro Station in
central Madrid
08
View of Madrid
Río Park
09
The town hall
and culture
centre in Plaza
de Cibeles

07   08

10
Entrepreneurs
with offices
at Madrid
Emprende
11
Calle Cava Baja,
a popular food
destination
12
Rocío Muñoz
of Real Fábrica
Española

09

10

11

12

On the ground

1 Speaking Spanish is still a must when dealing with people in a business environment.

2 Accept the local schedule and adjust yours accordingly. While many new businesses open all day, the best time to get anything done is usually between 10.00 and 14.00 and 17.00 and 19.00.

3 The relaxed culture of the city carries on into the business domain so don't be afraid to socialise with clients. A true *Madrileño* would never turn down the opportunity to have a *caña* (small beer) or a *vermut* (vermouth).

4 A flourishing network of co-working spaces have sprung up in the city in recent years. Save on costs and build up a good network with other active entrepreneurs under the same roof.

5 The quickest way to jet across town to an important meeting is on Madrid's extensive and efficient Metro.

13

13
Palacio de
Cristal in Buen
Retiro Park
14
Plaza Dos
de Mayo

15
Cervezas La
Cibeles bottles
are collected by
a worker
16
Calle del Espíritu
Santo

14

15 16

SENDAI
JAPAN

01
Staff at
Nagakansome
textile-printing
company
02
Dancers at
the summer
'matsuri' festival
03
Terrace at
Café Mozart
04
View of Sendai
from the city's
castle

Preface: Smart planning regulations and incentives for small businesses have helped regenerate the Japanese city most affected by the 2011 earthquake. Bucking the regional depopulation trend, Sendai is proving itself a success story against all the odds.

Population: 1.3 million
Key trades: retail, services, construction and manufacturing
Time to register a business: 1 business week
Annual hours of sunshine: 1,900
International flights: 9

———

Quote: *'Frequently cited for its creative industries, Sendai has the advantage of not being dependent on any one sector'*

Sitting at Café Mozart overlooking the Hirose River, surrounded by vintage furniture and students deep in conversation, it would be easy to forget that Sendai was the city closest to Japan's worst natural disaster on record: a magnitude nine earthquake followed by a tsunami that tore into the coast in 2011.

Yet Sendai has experienced something of a boom. Public funds have swelled with money for reconstruction projects as the city turns the catastrophe into an opportunity for renewal.

A green, compact city with a concentration of universities, Sendai has an unusually youthful atmosphere in a region stricken with depopulation. Although it is frequently cited for its creative industries, Sendai has the advantage of not being dependent on any one sector. Employers include everything from brewers and oil refineries to IT companies and workshops. Among the most established are the wholesalers, a powerful group who bring in a combined income of ¥600bn and even

have their own district, Oroshimachi. Aware that Japan's shrinking population will present challenges to their business, the wholesalers have embraced regeneration and are working with renowned architect Hitoshi Abe, who was born in Sendai and still has an office there.

To lighten the industrial feel of the Oroshimachi area, which is dominated by warehouses, the city has changed planning regulations to allow residential buildings along the main street. The wholesalers' HQ has been turned into a shared office space for 50 small businesses.

Sendai already had a financial incentive scheme in place to encourage new manufacturing and research facilities but since the earthquake the city has redoubled its efforts, offering a plethora of seminars, workshops and advice to both young and established firms.

One scheme pairs Sendai companies with designers to see how their products could be improved. Beneficiaries include Nagakansome, a family-run textile-printing business that has been operating out of the same workshop for decades. There are other examples of small businesses being nurtured by an impressive support system, such as a young coffee-roasting firm that was the recipient of a packaging makeover and a *kamaboko* (fish paste, a local favourite) producer that was given help to create a signature product that would stand out from its competitors.

New infrastructure, including the Super Komachi bullet train linking Sendai to Tokyo in just over 90 minutes, a new subway line and a rebuilt airport has added to the sense of a city on the road to recovery. — (M)

04

02   03

On the ground

1 Sendai has been an important commercial centre for hundreds of years and is well connected by road, rail and air. It has an international shipping network to cities as far afield as LA, Busan and Shanghai.

2 The city has a youthful population with 10 universities and nearly 50,000 students.

3 One of Japan's most creative cities, Sendai has an established jazz festival and an innovative cultural facility in Toyo Ito's Mediatheque. Tradition is important too: the Sendai Tanabata festival attracts two million visitors.

4 Sendai is known as the City of Trees (*Mori no Miyako*) for its green thoroughfares such as Jozenji Street and Aoba, which run through the centre of town.

5 Sendai rents are significantly cheaper than Tokyo and the government is eager to welcome new businesses and research initiatives, offering subsidies to incoming employers.

05

06

07

09
Local men carry a shrine at the summer festival
10
Exterior of the Sendai Mediatheque

05
Café Mozart
06
Makoto Takahashi at his restaurant Oyaji
07
Super Komachi bullet train
08
Live music on Jozenji Street

08

09

10

12

11
Library at
the Sendai
Mediatheque,
designed by
Toyo Ito
12
Masae Aoki at
her coffee-
roasting business
Mamebou
13
Ayumi Mori at
the Nagakansome
workshop

11

13

LONDON
UK

Preface: The British capital felt fragile in the wake of the financial crisis but has proved its resilience with an energetic regeneration powered by a new breed of small businesses – especially out in the East End.

Population: 8.2 million
Key trades: financial services, banking, retail, tourism and creative industries
Time to register a business: 2 working days (online)
Annual hours of sunshine: 1,600
International flights: 177 (Heathrow)

Quote: *'This melting pot still exudes a vitality so many other capitals lack'*

In 2012, just weeks before the London Olympics, *Der Spiegel* looked on scathingly at life and work in Britain's capital. It bemoaned the millions that squeezed into the clattering Underground to inhale "the melded odours of perspiration and perfume" in a wound-up city obsessed with money.

But big business too often takes centre stage when it comes to typifying London's working life. Another London has been busy working on a very different schedule: a version where a relaxed – or non-existent – commute takes precedent over a corporate pay cheque. In the shadow of the City of London, neighbourhoods that were at best artistic and scruffy and at worst downright grim, are flourishing with a healthy air of self-containment.

Under the rustling of enormous London plane trees, a not-so-quiet industriousness is underway at Hackney Downs Studios in east London. Here it doesn't matter if you're Japanese or Italian as long as you are designing, developing or sketching to your clients' requirements. Since 2011 the converted print works has been home to everything from record labels to architects and doubles up as a busy music and event space.

London's brute strength has always been based on the talent it attracts from all over the world. Despite cumbersome, sometimes shortsighted UK immigration policies, Argentines and Angolans miraculously rub shoulders in the galleries and bars of Shoreditch and Dalston. This melting pot still exudes a vitality so many other capitals lack.

London remains a city of craftsmen. Jack Trench set up a bespoke cabinet maker and architectural joiner in 2003 in an industrial quarter near Hackney Marshes. "The project was meant to last two days," he says. However, the company grew and gained clients in London, Sweden, Spain and beyond. You don't have to listen hard to hear the yards of east London humming with activity.

At Lockwood Umbrellas in Shoreditch, Edward Gucewicz and Moses Manley's workshop is keeping a London speciality alive. Snuggled against the Ace Hotel, the pair sell crafted umbrellas. On inspection, it's easy to believe that they learned these skills at James Smith & Sons, that icon of old London manufacturing found across town in Bloomsbury.

Long criticised for its urban management, London is finally shaping up. Its neighbourhoods are better connected and once-snubbed areas such as Hackney are now prime locations to set up shop – as the flow of creative talent testifies. Working in London has never seemed less like a necessity and more like a well-informed choice. — (M)

01
View from
Heron Tower
02
Six-legged run
on Primrose Hill
03
Netil Market
in Hackney
04
Rush hour at
Liverpool Street
railway station

05
Fitting a top spring in the Lockwood Umbrellas workshop
06
View from Primrose Hill

07
Edward Gucewicz (left) and Moses Manley, owners of Lockwood Umbrellas

03   04

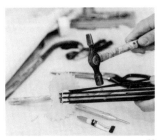

05

06   07

08
The Hackney
Empire
09
Artist Lauren
Baker at her
Hackney Downs
Studios workshop
10
Designer
Carles Rodrigo
at Broadway
Market

09

11
Camden Road
Overground
station
12
L'eau à La
Bouche café
in Broadway
Market
13
30 St Mary Axe
(also known as
the Gherkin)

10

08

11

13

12

14

15 16

17 18

Borough Market

20

19

On the ground

1 Businesses and entrepreneurs in London are used to having a huge amount of competition. If you cut your teeth here you'll have just about the sharpest gnashers going.

2 London might lack the finesse of its Scandinavian rivals but listening to the client and delivering promptly have long been core tenants of work life in London.

3 At Hackney Downs Studios, business tenants know full well that their workplace is on what used to be called London's "Murder Mile". But now an atmosphere of calm and serene creativity seems to dominate.

4 The old line about there not being a bus when you need one and then three come along at once might be a part of the mental image of the Big Smoke. Now huge infrastructure projects (Crossrail, east London/Overground network) are making the commute to work much more comfortable.

5 Nobody agrees on how to define a Londoner. At least five years of residence might do it. But what is clear is that place of birth isn't the issue. As with the famous cabbie test, being a Londoner is more about "the knowledge".

14
Lloyd's building
seen from
Leadenhall
Market
15
Russet café
at Hackney
Downs Studios
16
View from
London Bridge

17
London taxi
18
Shakespeare's
Head pub
overlooking
Carnaby Street
19
Borough Market
20
Café on Noel
Street, Soho

173

03/04

How to make it in the city
Why keyboards are out and tool benches are in
by Andrew Tuck

PREFACE: Cities used to be places where people made things. But as the service sector grew and the number of white-collar jobs increased, people soon lost interest in the handmade and the real. Now the tide is turning, with the 'made' movement rekindling the desire for artisan goods and reminding us what it is that cities are actually for.

It's good to make things in the city – and luckily that message can be seen, heard and smelt in an increasing number of metropolises around the world. Perhaps even in the city where you live. Go on, stand still for a moment. Can you see people scurrying around in their aprons? Hear the beat of hammer on metal or the snipping of wires? Can you smell fresh bread being pulled from an oven or the fragrance of juniper berries being added to a gin distillery, or perhaps the scent of prime leather being cut and trimmed in a luggage-maker's atelier? From the West Coast to Nordic shores and Asian hot spots to Australian beach capitals, something important is stirring. And you should be part of it.

The financial quake of 2008 left a lot of people feeling scared and dislocated. But also oddly awake. They looked around and saw the folly of believing that they, their city and their nation could get by on just the clatter of keyboards and the flickering screens of traders' computers. Service jobs are all well and good but to have a fully fledged and robust economy you also need people who know how to make things, who can use their hands and like to feel a bit of muscle ache at the end of the day.

Even if City Halls were slower than the people to react, there was just something in the air that made it clear that cities needed to start making things again. And it was also clear that if you got this revival under way, all sorts of other benefits would follow.

Lots of the freshest thinking about the joy of making things has come out of San Francisco, home to the so-called maker movement. It's a crusade that, as its name suggests, is about making stuff; rolling up your sleeves and doing it yourself. Some of its heritage goes back to the tech pioneers who made the early advances in computing by soldering wires in garages. However, today it's not just about the tech engineer but about a whole world of people who want to make bikes, food, anything. There's something about the pioneering vibe of the West Coast that's given it a deep resonance here. And its supporters have also been good at creating the shared spaces and events that justify the "movement" tag.

What's also intriguing is that in a city where people can become billionaires overnight by creating digital businesses there's a parallel world of people who crave the real, the artisanal and the slow. On a trip to Palo Alto I was speaking to someone high up in the city's tech aristocracy who told me about a wine shop where the owner plays proper vinyl records. It struck me how even the people who seem fixated by pixels and clouds hanker after the real. At heart both the tech world and the maker movement have a shared interest in making stuff. Stuff you can hold in your hands.

There's another reflection of this that you now find in several cities. Yes, in San Francisco but also Copenhagen. It's also a movement, one that celebrates localism and city provenance. It's the "made" movement that is part evangelical passion for creating things in cities, part eco-crusade (if you make the things your city needs in your city then goods travel shorter distances and cause less environmental damage) and part community building. Groups of makers coalesce and support each other in numerous ways, not least with some smart marketing. CPH Made, for example, states: "We are on a quest to celebrate great local craftsmanship. To show the world that not all products come with a 'Made in China' label." All of its members live within a 10km radius of Copenhagen and they make everything from chocolates to custom-built motorbikes. They also have an online shop.

That's not to say all cities are equal in their passion for supporting the makers and menders. Some city authorities have outdated zoning laws that push even the lightest of industry from the heart of the city to the fringes. And sometimes city authorities are too quick to back neighbours who have got used to an unnaturally quiet urban life and don't like it when they can hear a saw cutting wood or a sewing machine whirring merrily. Bad luck. Cities are

Urban landscape

1 Background noise
Make the most of your city location in your branding. People want to know your story and a key part of that is where you have taken root. It doesn't mean resorting to tourist clichés but something that quietly says Paris, Seoul or Sydney will help in a world of companies that are coy about their origins.

2 Seasonal cheer
Does your city lack a group that markets products proud of their urban heritage? Don't wait around: start one. Make the most of vacant spaces for pop-up or permanent stores, especially if you can gather together products that appeal to, say, visitors or Christmas shoppers. Seasonal works.

3 Front and centre
Even if you have a product that can be made and assembled out of sight, think how you could use retail as a literal shop window onto all that you do.

4 Worldly workforce
Cities are places of movement and migration so you will benefit from a diverse talent pool if you set yourself up in the right city. Numerous makers of luxury goods in Italy have taken on apprentices in everything from shoemaking to tailoring. Think how you can open yourself up to the world without leaving HQ.

5 Read the signs
Decide where is the best city for your business and move there. Don't invest in a city that lacks the elements you need for success.

better with clatter and trade. That's what they were devised for. If you want utter silence you are in the wrong place.

In a time before white-collar jobs became the norm, cities were alive with people making stuff. There are streets in London today that are silent and gentrified but which just a couple of decades ago were punctuated by car-repair shops, printers, knife sharpeners and furniture workshops. Slowly they vanished as the desire for the handmade was lost and we threw away anything that got broken. But we now see what we gave away and lots of entrepreneurs want to turn the tide back.

They are also being helped by a trend mentioned by CPH Made. People are happy to pay more for products that are authentic and have a genuine brand story behind them. Words such as luxury have become a little tarnished. Can a product made in China and assembled in Italy, all in bleak factories, be called a luxury product? This is where you come in. If you have a product with a clear and honest story then you can deliver something unique and special. Whether it's dresses or pottery, a modest city atelier can be the place to start something very special.

Even bigger companies are realising there's a shift. That's why we are seeing so much reshoring of production from countries that made their names and fortunes by offering up their people on low wages to manufacture the world's consumer goods. As salaries have risen in these nations and quality levels have failed to meet the demanding standards of consumers, so the appeal of producing everything in, say, Guangzhou has waned.

And this is helping bring about some big changes in some surprising urban spots. Take Los Angeles, a city with a global brand image that embraces the beach and Hollywood and little else. Well, the reality is very different. Central LA may not be the smartest address but in among the gritty bars and shelters for the homeless there's also a plethora of fun restaurants, artists' studios and a dense network of businesses making clothing, toys and furniture. Some of this is at the artisan level but there are also some bigger players here who have not been pushed, as in many cities, to the edge of town. As gentrification has advanced, the area has become a hotbed of craft-driven innovation. And the new companies that come here are actually spurred on by a rejection of some of the city's hollower values. Here are people who want to work for themselves and also employ the city's talented workforce.

But there are cities that have never lost their passion for making things – that don't really need any revival, thank you. Walk the *sois* of Bangkok or disappear into the alleys of Istanbul and you

will find that beyond the top tier of western cities the passion for making everything and anything flourishes as it always has.

This brings simple wins for a city – and wins that some of the most developed cities are warming to. If you make products where people also live it means that they don't have to commute to work and there's life on the streets at all times, which makes a place feel secure and allows people to develop a sense of pride for the skills that their city quarter represents.

It's a lifestyle that sits comfortably with many new young entrepreneurs who do not share the same values as their parents and have very different markers for what success looks like. They would prefer to have a fixed-gear bike sitting in the hall of their city pad than a hatchback on the drive of their suburban cookie-cutter home.

This is why you should consider anchoring your fledgling firm in the heart of your city. Be a part of a community; see how you and the people around you can flourish together. Know that there are people who will recognise you at lunch and ask how it's all going. It's one of the joys of going it alone – suddenly realising that you are anything but. So make some noise. Hit hammer on nail, rasp plane on plank and knead that dough with vigour. You are now a city entrepreneur of the new variety. And it's a variety that's here to stay. — (M)

HONOLULU
USA

01

Preface: Despite its remote location, Honolulu has become an important hub for Pacific trade and business. With impressive plans for public-transport renovation and a skilled young workforce, there's plenty going for Hawaii's capital.

Population: 390,000
Key trades: tourism and agriculture
Time to register a business: 2 to 3 working days if express, otherwise 7 to 10 days
Annual hours of sunshine: 3,200
International flights: 22

Quote: *'The city has become an attractive place for those looking to establish a second career'*

With its sun-soaked climate and laidback lifestyle, Honolulu may not immediately spring to mind as a top global business city. But positioned almost equidistantly between the US and Japan, Hawaii's state capital has become a hub for Pacific trade.

As one of the most popular tourist destinations in the US, it's perhaps unsurprising that Honolulu is an important centre for international air travel. From the charming airport terminal, flights leave for destinations across North America, Asia and Australasia.

A city that has long been dominated by cars, Honolulu will soon be a place where public transport offers an efficient alternative to bumper-to-bumper traffic. By 2019 the Honolulu Rail Transit project will be complete, predicted to remove around 40,000 cars from the city's congested roads. And with a 12-minute link from Honolulu's airport to the centre, the new rail transit link will make the city's global business ties even more efficient.

Infrastructure aside, setting up a business in Honolulu is relatively easy. While normal business registration takes up to 10 days, an expedited service is available to process applications within two days. And sourcing a talented workforce shouldn't be too hard either. With sun, sea and surf available pretty much all year round, as well as good schools and residential neighbourhoods, there's plenty to make relocating an experienced team relatively simple.

Hawaii's homegrown population is also a dynamic one. Over recent years, Honolulu has seen many of its young people returning home after university in mainland US. Setting up media companies, restaurants, organic farms and clean-tech businesses, young entrepreneurs are leading a generation that is reinvesting in its hometown, spurred on by the city's increasing global importance. Former furniture sellers Mark Pei and Travis Flazer set up Hound and Quail in 2011, selling an eclectic mix of curiosities from around the world.

But it's not just Hawaiians who have decided to move back to Honolulu. The city has become an attractive place for those looking to establish a second career in an environment where the standard of living is higher than many other US cities. Eric Rose left his restaurant business in Seattle to set up the Morning Glass coffee shop in the Manoa Valley. Waking early each morning, Rose roasts the beans and bakes the pastries himself before heading out for his daily surf. Serving customers at the breezy café located near the University of Hawaii's main campus, Rose's working day unfolds at Honolulu's easy pace, one with which few other cities are able to compete. — (M)

02

01
Downtown
farmers' market
02
View over
Honolulu
03
Hawaii
governor's office
04
Eric Rose, owner
of Morning
Glass coffee shop

03

04

05
Didi Robello,
who runs Aloha
Beach Services
on Waikiki
06
State capitol
building
07
Alan Joaquin,
the man behind
FarmRoof

05

06   07

08
Hound and
Quail's simple
shopping bag
09
Vintage furniture
and knick-knacks
at Hound and
Quail

08

11

09

12

10

10
Malakole
harbour, Oahu

11
Travis Flazer and
Mark Pei, owners
of Hound and
Quail

12
Kuhio Beach,
Honolulu
13
Lei maker in
Honolulu's
Chinatown

14
Aloha Rag shop
in Honolulu
15
Waikiki Beach
looking towards
Diamond Head

13

On the ground

1 Honolulu has the perfect blend of nature and urbanism with art galleries and museums never far from mountains, hiking trails and crystal-clear waters.

2 Local government-sponsored business incentives such as the Enterprise Zones Partnership and the Hawaii Small Business Innovation Research encourage entrepreneurs.

3 A tropical idyll yet still part of the US, doing business in Hawaii means becoming part of the world's largest and most diversified economy, as well as one with benefits such as intellectual-property protections and free-trade agreements.

4 Asians make up more than 50 per cent of Honolulu's population, making it the perfect place to set up a business that's looking west over the Pacific.

5 The city is taking advantage of its climate and investing in environmentally conscious practices. From electric-car charging stations to rooftop farms, Honolulu is a good base for sustainable business.

15

179

PALMA
SPAIN

Preface: Proving its worth as far more than just one of Europe's sunnier corners, the Mallorcan city of Palma has made itself a business-friendly destination with lighter legislation and a buoyant social scene.

Population: 407,600
Key trades: tourism (80 per cent of GDP)
Time to register a business: between 20 and 30 days
Annual hours of sunshine: 2,800
International flights: Palma de Mallorca Airport serves 35 international destinations

———

Quote: *'The council has reduced red tape and fast-tracked provisional licences for new businesses, making it easier to set up shop'*

Palma has long struggled to compete with the allure of Mallorca's coastal villages. But now there is a concerted effort to transform the city into a destination in its own right, cultivating terrain for entrepreneurs and prompting newfound confidence. It helps that it has one of Europe's busiest airports and that the city flourishes all year round – not just at the peak of summer.

The city council has reduced red tape and fast-tracked provisional licences for new businesses, making it easier to set up shop. Publicly funded body Palma Activa is pulling in a new generation of entrepreneurs, opening hours have been liberalised, permits granted for terrace seating on the pavements and more cultural spaces built, breathing new life into the city.

Start-ups have been appearing in unexpected places. Native food entrepreneurs Javier Bonet, Oliver Torrents and Perico Cortés opened their restaurant Patrón Lunares in a former social club for retired fisherman; today the tables are filled by locals and newcomers. "Many foreigners are looking to gain a foothold here, eager to invest in their second home," says Torrents.

Miquel Calvente and Toni Emazabel opened the island's first espresso bar, La Molienda, encouraged by cheap rent and the new licensing process. Calvente, who was a barista in Madrid, is establishing a similar coffee culture on the island. The café has steadily lured the crowds off the main shopping strip and into the small space in the heart of the old quarter.

There are also signs of recovery in the manufacturing sector. Since launching three outlets of men's fashion shop Addict, retailers Tony Jiménez and Suso Ramos have funnelled their profits into new brand Mews. Not far away, fashion designer Elia Riche's showroom houses womenswear label Aïle.

Perhaps one of the best indicators of the economy's health is the local art market. Swedish couple Stefan and Pärnilla Lundgren opened their private gallery Landings in a reformed palace. Exhibiting some of the world's best contemporary artists, their shows often sell out before even opening to buyers from across the world. "This island brings out the best in people," says Stefan, "mainly because people want to be here."

This pull, combined with smart local policies, has meant that people aren't just investing in Palma but are invested here, too, fuelling a refreshingly buoyant mood in the city. It's created real momentum for entrepreneurs young and old, giving the locals more reason than ever to sing their island's praises. — (M)

01

02

04

01
Avenida Jaume III
02
Toni Emazabel (left) and Miquel Calvente (right), owners of La Molienda
03
La Molienda aims for a new coffee culture
04
La Molienda's entrance on Carrer de les Caputxines in the city's old quarter

03

05
Terrace seating is
a new feature of
Plaça Del Cort
06
Elia Riche in her
new city-centre
showroom for
brand Aïle
07
Materials and
products by Aïle
08
Addict founder
Suso Ramos
09
Selection
of menswear
available at the
Addict boutique

06

05

07

08   09

181

10
Co-owner of
Patrón Lunares,
Oliver Torrents
11
Patrón Lunares
exterior
12
Inside Patrón
Lunares

13
Stefan and
Pärnilla
Lundgren in
their home
and gallery
14
Interior of Stefan
and Pärnilla's
Landings Gallery
and residence

15
Former
fishermans' club
Patrón Lunares
16
Tony Jiménez
with pieces from
Addict's new
Mews label
17
View across
Palma from
Santa Catalina

15   16

17

On the ground

1. Appealing to local tastes as well as foreign trends will lay the foundation for a successful business that isn't susceptible to seasonality.

2. Don't get the winter blues. Palma has become attractive all year round – your business should, too.

3. Park your car. Everything in Palma is so close that you can travel to most places on foot or using the city's new bike-share scheme.

4. Millions of people converge on Palma every summer so prepare to work hard over the peak season.

5. Clear your head. Close proximity to the beach and mountains provide the perfect opportunity for stress relief – and the headspace to plan your next venture.

REYKJAVÍK
ICELAND

Preface: Following the economic downturn in 2008 – in which Iceland suffered badly – a new breed of smaller-scale, local-focused companies that rely on each others' ingenuity for support are forming in the nation's capital.

Population: 204,800
Key trade: fishing
Time to register a business: 4 days
Annual hours of sunshine: 1,250
International flights: Keflavik International Airport offers direct flights to around 50 international cities on both sides of the Atlantic, including New York and London

---

Quote: *'My main interest is the collaboration of designers with other disciplines'*

Gudrun Lilja Gunnlaugsdóttir is sitting on a mid-century velour sofa at Stofan Kaffihús in central Reykjavík talking about the travails of family business. "My husband and I lost everything in the crash," says the former furniture maker who runs Studiobility, a consultancy, design studio and shop that works with local designers making modern Icelandic products. "With no loans, we started again. My husband Jón has launched a store called Kickstart [selling menswear]. I helped with the design. We have hosted lectures about creative leadership and we are planning a 3D printing workshop here."

The financial collapse in 2008 has spawned a generation of small, close-knit and distinctly Icelandic ventures but there is also room for outside investors. In 2010, Karl Sigurdarson was project manager at tourism firm Eskimos after his job at a car dealership became null and void in 2008. Today, he's working on film sets with Hollywood producers. Spurred on by the weak

Icelandic króna and favourable tax breaks, Hollywood directors are flocking to film in the island's uniquely ethereal landscape. "The weather also helps," says Sigurdarson. "We have 24 hours of [summer] daylight so it was great for continuity."

While sectors such as film and tourism are growing, many residents remain deeply indebted and borrowing from lenders for new business ventures is very difficult. Despite this, locals are now focusing on what is real and distinctly Icelandic.

"As the professor at the academy I came across all these projects that had great potential but were stuck as prototypes or simply ideas," says Sigurjónsdóttir. "My main interest is the collaboration of designers with other disciplines and Spark's focus is on local projects and initiatves."

Fishing is still a mainstay of the economy but companies are also looking to thermal power as Iceland's next chapter. Here, a collaborative culture is emerging. Carbon Recycling International (CRI) has opened a power plant that uses carbon dioxide emissions to make renewable methanol. Elsewhere, the Svartsengi Geothermal power plant, 40 minutes' drive out of the capital through a lunar landscape of lava fields, has become much more than an energy supplier.

"This has evolved into what we call a resource park," says the plant's manager. "Now we have spin-offs such as the Blue Lagoon – a multi-revenue tourist facility – and CRI is using our CO2. Up the road, a company is building a fish farm that will utilise our residual energy to heat seawater, where it will breed a fish called tilapia." Whatever next? — (M)

01

02

01
Local outside the Kaffismiðja Íslands café
02
David Robertson, Kría Cycles founder
03
Downtown Reykjavík

04

03

On the ground

1 The city hosts a series of events, from its Seed Forum to the Startup Iceland entrepreneurial conference. Get out there and meet your future business partner.

2 Investment is hard to secure so look towards friends and family or organisations such as the Startup Reykjavík business accelerator for initial funding. The latter, founded in 2012, offers funding in return for a 6 per cent equity stake.

3 Find the right scale: Iceland is a country of just 320,000 people. Businesses should start small and have a sense of provenance. Identify what the community needs and meet it.

4 There are unique resources in Iceland. At the moment much of the island's geothermal energy is sold to large foreign-owned aluminum factories in the country. If only someone could think of a way of exporting it?

5 Iceland has considerable cultural cache internationally. Any business in Reykjavík should seek to encourage local talent and keep brand Iceland progressive, hi-spec and individual: it sells.

04
The Blue
Lagoon uses
silica-rich water
from Svartsengi
power plant
05
Stofan Café

06
Port of Reykjavik
07
Fréttablaðið's
newsroom on
a Friday night

05   06

07

CHARLESTON
USA

Preface: Despite its languid air the small, conservative town of Charleston in South Carolina is rich in business acumen thanks to a young, ambitious population – and equally savvy city government – set on developing local industry.

Population: 125,700
Key trades: technology, tourism and higher education
Time to register a business: 1 day if business is registered to a home address; at least 10 working days if you are registering a commercial space as well
Annual hours of sunshine: 3,000

———

Quote: *'The first thing we did was make this a desirable place for creative people'*

"There's this young creative class that's bubbling up and moving the city into a new era," says Brooks Reitz, an entrepreneur and restaurateur who moved to Charleston from Kentucky. "We're being met with enthusiasm and a real 'attaboy' attitude from the folks who came before us."

There's perhaps no one better acquainted with the city's progressive spirit than mayor Joseph Riley, a septuagenarian native whose love for Charleston has won him 10 consecutive terms in City Hall. "The first thing we did was make this a desirable place for creative people," he says. "A physically beautiful, diverse, energetic place with a lively downtown and diverse cultural activities."

Riley's strategy of building a better city through rigorous preservation and wise civic investment forms the basis upon which young professionals have chosen to move here. Perhaps the most striking example of the city's progress is the Charleston Digital Corridor (CDC), a public-private initiative launched to house early-stage tech firms in a pair of smartly repurposed buildings. Overseen by Ernest Andrade, the city's director of business development, the CDC serves as the mother church for Charleston's digital businesses. Software firms such as Blackbaud laid the groundwork for the city's knowledge-based economy and Google's $1.2bn data centre in nearby Berkeley County has furthered Charleston's reputation, but it's the CDC that will drive innovation.

Walking the halls of the CDC's headquarters, Andrade points out offices occupied by people who have come from Austin, San Francisco and London. National firms such as People-Matter and BoomTown found their start under the CDC and have now grown to employ staff of more than 100 each.

Amid a charming mix of 18th and 19th-century clapboard homes Fuzzco, an award-winning design firm, has set up in a new structure on Cannon Street. Founded by Josh Nissenboim and Helen Rice, the firm's clients range from Mario Testino to a Charleston soda maker. "It's a great place to start your business," says Rice, a Charleston native. "There are fewer distractions than in a bigger city so you can really focus on the things you're interested in."

Whereas many US cities dangle fiscal bait to bring new business to town, Charleston has taken a relatively restrained position on corporate welfare. "We have a local development corporation to assist with financing when needed but no portfolio of incentives," says Mayor Riley. "Really, what we have that is of greatest value is the place itself." — (M)

01

02

03

01
Employees in the office of Fuzzco
02
Five Loaves café on Cannon Street
03
Fuzzco owners Josh Nissenboim and his wife Helen Rice
04
View of King Street in Charleston

05

06

07

08

05
Patrons eat on
the second-floor
deck at Husk
06
Cyclist in the
Elliotborough
neighbourhood
07
Celia Gibson and
Michael Moran
of Moran Wood-
worked Furniture

08
Shoes at textile-
design company
Proud Mary
09
Furniture
awaits delivery
from Moran
Woodworked
10
Harper Poe,
owner of Proud
Mary, at home

09

10

On the ground

1 The city is shaking off its patriarchal insularity and welcoming entrepreneurial newcomers.

2 Charleston's big opportunities lie toward the north end of the peninsula. Upper King Street and Morrison Drive, plus neighbourhoods such as Elliotborough and Cannonborough, provide a pleasant alternative to the more touristy downtown.

3 This is no Palo Alto but Charleston has a growing software industry. A reasonable cost of living and high quality of life will see new industries develop.

4 Don't let the city's strict historic-preservation standards scare you away. Charleston's Board of Architectural Review is balancing progress with preservation, proven by ongoing revitalisation of businesses throughout the peninsula.

5 While the city's culinary offerings have become a major draw, the same can't be said for Charleston's hotels. Entrepreneurs with a focus on hospitality could locate a charming, smartly designed hotel a few blocks off King Street.

11   12

11
Brett Carron
(left) and Chip
Cracraft at men's
clothing shop
Indigo & Cotton
12
Courtney
Rowson (left)
and Amy Pastre,
owners of Stitch
Design Co
13
Marion Square
at the corner of
King Street and
Calhoun Street

13

CAMOGLI
ITALY

Preface: For those who dream of switching square mile for start-up, the Ligurian fishing town of Camogli – complete with favourable property laws, a bustling art scene and olive tree-lined slopes – offers a more authentic take on la dolce vita.

Population: 5,400
Key trades: tourism, fishing
Time to register a business: 3 days
Annual hours of sunshine: 2,200
International flights: the closest airport is near Genoa, with direct flights to 10 European cities, including Munich, London and Paris

Quote: *'Buying property in Camogli is a straightforward process for both Italians and foreigners'*

Set on the spectacular Ligurian coast against a backdrop of mountains about 20km from Genoa is the fishing town of Camogli. Today it is attracting a growing number of artists, architects and hoteliers looking to start anew away from the big cities in the north – causing others to take note of what makes the perfect town for running the small hotel, bistro or gallery you've always dreamed of.

"I moved here because it's a very traditional fishing village," says Mario Pietraccetta, who owns Villa Rosmarino, a secluded escape on Mount Portofino. "Camogli has become a refuge for international intellectuals while remaining true to its roots. People respect your private life and newcomers are welcome."

In front of the small harbour from which fishermen and boats for San Fruttuoso and Punta Chiappa depart is Locanda I Tre Merli. This quaint hotel has just five rooms and is owned by Eleonora Bozzi. "I love Camogli. You are surrounded by tranquility and the beauty of Monte di Portofino," she says of the town's charms.

Local editor Rosanna Massarenti says: "It's a small village with a very active and respectful social life. Camogli is at the heart of the Ligurian artistic scene."

Among the entrepreneurs who've bet high on Camogli's cultural spirit is art collector Natalina Remotti. She and her husband launched Fondazione Remotti out of a former church. "We liked the intellectual atmosphere in Camogli – that's why we started our foundation," says Remotti of the venture, which specialises in exhibitions by Italian artists.

True to its Italian ethos, the town boasts small cafés, wine bars and restaurants along its steep streets and narrow paths. There's the traditional focaccia bakery Revello on Via Garibaldi, which has been around since 1964, and Gelato & Dintorni, a small *bottega* perfectly situated on the waterfront and offering 20 homemade flavours.

New residents and entrepreneurs are investing in the faded country houses that dot the town and offer views onto the Paradiso Gulf that stretches from Savona to Portofino. Some of them have been magnificently restored by architect Guido Risicato. Camogli-born Risicato has been making a name for himself with his airy, sympathetic renovations, mixing new design with traditional style.

And to make things even more irresistible, buying property (whether residential or commercial) in Camogli is a straightforward process for both Italians and foreigners. It takes roughly a month to become the proud owner of one of these warm-hued villas that were once home to sea captains. — (M)

01

02

03

04

01
Camogli
Harbour
02
Water taxi
03
Editor Rosanna
Massarenti
04
Trattoria do
Spadin

On the ground

1 Camogli has a growing number of artists and intellectuals moving in or visiting the town – betting on a cultural venture (be it a new art gallery or bookstore) would surely be a success.

2 If you're into retail, the town would benefit from more quality clothing stores to cater for increasing visitor numbers.

3 Most of Camogli's houses were built during the 17th and 19th centuries – skilled architects and designers are always welcome for the restoration of these residences.

4 As a secluded tourist gem, the town needs better-stocked newsstands. So if print is your thing, Camogli is the place.

5 If you have a business idea for a year-round venture, opt for the Boschetto neighbourhood. A short drive from the centre, temperatures are a little cooler than the waterfront so it's comfortable in all seasons.

05
Garden at Villa
Rosmarino
06
Via Garibaldi
07
Focacceria
e Pasticceria
Revello

05

06

07

08

08
Apartment
interior on
Via Garibaldi
09
Fruit and veg
outside a
Camogli shop
10
Caffè Mangini

09

10

191

GOTLAND
SWEDEN

Preface: Out of sight, out of mind? Not so on the Swedish outpost of Gotland, where an outward-looking, vibrant craft industry is just one indicator of the island's burgeoning entrepreneurialism.

Population: 57,300
Key trades: fishing, tourism, cement-making and crafts
Time to register a business: 16 days
Annual hours of sunshine: 1,900
International flights: Visby Airport serves 36 regional cities; you can also fly to Stockholm for more international options

———

Quote: *'Many people come from the big cities and bring great networks with them'*

For most people Gotland is best known as the setting for many of local director Ingmar Bergman's films. But the island is also home to a thriving craft industry, a tradition rooted in the island's materials: wool, limestone and wood. Gotland's craft community isn't just surviving, it's booming. With more than 50,000 residents, the island is one of Sweden's leading regions for entrepreneurship, especially among designers and craftsmen.

One reason is the quality of the raw materials. Barbro Lomakka arrived in Gotland in the early 1990s and ended up staying after finding working with the island's wool so rewarding. Asked by the handicraft society to find out if Gotland wool could be used commercially, she began experimenting. Twenty years later her designs are used by architects across the world.

It's not just materials keeping craft alive. Designer Stina Lindholm runs Skulpturfabriken, a studio specialising in furniture made from concrete. "After I

arrived, many ceramicists, designers and artists moved here," she says. "It's the sea and the light. It's magical, somehow."

Aside from the magic, the cost of living and local resources are a key factor in attracting talent; work spaces such as Lindholm's are cheaper than in Stockholm and the island's skilled craftsmen are all on hand. Kristian Eriksson's GAD is one venture that makes the most of the island's skills. The wooden-furniture company, known for the exquisite finish of its pieces, has a carpentry factory in southern Gotland.

"When we started, everyone was trying to do things as cheaply as possible," says Eriksson. "We said, 'Let's do the opposite, let's do the best possible. And not cheat.'"

"The flow of people is a great breeding ground for entrepreneurs," says Helena Bloom, co-owner of Leva Husfabrik, which designs and builds environmentally friendly houses made out of the island's wood.

Tourism is another key force keeping Gotland's vibrancy alive. Around 800,000 visitors come here every year and these connections with the mainland help in marketing products to a wider audience. Many people moving here come from the big cities and bring great networks with them. Much of Gotland's products are thus exported outside of Sweden; Lomakka and Skulpturfabriken, for instance, export to the US, Germany, southern Europe and the other Scandinavian countries.

Lomakka says that it's crucial to be a player in the big markets, not just in little Gotland. "One has to be vigilant with the quality and not settle. You need to reach out from Gotland and put your products to the test." — (M)

01

01
Fog in the fields of Gotland
02
Marie-Louise Malmros at Skulpturfabriken

02

03

On the ground

① Check out the services of Almi (*almi.se*), a state-owned organisation that offers advice, loans and venture capital for budding start-ups.

② Be creative when looking for a location: an old farm, warehouse or a petrol station can make an original workshop, store or office.

③ When buying a property, don't settle for the asking price – there's often room to bargain.

④ In the summer Gotland fills with tourists so starting up a café in connection with your business or keeping part of your workshop open to visitors might be a way to boost earnings and market your brand.

⑤ Source your materials from Gotland and hire local carpenters and craftsmen; quality is high and you also support the community.

04   05

06   07

FOGO ISLAND
CANADA

01
Architects of
the Inn (left to
right): Kingman
Brewster, Joseph
Kellner, Eric
Ratkowski and
Nick Herder
02
Fogo Island's
coastline
03
Ladies of the
textile guild

Preface: Her money was made in California but Zita Cobb put it to work on the island she left as a 16-year-old. The result has been Fogo Island's startling revitalisation and a heady lesson in localism. And it goes to show that with determination almost anywhere can be your base.

Population: 2,400
Key trades: geo-tourism, fishing and hospitality
Time to register a business: 1 day
Annual hours of sunshine: 1,600
International flights: Gander International Airport is an hour's drive away and offers several daily flights to Toronto's Pearson international airport, Canada's busiest hub

Quote: *'There was a time when people wondered what they would do if they couldn't fish'*

Forty-five minutes from the coast of Newfoundland proper, Fogo island is home to 2,400 people and is a perfect case study in entrepreneurial determination that other rural communities can take a cue from.

The island's regeneration is thanks to a returning native's vision and grit. Her name is Zita Cobb and what she has done is proof that the best ideas can bear fruit in the rockiest of ground. Cobb left Fogo Island at 16 and eventually became CFO of hi-tech company JDS Fitel in Ottawa. She retired early in 2001, returned to Fogo Island and established the Shorefast Foundation, a charity that uses her earnings for the island's future. "I had more money than I needed to live a life. How could I set it free?" says Cobb.

First she founded Fogo Island Arts, a series of residencies in four modernist studios dotted around the area, built by Bergen-based architect Todd Saunders. Artists and writers visit, mingle, get inspired and create.

Next came the Shorefast Business Assistance Fund, a micro-lending scheme to help create small businesses and alleviate the reliance on fishing as the sole economic provider. Applicants include Nicole Decker-Torraville who started a successful café before taking over the lease of a shop and converting it into Growlers ice-cream parlour. Her ingredients and recipes are sourced locally, her proud contribution to the island's industry.

Other businesses helped by the fund include bed-and-breakfasts, a taxi firm and greenhouses that extend the farming season. "There was a time when people wondered what they could do if they couldn't fish," Decker-Torraville says, referring to the stoic fishermen displaced by changes in regulations who chose to stay anyway. "But now when I see these people who have stayed, their faces are not sad anymore. They're happy."

Fogo Island Inn is Cobb's latest venture. It is intended to pull together the smaller businesses, offer consistent employment opportunities for islanders young and old and open up Fogo Island to the curious, intrepid tourist. Long and timber-clad, it features 29 sea-facing rooms, a rooftop sauna, cinema, library and art gallery. Its structure is a nod to the island's architectural vernacular.

The inn has even drawn new residents to Fogo Island. Among them is Curtis Burns, who started up Flat Earth Coffee. "It's a new skill I can bring because Fogo Island is traditionally a tea-based community," he says.

Or as Cobb puts it: "The goal is not to take anything away from the island but only adding to it." — (M)

01

02

04
Miniature
fishing stage in
the community
of Tilting
05
Squish Studio
artists' residence
06
Zita Cobb of
the Shorefast
Foundation

06

On the ground

1 Engage local communities. Because of its far-flung locale, local residents have had to do things on their own. In the process they've developed useful skills from making furniture to quilting.

2 Returning residents and creatives have opened up Fogo's world view. They are receptive to new ideas, drawing the best from around the globe and adapting them to the local context.

3 Band together. Thanks to a small population and guilds, people from different parts of the island have a long history of working together. Tap into these community structures and networks.

4 It's not just the artists who have to be creative; entrepreneurs must take an imaginative approach, too. Look for gaps in the market and fill them.

5 Think about the seasons. Winters can be harsh and worth keeping in mind in the longer term when developing your business.

03

04   05

OBSERVATIONS

Entrepreneurial lessons to be learned

Preface

How do you do business with a Finn? What could a PA really do for you? How do you hire – and fire? So many things to think about. And that's where this chapter comes in. We have asked the great and the good, the fledglings and the big players to give us their mini manifestos and sometimes contemplative, sometimes witty views on every angle of the business world. We hope their words will not only give you a shove in the right direction and open your eyes to some things that you would just never have thought of (is it OK to go to a sauna on a first business meeting? Well, yes, if you are in Helsinki) but also entertain you.

Because the world of work is never dull, and you should be able to sport a negotiator's poker face or a smile when needed. Have both ready for this fast-paced ride down the flume of entrepreneurship; we did tell you it might be a bumpy ride every now and then.

Contents

WORDS OF WISDOM
GLOBAL

Preface: From alternative workspaces to contemporary customer service, attention to detail can make the difference between a business sinking or swimming. Here are our mantras for a new industrial age.

O1

The secret of a good staff uniform

There is an expensive bar in Ginza in Tokyo – one of many such bars in this upmarket neighbourhood – where the barmen move discreetly in the semi-darkness, deftly turning out cocktails with confidence and skill. The head barman is an award winner and the drinks are exceptionally good.

It's the attention to detail that makes this establishment such a pleasure to drink at: the hand-hewn ice cubes, the polished wooden counter and the thin glass tumblers. And not forgetting the staff uniform: a white tuxedo jacket, slightly frayed but always clean and pressed. This agreeably worn garment conveys a message to the Ginza customer: that the wearer is a man of experience who knows how to make a proper martini.

And here is the secret to a good uniform: it should be part of a bigger picture, not a talking point in itself. Doormen in extravagant national costume or waiters in startlingly fashionable attire seem to miss the point. In hospitality – unlike, say, the military or the emergency services – the best uniforms are those that barely register. Much more important than a fussy outfit is the overall impression of a job well done.
Fiona Wilson MONOCLE WRITER

O2

Why lunch is the most important business meal of the day

The "work breakfast" is a hellish overeating of sugared dough; time spent fending off the night before. Dinner, on the other hand, is far too intimate an affair to be spent in the company of someone you aren't going to sleep with. One of the best things about work, however, is the working lunch. The business luncheon is your break from a day during which you've been primed by a couple of morning coffees but have yet to nod off during the postprandial lull. But for the working lunch to be successful, you have to get a few key aspects right; the most vital is the balance between the "working" and the "lunching".

First of all: who are you having lunch with? Choose wisely. Only accept the invitation of someone you know to be fun or someone that's taking you somewhere decent. A stilted affair at which a stranger talks about contemporary dance while nursing a dressing-free salad and sipping "tap" is a disaster area. An all-guns-blazing, old-fashioned Fleet Street piss-up at which you promise the impossible and lose a tooth after proposing to someone's wife is no good either.

Ideally, get invited to lunch by a European; this lot always know a good local joint and they will share a bottle of wine without feeling – as Americans do – that this is only possible as a prelude to a stag night. And food? Although someone else might be footing the bill, don't go bananas. It's bad manners and highly impractical to work through an aged steak with all the trimmings or a range of rare sea urchins while talking to someone you don't know that well. Brasserie French is good or tapas, so that you can share. Think of it as a sort-of date.

Drink. It's important to have enough to get into the spirit of things without having so much that you change that spirit into something akin to bacchanal. A heart-starter – a briskly dispatched negroni, for example – isn't a bad idea but don't have more than two because the wine is next, it's only 13.30 and, frankly, who are you kidding? It's not *actually* a date.

When it comes to the business part, take it easy. Don't hard sell or be hard sold to. If you're being invited, start the work bit of the conversation yourself instead of evading the subject like a girl that's read *The Rules* (again: it's *not* a date). Phones are far more offensive on a table than elbows. Endlessly trying and failing to name the friend that you're sure you both have in common is tedious. Stick to the reason you came.

Finally, and this might sound a bit odd: use the right tense. The present continuous is useful for vaguely promising things while complimenting the sancerre. Shall we say Thursday at one? It's a date.
Robert Bound MONOCLE CULTURE EDITOR

For the working lunch to be successful, you have to get a few key aspects right; the most vital is the balance between the 'working' and the 'lunching'
— 02

03

Pride in precision: perceptions of a PA

Getting from A to B is easy – thinking about C and D while arranging E is what you sign up for. The position of PA to the CEO is a job that requires attention to detail. Scheduling meetings and setting up conference calls in a series of countries demands a passion for time.

As a PA, you not only create time but you also look out for it. You are the watchmaker and the timekeeper. You straighten the bumps on the daily road travelled by the CEO to provide overview, clarity and efficiency.

The image of the gate-keeping frown is to be replaced with the welcoming face. The care taken in precision is reflected in the company's image. This is the pride of the PA: the seamless days where everything runs as smoothly as the Mercedes E class your CEO is going to the airport in.
Kristoffer Parup
MONOCLE PA

04

Searching for that USP

From charming hotels and crafty restaurants to smart retail operations, new businesses seem to be sprouting up around us with hopes of carving out their niche in long-battered yet resilient consumer markets. And now, perhaps more than ever, businesses seem determined to sell potential customers on their brand story. In other words, who are we and why is our business different to the ones down the street? What makes us unique? And what can we offer you that you've been missing for so long?

This sort of storytelling in its most basic form is indeed an essential part of explaining why people should open their wallets. If you're a bricks-and-mortar shop, you'll probably tell us that you're all about service, filling some sort of gap in the market. Perhaps you've even got a "well-curated" product selection that everyone seems to be clamouring for. And if you're a hotel, it's a good bet that service is paramount in the pecking order of your mission statement. You're probably also focused on quality food and drink, good design and a general belief in making sure guests feel at ease.

Regardless of what business you're in, it's safe to assume you've gone to great lengths to envision your operational points of pride. Maybe you've paid some talented advisers a nice sum to help you shape the language so customers understand what you're about.

But, too often, crafting this identity comes without any sense of commitment from those who tell the story. In other words, you start communicating what sets your business apart from the rest but fail to live up to the standards.

To give an example, I was in a small, independent clothing shop in New York that had been talking a lot about its service and its promise of a smart product selection. But when I entered the doors of this much-lauded establishment I wasn't given more than a split-second glance before the employees returned their attention to a YouTube video of a baby monkey riding on the back of a pig. Or that's what I imagined given their laughter and unwillingness to acknowledge my presence in the shop. What was that they had promised about exemplary service? Hmm.

As I walked around the shop and thumbed through a handful of truly nice garments I couldn't help but notice that they seemed to resemble the same things I'd find in every other menswear retailer in the city. Well-selected products, yes – but just what you'd find anywhere else.

In retail, good service and a unique product selection is sort of expected. And if you codify these things in your brand story, it's worth taking them seriously. Don't promise service if you or your staff haven't committed to providing it. And if there's nothing unique about your business, you shouldn't make too much of a fuss suggesting that there is.

Now, more than any time in recent decades, there's an opportunity for new businesses to flourish if they're willing to live up to their stated mission. But not living up to the basic tenets you set out for yourself is a recipe for failure.
Barrett Austin MONOCLE WRITER

05
The rise of corporate playgrounds

How often do you show up for a meeting in unfamiliar territory and find yourself suddenly slammed with an extreme case of office envy? Do you sense that you're in for a bit of a treat the second you glide into a lobby or is it more a case of emerging from a lift and finding yourself transported into a heavenly environment? Can you remember the last time you experienced that odd mix of elation and jealousy after drifting through a beautifully designed, serene environment?

I have a few offices on my circuit that I always enjoy visiting. I never fail to walk away thinking next time I need to install this type of door, fit those type of floors and design my reception like that. In Stockholm there's always been something about the smell of the wood floors and the handsome yet practical furniture that's made it a joy to visit the offices of Thomas Eriksson. In Copenhagen you can't find a tighter ship than Maersk's global headquarters with its subtle nautical touches, razor-sharp branding and perfectly appointed furnishings. In Tokyo I could happily move into the mansion-cum-office of Wonderwall architects *(see page 232)*. And in Milan, the Diego Della Valle HQ is always a pleasant environment to enjoy a cup of coffee and a pastry. In all of these environments there's comfort, attention to detail, fine materials, design for purpose and a calm sense of commerce.

As most corners of civilised society have been working from some form of orderly office set-up for many centuries now,

I'm perplexed as to how some of the world's largest – even smartest – companies can get it so wrong. More worrying is the frightful trend of turning corporate offices into play schools for adults.

Anyone who's spent a little bit of time in and around San Francisco, funkier corners of Berlin and Munich, warehouse spaces on New York's lower west side and any other environment that might use the words "tech" or "digi" to define what part of the light-industrial food group it falls into will know exactly the type of environment I'm talking about. For a sector that likes to fancy itself as creative it's remarkable how many fall for the same design clichés to show how "down" they are with the market and why they're the right choice for grads looking for just the perfect home to amass a load of share options for a potential IPO. Without fail there will be skate ramps in reception and "kray-zee" furniture for otherwise dignified people to fall off while they wait to be collected. And there's a very good chance that there'll be lurid green AstroTurf underfoot.

Once beyond reception there will be basketball hoops and maybe jogging lanes and tennis boundaries painted on the floor. Along one wall will be a bunch of plush animal heads mounted trophy-style; there'll also be lots of eating stations where people will be filling up their 500-litre Thermoses with various free beverages. And as you weave your way past half-finished walls made out of particleboard you'll pass lots of young men who'll never glance at you but will

knuckle bump their colleagues and shout, "Yo, man!" when they pass along the kooky zig-zag corridor. Somewhere just beyond the bathrooms – that have been spray-painted by a local graffiti artist – you'll come to a screeching halt and ask yourself five rapid-fire questions:

1 When is this infantilisation of the workplace going to end?
2 Who is responsible for it and can they be prosecuted?
3 Do shareholders really endorse all of these extra-curricular add-ons when staff should be working rather than "brain-jamming" while throwing around a spongy football?
4 Do these fun diversions really keep people in the office longer and see them put in more productive days?
5 Does all of this nonsense mask the fact that working with algorithms and developing apps is hugely unrewarding and therefore requires airlock-style soundproof rooms so that staff can sneak away in search of more meaningful employment?

Perhaps, like me, you'll come to the conclusion that these sophomoric playgrounds are not the indulgent "grand projects" of benevolent tech billionaires but little more than upmarket versions of Foxconn manufacturing compounds. Who needs guard houses and razor wire when all you need is round-the-clock free soda and crisps?
Tyler Brûlé MONOCLE
EDITOR-IN-CHIEF

> *Do these fun diversions really keep people in the office longer and see them put in more productive days?*
> — 05

> *We need some places, some escapist spots, where we can be not at home with the humdrummery and not at work with the brain set on frenetic*
> — 06

06

A place to switch off

So the "third place" is somewhere that's free, that often involves food or drink, that's welcoming and where you can meet friends. It's a spot in between work and home. It all sounds well and good – it also sounds like the description of any London pub – but it ignores one brutal fact: for most people, nowhere is actually away from work. That vibrating, ringing, flashing phone in your pocket can capture your attention and pull you back at any second. It's like Gollum's precious ring: it demands your attention.

There was probably no golden age when the day of work was really done – no doubt in Charles Dickens' time some urchin would run in with the age's equivalent of the text message – but surely it was never like this.

Today, work sits on our shoulders like a pirate's tweeting and squawking parrot. (Gosh, there are a lot of metaphors here.) But we need some places, some escapist spots, where we can be not at home with the humdrummery and not at work with the brain set on frenetic.

The pub? There's bound to be someone updating their Facebook or partaking in Snapchattery sat next to you. The café? What about all those people bathed in laptop light? There is an alternative: the museum.

Take London's British Museum. You will look like a fool doing your work while surrounded by Egyptian mummies. You will feel out of place even talking on your phone. You will be forced to engage; find yourself lured in by Mesopotamian treasures and Roman coins. Work and home, like two squabbling children, will be pushed away and silenced. Your brain will clear. And then, yes, after that you can go back to the office – or the pub.
Andrew Tuck MONOCLE EDITOR

07

Why good design should speak for itself

Sophisticated branding is, of course, brilliant. But it's getting out of control as far as young designers are concerned. Does, say, a table really need a book and a short film to explain why it's good design? Shouldn't it be able to speak for itself?

It's not just the fact that there's a lot of material to wade through that's the problem; it's that young designers feel it's necessary – and enough – to sell their design. After presenting a mildly amusing animation of some dancing cutlery, one young graduate was asked why his cutlery was an improvement on what exists already. It might sound harsh but he couldn't answer. So how would he be able to persuade a flatware manufacturer to invest in putting his prototype into production? What is the point of the animation, the logo and the packaging if the designer can't speak simply about why their design is valid?

Clever, creative branding should be supporting material, not a substitute for human communication; nor something for designers to hide behind.

I mentioned this to a designer whose company has taken the furniture industry by storm. "Where's your animation and coffee-table book that explain the idea behind what you do?" I asked. He agreed that collateral material and branding has become excessive. Instead, he credits his time spent at the San Francisco Academy of Art University, where – rather than learning graphic design – they were given acting and performance classes, providing him with a better way to promote his work. At the time he said he thought it was a complete waste of time. It's taken 20 years for him to understand what a blessing it was, granting him the gift of the gab, the power of the pitch. What he might be lacking in the finer nuances of Apple's Final Cut Pro, he makes up for in being able to talk straight about what he's creating and why it's important. And that translates to success.

Young start-ups take note: if your product doesn't speak for itself and if you can't speak for it, an accompanying Manga comic is unlikely to do the talking for you.
Hugo Macdonald WRITER

08

Choosing the vocational route

I took a look behind the elegant curtain of The Peninsula hotel on a walkthrough of the Hong Kong icon's kitchens. Bustling with staff in pressed uniforms, the area was filled with everyone from cooks with simmering stock pots to stewards polishing silver, and white-jacketed waiters preparing for lunch.

One of the people I met was Johnny Chung, the hotel's senior bartender. Chung has been at The Peninsula since the 1950s, having joined his father there while still a teenager, and he claims to have served the city's first screwdriver cocktail to none other than Clark Gable.

Hotels, jobs and opportunities have changed considerably since Chung started but The Peninsula's busy back-of-house poses an attractive alternative to university. Yet while admission to hotel schools is competitive, fewer teenagers choose to take the vocational route into hospitality. Attracted to roles with quicker promotion prospects, many job hunters turn their nose up at a front-desk or housekeeping job in even the starriest five-star hotel.

But it wasn't hotel school where all of today's most established hotel managers started out. Apprenticing provided the beginning of many careers where dedication can be rewarded with jobs all around the globe.

At The Peninsula, nearly 40 per cent of new staff come from vocational schools and the hotel works hard to ensure the speciality jobs that its guests rely on will be filled for years to come. Despite being consistently popular with diners, the art of dim-sum making is set aside by many of today's young chefs in favour of more glamorous paths in pastry kitchens. But a good dim-sum maker could still have a job in 50 years' time. Just like Mr Chung.
Aisha Speirs MONOCLE WRITER

09

Chaos at the front desk

If you want to know what a company thinks of its customers and the outside world, take a look at its reception – if they actually have one. Just as first impressions count for people, so they do for businesses, whatever their size or sector. But, judging by some of the lobbies you might find yourself in, there are a lot of enterprises that may have glossy smiling faces on their billboard campaigns but back at HQ they are revealed as scruffy, unthinking and pretty useless.

1 **Scene one:** a lobby at the HQ of a major hospitality company. You arrive on the 20th floor but, while there is a reception, there is no receptionist and all doors in every direction are sealed and frosted. On said reception you spot a phone and a sheet of instructions. Your task is to key in the name of the person you are meeting and dial their extension. Fine, except the person you are meeting is not on the list. At that point the receptionist returns from her lunchtime run dripping in sweat but darts through the door and will not be seen again. Finally, by dialling random numbers, you find a live person who agrees, reluctantly, to search out the colleague you're meeting. You do not wish these people well.

2 **Scene two:** the reception for a global brand where you are due to meet the CEO. There is a receptionist but she is not there to work – you are. On the counter is a dirty old Dell on which she tells you to type in a vast list of details. You are with two colleagues and have to do the same for them. Meanwhile she stands there with nothing to do and not a smile on the horizon. No wonder it is a struggling business these days.

3 **Scene three:** a sunny day in California. Now, here the reception bit works a treat and the receptionist is a camp, older woman who would be as at home in a diner as in this sparkling office. You go to the windowless meeting room and you wait... and you wait. You have flown thousands of miles but the journey from their nearby desks to this soulless bunker seems trickier for the locals. But then the best bit: they all arrive carrying giant teat-topped water bottles that they proceed to suck on for the next 40 minutes. It's a good meeting but, as they press lips to nipple, do they never wonder if visitors to this tower should at least be offered a glass of water?

Luckily there are companies that get it right and it's funny how it's those businesses you usually end up wanting to work with. You can be half sold on a deal if you find yourself content to sit and wait in the lobby.

A few tips for CEOs from the successful welcomers: have a nice space for visitors to wait in with magazines and wi-fi. Offer water and good coffee. Make sure you've booked a meeting room. Oh, and have a receptionist who likes their job and realises they are the first experience that visitors will have of your brand.
Stuart Lawrence WRITER

You have flown thousands of miles but the journey from their nearby desks to this soulless bunker seems trickier for the locals

— 09

10

How to choose your craft

I was not a practically minded boy growing up. I read books, acted in plays and generally daydreamed about what I considered to be lofty ideas. I didn't often get my hands dirty, unless I was making "art". To enrol in a vocational shoemaking course in my last year of school seemed like the perfect rejection of the institutionalised education I was fed up with. At the time, I don't think I really considered that it might be what I'd do for the rest of my life.

My paternal grandmother is pretty much the embodiment of the intellectual side of my family so I was quite surprised at her enthusiasm for my new pursuit. Even more so when she told me that three generations before her, a line of 18 Polish shoemakers in our family had ended – the last of whom had regularly taken commissions from the Tsar of Russia.

I don't know if it really is as simple as being in the blood or if I was always going to find something that feeds my passion the way shoemaking does. It is definitely in part the application to the task that satisfies me, the working with slightly elemental materials in complex ways. There is something of overcoming, of the wrestling with a block of wood to make the last that represents someone's foot, or the strain of pulling over the leather upper to create the desired shape. I like that this work requires a conscience because a man's relationship with the shoes he wears means he can't ignore a fault and will return to tell you if the fit doesn't feel right.
Sebastian Tarek SHOEMAKER

11

Why hard work always pays off

Finding north London's Oslo Court restaurant for the first time feels almost invasive. A very discrete sign leads you to enter a 1930s block of flats to be met not by a maitre d' but a concierge. "The restaurant is to your right," he says. Then, through the door, a narrow hallway leads you past the kitchen to the dining room.

Inside, elegantly dressed patrons sit at tables draped with salmon-pink tablecloths, part of Oslo Court's signature décor. Tony and José Sanchez, the owners, zip between taking a seat with some of the regulars and directing smartly suited waiters.

But the true star of the show is Neil – no last name needed. Neil is Oslo Court's 60-plus dessert waiter. Having moved to London from Egypt at the age of 18 he's been doing the same job since his twenties. He is one of the main reasons that people keep coming back.

What's striking about Neil is that he flies in the face of what we're taught to recognise as success. Dishing out raspberry torte daily, no matter how divine it may be, doesn't often make it onto a list of aspirational careers. But what Neil does he takes pride in and does with care. He is, of course, just one example of Oslo Court's entire staff, dedicated to detail and service.

It's a good lesson learned. We needn't all break records, make headlines or change jobs to feel like we're getting what we should from our careers. Neil's hard work isn't driven by unbridled ambition – just self-worth found in a job well done.
David Michon MONOCLE WRITER

12

When to mix business with pleasure

Looking for the right person to launch a business with? Often they can be closer than you think. My business partner Kristo Käärmann and I were once just friends – we were two Estonian expats living in London. A few years ago we quit our jobs to build TransferWise, an international money-transfer platform, from Kristo's kitchen table.

Social dynamics don't always translate well into business ones. There are some important factors you should think about when considering a partnership: do your skills complement each other? Do you share the same vision for the product? And will you be able to easily switch back and forth between friendship and business? Being in a position to voice opinions and concerns at all times is absolutely key.

Kristo is a great business partner for me because we bring different things to the table. With his consulting background he's our operations and compliance man, while my experience as part of Skype's early team means that I can push our marketing and product development.

Our friendship has certainly helped the business to thrive. Our one goal was to disrupt the financial-services sector and fix a problem that we both faced: we wanted to make international money transfer as low-cost, quick and transparent as possible.

A few years and £1bn transferred down the line, this unified vision remains a key driving force in our business partnership – which we now share with 85 team members who've joined our little revolution.

Taavet Hinrikus CO-FOUNDER, TRANSFERWISE

> *Will you be able to switch back and forth between friendship and business?*
> — 12

> *Rain or shine, with a small investment in waterproofs, any cycling employee becomes master of the city*
> — 13

13

On your bike: the joy of cycling to work

The dreaded commute to work: in London, more dreaded and more despised than elsewhere. Delays, diversions and daily transport dilemmas are the rule, not the exception. Except for the cyclist, that is, speeding past bottle-necks and the heaving pavement masses.

No two rides are the same through the urban rhythms being acted out all around. A scaffold goes up or a piano is delivered; here a café opens, there another pub closes. They are all fragments embedded in the cyclist's memory.

With its shortcuts and clandestine conduits, London seen from the saddle is a world away from the parallel realm of freesheets and clanking escalators. Entirely safe? Definitely not, but cycling has become a mainstay of our cities. It keeps the traffic moving.

It is also a pre-work tonic. Part adrenaline rush and part therapeutic meander, the two-wheeled commute is addictive. So much so that, deprived of his bike, the London cyclist is a lost, fumbling Tube illiterate.

Rain or shine, with a small investment in waterproofs, any employee becomes an agile master of the city. Breakfast meeting by the canal? A quick lunch on the other side of town? A bike makes what is unfeasible by Tube (and maddeningly slow by cab) a carefree reality. So whether your bike is Dutch or mountain, hybrid or fixed-gear, city or racer – be brave, jump on and get moving. Your commute may just become the most inspiring part of your day.

David Plaisant MONOCLE 24 ASSOCIATE PRODUCER

14

The art of hiring

The advertisement has gone out, the CVs have come in and you've got the list of candidates down to just six. And then they arrive. Six people all hoping that you will give them a job. You want to be kind and fair, to dwell on their academic careers. But there are limits. Especially if you are running a small business. Because your first thought is, "I am potentially going to sit next to you for years to come."

It's fine if you are the head of HR in a giant company because after you employ the very talented but perhaps grumpy, over-familiar or needy candidate you may never see them again until the day they leave. A distant department will have to deal with their oddities. But when you have just a couple of employees, hiring a new team member feels similar to choosing a life partner. If you are honest with yourself you'd like to know about their eating habits, their sense of humour, their bathing regime.

There are lots of traps that most countries have laws to cover: employees should not be picked – nor rejected – because of race, faith or gender. But no country says you have to employ someone who, while potentially good at their job, is going to make life less fun.

And you spot them so quickly – the person who needs too much mental stroking, who doesn't let you finish your sentences, who turns up late, whose dress sense may panic clients.

Take your time. Choose staff who will get the job done but whose egos are neither puffed up or delicate, who can be funny but know when to be quiet, who want your business to grow and are not there to get ideas for their own. Being nice is important. Hire the person you'll get on with. Because, with staff, a divorce can be messier than the real thing.
Ken Warduct WRITER

15

When meetings get hot and steamy

You are en route to a business meeting in Finland. Want to imagine what it might be like? Just add up all the stereotypes you associate with the distant Nordic country. What do you get? Santa Claus is probably too busy to join you but excessive alcohol consumption and the sauna may well be on the agenda once the plane touches down at Helsinki-Vantaa Airport.

Finnish business etiquette has changed dramatically since the 1990s. EU membership, the collapse of the Soviet Union and the rise of Nokia have all contributed to Finland finally becoming a place for global business. Finns have found themselves dealing with people other than themselves or the Russians. As a result, the Finnish business culture is now an interesting mix of western and Finno-Ugric traditions. But some peculiarities remain so, being a Finn myself, I have compiled a list to help you fit in to our unique business landscape.

Firstly, don't be intimidated. The Finnish way of speaking is something that may come across as rude or awkward. You have to understand the background. We value words. We mean what we say and say it as economically as possible. We don't use superlatives without good reason and we have an astonishing ability to tolerate long silences.

So if your Finnish business partners seem quiet, don't freak out. They don't dislike you – they just feel that at that very moment it is not necessary to say anything. They probably secretly admire your business outfit and impeccable taste. But, of course, us Finns won't flatter you by saying that aloud.

Also, though our education system may be the best in the world, it does not teach English intonation. Consequently, my countrymen and women speak English with a Finnish flat, low, tone. This means that they can easily sound bored, unintelligent and as if they couldn't be less excited about you as a business partner.

Finns love order and precision. They will state their full names when introducing themselves to you and so should you. Also, following the principle of precision, never be late for a meeting.

Sometimes there is a real treat in store (well, that's how the Finns feel at least) and they may have organised a *saunailta*, or sauna evening, for you. Instead of a business suit you are expected to wear nothing. You really are meant to be naked. Fully naked. Try to go with the situation because, for Finns, getting red and sweating together is a bonding moment.

And if you really want to impress, stay in the sauna until the very end. This will garner a huge amount of respect from us Finns and, whatever deal you are trying to close, it will already be in the bag. One word of warning – I have never heard of a *saunailta* that has not continued in a bar with excessive drinking.
Markus Hippi MONOCLE 24 PRODUCER

16

Right on trend

The hipster of today is a mutation of the 19th-century English dandy, choosing to take on both work and leisure with the same broad aesthetic brushstroke. Just like the dandy, the hipster dream is to not work at all – but, if you must, work should fit as seamlessly as possible with the rest of life.

On top of this, hipsters seem to hold the destiny of the urban environment. Entire neighbourhoods, or even cities, are being devoted to or consumed by their lifestyle. Set yourself down in the middle of the trendiest postcodes of London, New York, Melbourne or Portland and dare yourself to find a coffee shop without a barista sullenly standing behind an imported La Marzocco espresso machine, offering up a flat white.

They are agents of change. The hipster dream has driven many to eschew their jobs, invest in a Heidelberg press and have a crack at printing limited-edition vinyl-record jackets. But this is no rant. Cities are vibrant places because of their many subcultures; hipsters happen to be the loudest at the moment, securing most of the cool capital to be had. However, they are by no means the only one that matters.

What we celebrate about cities such as Beirut or São Paulo is that they have their own way of doing things. The metropolis should have a social terroir. This means that we keep space for the unselfconsciously quirky, the "mom-and-pop shops" and the grit.

Despite the increasing clatter of Rob Brandt coffee cups throughout our cities, there is a limit to the flat-white economy and, eventually, a natural end to it. So, before you choose to set up yet another coffee shop, letterpress workshop or craft brewery, think about the natural ecology of your 'hood and the social and business prospects your new venture can foster for all.
Michael Davis WRITER

> *Just like the dandy, the hipster dream is to not work at all – but, if you must, work should fit as seamlessly as possibly with the rest of life*
> — 16

17

In the blood

Take a plane to Milan and drive northwest. In the foothills of the Piedmont Alps you'll observe Italy's textile heartland through the window of your Fiat Panda. Factories pepper the landscape.

The area around Biella is known for its refined cloth industry and the world's finest wool is still washed, combed and spun here. This output is largely produced by small to medium-sized businesses. And most are family affairs.

Skills are inherited, as is leadership; interviews and formal applications are less common. Economists have suggested this rigidity hampers national reform of the business world. The sense of obligation between fathers and sons, mothers and daughters, uncles, aunts and cousins might even drive firms into trouble.

But family loyalty is also one of Italy's strengths. At Reda, one of Piedmont's oldest clothiers, the ethos of a family business drives innovation. The owner, Francesco Botto Poala, says he is determined to push on because of his responsibility to his workers and to his family, recently upgrading the looms and setting up a knitwear line to diversify the business.

In the old mill Reda moved into several years ago, a portrait of Poala's grandfather hangs in the boardroom. The factory administrator, Frederici Raffale, wears a three-piece suit to show visitors around – he has worked here for more than 30 years. Reda is an example of how a sense of loyalty and lineage can make for healthy businesses.
Sophie Grove MONOCLE SENIOR EDITOR

18

Setting up shop

The shopkeeper. Not an occupation that's often championed, hailed or admired. Yet to run and own a shop – whether you are a purveyor of high fashion, pots and pans or apples and pears – can be one of the most noble and fulfilling occupations. Of course, it's not a calling for everyone. There is that element of chance: there are the time-wasters, the ditherers, the difficult neighbours and the greedy landlords.

But there is great art and skill involved, too. My first ever job as an assistant in a small boutique in Cambridge has never left me. The proprietor, Rosalind Bown, sold cashmere knits and frocks with the skill of a veteran diplomat. She was style adviser, salesperson and eventual friend and confidant to each customer, no matter what their ilk. She galvanised the local economy, set the tone for the (somewhat motley) retail in the street and became a focal point for like-minded people in the area. Fifteen years later she's still there and as spirited as the day she opened.

So before you dismiss him as a mere retailer of goods, remember the lone shopkeeper is steward of the public-private threshold, a master of his own kingdom, a building block in the local economy and a linchpin in society.
Sara Gover WRITER

19

The circle of (business) life

Entrepreneurs are volatile creatures. Their journey is an emotionally draining one, with continual crescendos of hope and nadirs of despair. Life is a continual grapple with uncertainty as we struggle to keep up with the world's dynamic whims. And sometimes it seems the only way ahead is to plough on blinkered, focused on a distant goal that few others can understand, foolish as it may seem. In short, it is the most naked expression of what it is to be human.

The financial turmoil of the past few years and the continuing worries about economic growth have done little to encourage those of us who choose this road less travelled. Commentators make hyperbolic comparisons, most notably with the 1930s – a decade seared in cultural memory as the Great Depression and a traumatic time of economic distress as well as mass unemployment.

Less known is that it was also one of the most successful periods for entrepreneurs in US history, with more fortunes being created than in almost any other comparable period. Ruth Wakefield invented the chocolate-chip cookie, while well-known names today such as Motorola (1928), KFC (1930), Tampax (1936) and Hewlett-Packard (1939) sprang into existence.

The conundrum reveals some interesting truths. First, no country ever went bust forever. In the midst of even the most troubled economic environment there are embers waiting to spark into life and produce future growth.

Second, innovation is in our blood. Capitalism is a continual process of creative destruction, where markets periodically clear out the old and replace it with the new. This agnostic dynamism is fundamental to our ability to adapt to a changing world and find ways forward.

I cannot read the tea leaves of the future but I can read the pages of the past. And the lessons of history are clear.

Life is simply too short to be truly rational. Looking through the narrow lens of human speculation, the ability to make quick decisions, and myopic ones at that, is key to our growth. The blinkered taking on of risks, the relentless focus on the here and now, the ability to persuade peers into your vision and so on: these may all be qualities that we deride in speculators as causing financial contagion. But they are also all qualities that led to the creation of successful empires, fed innovation, built economies and allowed us to progress from lone hunters in caves to the sophistication we have today. Any delineation is merely the result of taking snapshots of the same person at different times.

History concurs. Progress is often linked to the capacity for error. It is the taking of imprudent risks that leads to many advances. The rise of the internet spawned an infamous dotcom bubble. However, that same bubble also financed a paradigm shift in the global exchange of information and social interaction that defines our world today.

As George Bernard Shaw noted, all progress depends on the unreasonable man. And as entrepreneurs we would be wise to hold that maxim close on our journey into glorious uncertainty.
Bob Swarup INVESTOR AND AUTHOR

20
Taking your
business outside

The Inner Hebrides is one of the most northerly parts of the UK. To get there from London involves a plane and a three-hour taxi ride. And to get to the beautiful Ardlussa House, which sits on a remote hill on the small Scottish Isle of Jura, requires a small boat through the craggy isles past the Corryvreckan whirlpool – skirting nesting sea eagles.

Jura is an escape. George Orwell, who stayed here to write *Nineteen Eighty-Four*, called it "an extremely un-get-at-able place". At the last count there were 5,500 deer on the island and only about 200 people. Many are locals and some are just visiting for the summer. Others are here in retreat from careers in the city. They have left their desks and taken up tools, reins and fishing rods to make their way in the wilderness. Just as workaholics seek to purify themselves through hard work, Jura's severe, windswept landscape is both a challenge and a cure.

Until a few years ago, Claire and Andrew Fletcher had lived in London and then Glasgow – they were seasoned, chic urbanites. They left their urban careers to run the Ardlussa Estate with its vast expanse of bracken and heather-covered land. Now they grow their own vegetables and eat wild venison and fresh eggs from their chicken run. They wake up to the cockerel crowing and have no need for a watch. Their house is filled with roses from the garden and they host visitors in front of big log fires.

Andrew takes parties out deer stalking and drives an all-terrain Argocat around uninhabited parts of the island, maintaining the estate. Claire rides ponies around the fields and runs the guest house.

To see first-hand proof of the agrarian dream is bad news for me. Like so many people, I have nursed an urge to live off the land and often reassured myself that it wouldn't really be so peachy. Of course, it's not just me. It is well known that agriculture and life on a working farm is hard and that we would quickly miss the amenities of our urban lives. But still we yearn.

Land lust has been around for aeons of course, since Marie Antoinette built a retreat in the park of the Château de Versailles. Think of Tolstoy, who cultivated an alternative life surrounded by Russian peasants and yearned for the purity found in the fields.

But for a growing number of entrepreneurs, farming the land is not about rustic aesthetics, remote retirement plans or literary aspirations: instead it has become a modern business reality. In the US, for instance, the Department of Agriculture counts about half a million "beginning farmers" – those with under 10 years of experience. (They are more likely to be college educated and less likely to receive government subsidies.) These entrepreneurial land lovers are finding ecological and clever ways of working the land, living in the wilderness and making a profit.

For many, hot days in the office are over. They are not just lusting after or even reading about the land – they're ploughing, fishing, sowing and stalking it instead. Here's to that.
Phoebe McKenzie WRITER

> *For a growing number of entrepreneurs, farming the land has become a business reality*
> — 20

> *Increasingly, establishments with nice older staff win out over places with the cute but useless*
> — 21

21
Experience is
everything

Older is wiser. There's a small Swiss hotel in the mountains where they do everything well. We are not talking grand or five-star but simple larch-clad rooms, bathrooms that work, good coffee and a welcoming fresh duvet. In some places it borders on the spartan. One of the highlights, and one of the reasons people look forward to coming back, is the woman who takes your breakfast order. She's in her sixties, homely and has a cheeky smile. She even gives you a hug on the first morning.

Increasingly, establishments with nice older staff win out over places with the cute but useless. It says something about a business's loyalty to its staff and ideals. And that's what builds customer loyalty.
Daniel Croft WRITER

22
Rethinking hospitality

Since I joined Noma as director of business development, my desk has been just steps away from the kitchen. My vantage point has allowed me to keep in mind the key to this restaurant: 60 employees devoted entirely to making people happy. In an increasingly digital, impersonal world they work with their hands, they move non-stop and they smile.

It has been clear from the very beginning of my tenure here that the typical PR strategy won't ever work for us. Instead we focus our resources on treating our diners as guests, not customers. Noma might be known around the world for pushing boundaries and discovering new flavours but at its core the restaurant is grounded in a timeless sense of hospitality.

We try to know our guests before they arrive. At each service meeting, the staff discusses the 40 diners that will soon enter the restaurant to figure out where they come from and why they've chosen to join us. Have they eaten at Noma before? Do they have any preferences or dislikes? Is this going to be the meal where he's going to pop the question?

Getting to know your customer like this shouldn't just apply to the restaurant trade. It's a powerful way of gaining trust and reputation.

We only serve 80 or so guests a day. But if you consider that we do 10 services five times a week, hosting diners from all over the world, the reverberations from creating a unique, personalised experience can be more powerful than any advertisement and certainly more lasting. If you give someone an unforgettable meal they will let others know and they can attest to the fact that it's not hype. It's real. That's what we try to do at Noma.
Peter Kreiner DIRECTOR OF NOMA

23
The importance of lists

1. Write a an essay about the importance of lists.
2. Explain how impossible I find it to start the day without first writing a list of everything I need to do.
3. Mention the different styles in the office – explain how I type mine out and print it every morning, the editor scribbles his on Post-it notes and everyone under the age of 30 has some sort of app.
4. Reiterate that pen and paper are far better and that everyone under the age of 30 is wrong.
5. Remember to add a couple of easy tasks so that I can feel good about ticking things off.
6. Check emails.
7. Make coffee.
8. Cite some examples of great authors from history writing lists to lend unearned intellectual ballast.
9. Hemingway.
10. Add at least one item that has nothing to do with work.
11. Pick up dry cleaning.
12. Always include one item that has been on the list for months but I still haven't got round to doing.
13. Come up with serious idea for an essay.
14. Talk about why, despite the flippant tone, this actually says a lot about the way we work effectively; put forward the argument that most of us organise our time badly and it is a constant struggle to keep on top of things; suggest that the act of writing the list is more important than ticking things off.
15. Describe the thrill of ticking things off.
16. Unnecessarily break up bigger tasks into several smaller ones so that there is more to tick off.
17. Like this.
18. See?
19. Wonder why I feel more comfortable writing lists of 10s and 20s – ending on an odd number just feels wrong.
20. Think of a suitable ending.
Steve Bloomfield MONOCLE FOREIGN EDITOR

Contents

Preface

A good office interior should say something about you and your company. That doesn't mean being tricky or dizzyingly fashionable (unless you want to give the impression you are the season's hot thing). The first impression you give to potential employees and clients will stay with them for a very long time.

A good office interior should also be practical: choose materials that will survive some knocks and look good with a few layers of age because you do not want to be refurbishing every few years.

You also need to think beyond aesthetics. How is this space best divided, what will be the rhythm of the day, can you make the most of open windows in the summer for some cross breeze and where will you sit so that you have privacy but still feel connected to daily goings-on? This is the human bit of office design and is as vital as paint colours and fabric swatches. You need to consider lighting and good chairs, furniture systems that can expand with your business and the kit that makes a good office tick along nicely. Go from function to form and all will make sense. Oh, and try to avoid brutal overhead lighting. Nobody looks good in a white glare.

6
BUILD
AN OFFICE

How to create the perfect workspace interior

AT YOUR SERVICE
PLAISIR

Preface: Outdoor-advertising giant JCDecaux, based near Versailles in France, has its roots in providing essential services such as bus shelters and amenities for cities. This uniquely down-to-earth business model within a family-run company means its headquarters are impressive yet welcoming.

Company: JCDecaux
Location: Plaisir, France
Founded: 1964
Number of employees when founded: 1
Number of employees now: 12,000
Family members involved: 4

———

Quote: *'For a company like us it's important to remember the fundamental needs cities have'*

In the vast grounds of the headquarters of JCDecaux in Plaisir, close to Versailles, sits a building made of huge slabs of marble-like concrete. Its handsome façade is marked with two plaques scored with a list of cities, ranging from Aachen to Yokohama. It could be a town hall or the head office of an elite financial institution. Open its glass doors though and it's not the lobby of a conglomerate that appears. Instead it's women in overalls running off posters and blue-collared men tinkering away at vast printing machines. It's a factory.

Making the mundane appear good-looking is something that advertising giant JCDecaux has excelled at in its long history. The family-run company provides the essentials of urban life: bus shelters, automatic public toilets, lampposts, bins and self-service bicycle schemes. It operates in more than 60 countries, controls advertising in more than 145 airports, is the world's number one company of its kind – with 1,082,400 advertising panels – and employs 12,000 people.

The company was started in 1964 by Jean-Claude Decaux in Lyon. The young entrepreneur's idea was simple: to provide municipalities with much-needed bus shelters. He would clean and maintain them at no expense to the taxpayer or the city authorities and in return

make money from the advertising placed on them.

The campus, about 45 minutes from Paris, is all manicured lawns, beehives and sculptures plus an artificial lake. The senior management and HR departments work in a low-slung international-style masterpiece designed by Jean-Pierre Vidal. It's little wonder that some of the world's best architects – such as Norman Foster, Philippe Starck, Mario Bellini and Philip Cox – have been inclined to work with JCDecaux, such is the company's commitment to the way things look.

Although tastes and technology may have changed, it's striking how little JCDecaux's core model has altered since the company began. Jean-Claude's three sons are now running the show. "For a company like us it's important to remember the fundamental needs cities have and will still have in 30 years' time: the loo, the bins, the benches, the bus shelters, the bicycles," says the youngest, Jean-Sébastien. "They are fundamental material needs and we are not to forget them." — (M)

Why it works:
Jean-Claude Decaux's original far-sighted investment in the way things look is not only defined at his company's headquarters in Plaisir but now also influences streets and airports in all corners of the globe.

01

Previous spread:
01
Head office at
the JCDecaux
campus

This spread:
01
Beehives on site
provide pots of
honey for visitors
02
On-site fitness
03
Beekeeper
tending the hives
04
Maintenance
keeping things
in check
05
Posters awaiting
transport

06
Making posters
07
Philippe Starck's
'Sunflower' lamp
post
08
Column
designed by
Norman Foster
09
Great attention
to design is a
common theme
throughout the
site, even in the
printing rooms
10
Panoramic view
of the campus
11
Ready to go

01

02   03

04

05   06

07

08   09

10   11

OPEN HOUSE LONDON

Preface: When tiemaker Drake's moved to new premises it wanted a place that would reflect the company's ethos. That meant tearing down the physical partitions that divided staff and creating a space in which clients could see the manufacturing process unfold for themselves.

Company: Drake's
Location: London
Founded: 1977
Number of employees when founded: 6
Number of employees now: 50
Number of premises: 3 (a shop, the office/warehouse/factory and a shirt factory in Somerset)
Family members involved: 1 (the co-owner, Michael Hill, is the son of the first Drake's tiemaker)
Bestselling product: navy grenadine tie

Quote: *'People feel like they are working together'*

01

"We are not hiding the manufacturing process like some companies; if anything, we're celebrating it," says Michael Hill, director of Drake's. Fittingly situated on Haberdasher Street in London's East End, Drake's …is a British menswear manufacturer and acclaimed maker of handmade ties. Since April 2013 the entire company has been housed in this bright, open-plan building: the factory, the commercial arm and the distribution centre. There is even a small on-site shop.

The factory is on the first floor. Here, 25 craftsmen and women and three designers work alongside one another making up to 2,000 to 2,500 ties a week. Of the 13 stages of the production process, only one involves the use of a machine; the rest is done entirely by hand. This is a great source of pride for the brand. "Wholesale customers can simply go upstairs and see exactly how the ties are made," says Hill.

The company could easily have moved out of London in 2013 and saved money in the process but, as Hill explains, that was never really an option: "The brand was always about 'Made in London' so it would have been disingenuous if we hadn't been here." The central location benefits everyone; many of the factory workers live in east London and can get to work with relative ease.

A great deal of thought went into the design of the new space. "This building dates back to the 1930s," says Nicola Rutt, partner and architect at Hawkins\Brown, the firm tasked with the renovation, "but when we came in it was being used as storage by a courier company. It was all low ceilings and drab ceiling tiles; there were lots of partitions making it very dark." The Hawkins\Brown refurbishment removed inessential partitions to open up the space and installed large, steel-framed windows made by Crittall, a family-owned business based just outside London in Essex. Those partitions that had to remain were remade out of Crittall glass.

The light, capacious and airy factory floor is a far cry from the urban sweatshops associated with many clothing manufacturers. The openness of the architecture reflects the company's nature. "People feel like they are working together," says Hill. — (M)

Why it works:
The craftsmen and women take pride in their product and the company, in turn, looks after their wellbeing. The factory floor is open and bright but feels intimate due to the small size of the team. An egalitarian ethos is evident in every aspect of the factory, from the shared cafeteria to the design of the building.

02

03　04

05

01
Factory floor
02
Paper patterns
for cutting fabric
03
Traditional
pattern cutting
04
Skilled cutter
05
Showroom

06
Drake's on Hab-
erdasher Street
07
Each tie is
stitched by hand
08
Drake's labels
09
Design assistant
10
Up to 2,000 ties
are made a week

11
Pattern maker
12
Every tie is hand
sewn

CRAFT WORK SOLOMEO

Preface: Translating inspiration into soaring profits is an imperfectly understood art but cashmere specialist Brunello Cucinelli has cracked at least part of the code. And by putting the skill and contentment of its artisans at the heart of the product, it is remaking and re-energising the notion of the factory.

Company: Brunello Cucinelli
Location: Solomeo, Italy
Founded: 1978
Number of employees: 1,000
Number of premises: 2 (Solomeo's castle and an industrial cluster of restored buildings)
Start-up cost: 500,000 lire to produce the first samples
Family members involved: 4 (Brunello works with his wife Federica and daughters Carolina and Camilla)

———

Quote: *'We are a source of inspiration for new entrepreneurial generations'*

At the Brunello Cucinelli factory in Umbria, lunchtime for workers is an hour and a half long. In the canteen, a former farmhouse, the staff sit down at a long wooden table to a subsidised meal of regional produce. The owner, who shares his name with the factory, believes that lunch is a sacred ritual – *il pranzo è sacro* – and one that ups the creativity and fosters familial cohesion.

It is an unusual set-up for a luxury clothier listed on the Milan Stock Exchange with a worth of over €1bn. But while turning a healthy profit, Brunello has crafted a business with an overtly humanist ethos. "Ethical capitalism means that we have to respect workers' dignity, culture, art and beauty," he says. "This is a founding principle of our collections. We believe that giving economic recognition to the people who work for us allows us to preserve the high level of craftsmanship and quality of product."

The village of Solomeo, the company's headquarters, has about 750 employees working in its restored interiors. Its buildings house production of the ready-to-wear collections; a 14th-century castle complete with wooden beams, stone fireplaces and frescoed walls is home to workshops and the quality-control facilities for cashmere production. Every element of the environment has been chosen to "elevate" staff.

The project includes a theatre and there is a school of craft, a vital part of Brunello's long-term plans, that teaches everything from mending to cutting and assembly. The aim is to usher in what the company calls a "neo-renaissance" in Italian manufacturing: to regenerate the status of craft as a noble profession and inspire a new generation of artisans. In pursuit of this vision, Brunello believes a high wage is crucial to changing attitudes and pays his staff accordingly.

He also sees the way the company operates as setting a precedent: "We are a source of inspiration for new entrepreneurial generations," he says. "This business model – based on authentic Italian craftsmanship – is thanks to contemporary creative artisans. It can be replicated and it can have a significant future." — (M)

Why it works:
Striving to elevate and inspire your workers can, in turn, help elevate the product. Brunello Cucinelli's share price is proof that beauty and ethics need not hinder growth. The company's strength is in its artisanal talent, which is why it is committed to training and longevity. The school of craft and favourable working conditions enjoyed by staff ensure that, once skilled, the workers who have developed within the firm stay with it for many years.

01

01

03

02

Previous spread:
01
Class at the
school of crafts

This spread:
01
Employees head
to the canteen
for lunch
02
Meeting room
in the factory

03
Student and
teacher in the
school of craft
04
Lunchtime in
the canteen
05
The experienced
team gets to work

04

05

HARBOUR INTENT SYDNEY

Preface: Being chained to your desk is so passé – Sydney's most forward-looking company owners are broadening their horizons by letting their workflow dictate their workspace.

Companies on site: cafés, restaurants, a dance studio, a diving school and investment firms
Location: Sydney
Founded: 2010
Number of premises: 78
Size of premises: a total of approximately 14,095 sq m
Number of visitors: hundreds of people visit and work at Headland Park every day
Annual rent: up to AU$650 per sq m

———

Quote: *'A rising breed of workers are looking for a fresh take on the nine-to-five'*

Flexible business environments have become the new focus the world over for both freelancers and staffers. What started as an opportunity to reduce rents by sharing space with others has morphed into a new take on working life. In Sydney a group of architects, interior designers and bespoke-furniture manufacturers have risen to the challenge of this new culture. They have set about creating layouts and furnishings that meet the particular needs of this rising breed of workers looking for a fresh take on the nine-to-five.

Geoff Bailey, executive director of Sydney Harbour Federation Trust, oversaw the renovation of a former First World War hospital and women's army barracks into shared office spaces at Headland Park on the harbour's edge. "We decided we could better enrich the life of this part of the city by repurposing rather than bulldozing these buildings," he says.

The aim was to ensure a wide range of uses and the buildings on site include a gym, cafés, a bookbinding service, dance studios and a childcare centre, in addition to studio spaces for artists. "It was important that the site would appeal to a range of businesses," says Bailey.

South African-born interior designer Marni Burger runs her business from Headland Capital's office space. As the "creative in the corner", she specialises in high-end residential interiors, such as the Canberra residence of the former Australian ambassador to Denmark, James Choi.

Down the hill, Hut 32 is the Sydney base for customer-experience consultancy Proto Partners. Staff work across areas shared with external consultants. "Having the use of several spaces means we are not limited by the confines of a normal office," says company founder Damian Kernahan.

Meanwhile, corporations in Sydney's more traditional office buildings, from international auditor giant KPMG to financial specialist Macquarie Bank, are also embracing greater flexibility, moving to bespoke headquarters and implementing an ABW (activity-based working) model. Employees are no longer allocated seating or desktop computers but work instead on mobile devices and sit wherever their activity is taking place. The emphasis on hot-desking is far from ideal but it does shows that people will always like working around other people. — (M)

Why it works:
By making diversity a priority, Headland Park reaps the benefits of unplanned but serendipitous synergies. This sets the stage for inter-disciplinary learning and the fertilisation of ideas. Spectacular views of Sydney Harbour means there's plenty to be inspired by.

A PERFECT BLEND
NEW YORK

Preface: Coffee shops are the most social of places so it's only right that the behind-the-scenes preparations for selling good coffee carry some of that appeal. The Pulley Collective is a communal location in Brooklyn where coffee-shop owners can come to roast their beans and share some good ideas.

Companies on site: coffee roasters
Location: New York
Founded: 2013
Number of members that use the site: 10
Number of employees on site: 4 or 5 at a time
Number of spaces: 1 (there are 2 coffee-roasting machines and a test kitchen for coffee cupping. In addition, those who roast at Pulley store their raw beans in military surplus lockers arranged throughout the space)

Quote: *'The community aspect of the member set-up is just priceless'*

Steve Mierisch runs Pulley Collective, a shared space for coffee roasting that taps into the same ideas that have made shared workspaces take off.

"I wanted to create a space that people feel like coming to," he says, looking past a kitschy yet somehow appropriate chandelier towards a brick fireplace. More akin to a hidden-away supper club than a coffee-roasting warehouse, Mierisch's set-up is comfortable, well equipped and affordable for people to use.

That's the basic premise under which he started the venture in Brooklyn's Red Hook neighbourhood. "I created Pulley to lower the barriers to coffee roasting," says the soft-spoken Mierisch (*pictured middle, on MacBook*). Originally from Nicaragua, he has held jobs with coffee exporters in Latin America and importers in Italy, a New York commodities hedge fund and Chicago-based roaster Intelligentsia Coffee. It's a career that has provided him with a deep knowledge of the coffee world and solid relationships with entrepreneurs looking to take the next step: investing in a coffee-roasting facility.

The members of the collective pay a monthly fee for four six-hour slots with Pulley's coffee-roasting machines. In addition, they get access to a well-looked-after collaborative space. "The community aspect of the member set-up is just

priceless," says Ed Kaufmann, who oversees the roasting operations at Joe, a small coffee outfit with eight shops in New York and another two in nearby Philadelphia.

Kaufmann says the reduced up-front investment and the knowledge-sharing with other roasters make this establishment unique. He estimates that a single company would need to spend a million dollars to start its own roasting operation.

Mierisch adds that his members all benefit from not having to worry about the cost of water, electricity, equipment maintenance and space rental; they only have to think about getting the beans just right. Members also have the option of sourcing their raw coffee beans directly from Mierisch, whose family has been growing coffee in Nicaragua since 1908.

Mierisch thinks this model can work in other cities. The Pulley Incubator programme is giving novice roasters a chance to use the facility by the hour. The hope: to inspire those who might not otherwise have the means. — (M)

Why it works:
Drawing on the shared office-space set-up, Steve Mierisch's collective creates a community for café and coffee-shop owners to exchange insightful knowledge about their businesses.

MASS APPEAL AUCKLAND

Preface: Cities are learning that you can benefit from seemingly redundant industrial buildings as part of a new co-working age. Auckland's City Works Depot is one such building, having been given a new lease of life by ambitious creatives.

Companies on site: design studios, cafés, architecture firms and marketing and production agencies
Location: Auckland
Founded: 2012
Number of businesses: 30
Number of spaces: 42

———

Quote: *'The city has learned that its ruins are treasures and the City Works Depot was probably one of the greatest ruins of them all'*

Originally built by Auckland's city council in 1968, City Works Depot was a near-derelict collection of sheds, abandoned for almost 20 years despite being just a few blocks away from the city's commercial hub. In 2012, two unlikely saviours emerged: Simon Rowntree and James Brown, owners of one of New Zealand's largest parking companies, Tournament. They saw an opportunity when the three-hectare site was put up for sale and they jumped.

"A lot of people tendered but not one person understood the architectural merit of the place," says Rowntree. He and Brown brought in Nat Cheshire of local firm Cheshire Architects early on. "It had been invisible for so long that it just wasn't on people's radar," says Cheshire.

The space has become a converging point for the city's creative classes. Design studios, advertising agencies, architects and production firms have all made the place their home, attracted by its lofty metal-framed structures with their soaring ceilings, generous spaces and mid-century modernist touches.

Leon Kirkbeck, co-owner of Augusto, a production company and design studio, was the site's first tenant. His office is a former water-testing laboratory, traces of which can still be found in now-defunct 1960s control boards that look like something

out of *Dr Who*. "It's spaces like this that make a city feel special," says Kirkbeck (*right, with co-founder Michelle Walshe*).

"It was pretty rough and ready and raw," says architect Matthew Godward. He and business partner Julian Guthrie (*opposite page, in blue jumper, with Godward*) shifted their practice into a high-ceilinged bunker lined with plywood and lit from above by a long line of windows. Godward designs commercial spaces including restaurants and cafés, while Guthrie builds timber houses; both are united by a love of honest materials. "It's perfect for the way we work," says Godward.

Jewellery designer Zoe Williams (*opposite page, bottom left*) of Zoe & Morgan has a space that's part office and part showroom. "It feels really creative," she says. "It's the best space I've ever worked in."

The site's revitalisation is emblematic of Auckland's resurgence. "One of the critical things the city has learned is that its ruins are treasures," says Cheshire. "And the City Works Depot was probably one of the greatest ruins of them all." — (M)

Why it works:
City Works Depot shows that unique architectural features in once-abandoned structures can give a site new purpose.

WORK COMFORTS LONDON

Preface: An office might be somewhere you work but that doesn't mean it can't be comfortable. That's the philosophy of Ilse Crawford, head of design company Studioilse, which is demonstrated by the layout of her studio with a kitchen at its heart.

Company: Studioilse
Location: London
Founded: 2002
Number of employees when founded: 2
Number of employees now: 25
Number of premises: 1
Start-up cost: savings from a year spent setting up Donna Karan's homeware line in New York
Bestselling product: it's more of a mindset or a message: that design can be warm, not cool

Neckinger Mills, a grade II-listed Victorian building in Southwark, was once a paper mill and then a tannery before being converted into mixed residential and studio spaces. With iron columns and Crittall windows, plenty of natural light, an open-plan set-up and occupying a spot a stone's throw from Maltby Street food market, it ticked all the boxes for Ilse Crawford and her design team at Studioilse.

From retail to transport, Crawford's team has a simple mission: to make spaces where people feel comfortable. When it comes to an office she believes that just because it is a place of work it doesn't have to look like one.

The 25-strong team works on a number of projects at any given time so flexibility of working and presentation areas was key in determining the layout. The main studio space is anchored with three oak worktables where the team moves around depending on what they are working on. Sliding walls divide the studio from a library and act as handy presentation boards. Glass screens section off another area for more formal presentations at a large Saarinen tulip table.

The heart of the studio is the kitchen. The team cooks and eats lunch together here every day and on a Wednesday, Crawford's housekeeper and former chef Patrizia cooks for the team and a handful of guests. For a few hours the studio feels more like a party and guests get to watch as the space seamlessly transforms from work to play – and back again. — (M)

Why it works:
The studio uses wood, brass, leather and skins together with built-to-last furniture to convey a sense of permanence; greenery adds life. Though the main studio has large desks where the bulk of the work is done, flexibility for different needs and moods has been written into every detail.

01

02

03

01
The library has a sliding wall making it a handy space for small workshops and client presentations
02
Architectural models and product samples from former projects
03
Woody corner of the materials library
04
Main workspace, anchored by three long oak workbenches

05
Bathrooms
have been
given as much
attention as the
rest of the studio
06
Saarinen tulip
table, a set of
Hans J Wegner
chairs and an
original Aalto
pendant set
the tone for
the meeting/
dining room

07
Glass screens
and doors
divide the space
into different
function areas
08
Vitsoe shelving
in the meeting
room holds
favourite books,
previous pitch
material and
product samples

05

06 07

09
The Studioilse
team cooks
and eats lunch
together
every day

10
Aalto's Stool
60 is handy
for perching,
while pendant
lighting is perfect
for late-night
working

08 09

11
Looking towards
the meeting
room from the
kitchen
12
Hardware
samples and
the wo84 task
light, designed
by Studioilse for
Swedish lighting
firm Wästberg
13
The original
Crittall windows
and cast-iron
supporting
columns have
been paired
with a reclaimed
Carpathian
oak floor

10

11

12

Six brands all office builders should know

1 **USM** The powder-coated modular Haller shelving system (*see page 272*) smacks of Swiss functionality: available in 14 different colours, it will take everything you can throw at (or in) it. *usm.com*

2 **Vitra** We'd keep it Swiss for meeting-room furniture, too. No one does a task chair better than Vitra. For comfort and style, Charles and Ray Eames's aluminium series is hard to beat (*see page 274*). *vitra.com*

3 **Artemide** The Tolomeo lamp (*see page 260*) by Michele De Lucchi is the best way to keep nightowls well illuminated and desks looking good. *artemide.com*

4 **Novex** The Mecono range by Novex, made of aluminium, steel and wood, is a highly versatile choice for desk tables. The timber surface will help warm up any office environment. *novex.ch*

5 **Unifor** The workplace furniture arm of Italian manufacturer Molteni&C, Unifor works with a roster of collaborators that includes Jean Nouvel and Pierluigi Cerri. *unifor.ch*

6 **Crittal Windows** Based close to London in Essex, Crittal uses recycled steel from Switzerland for its fenestration and has fitted everywhere from Universal Studios in LA to the Ace Hotel London. *crittall-windows.co.uk*

13

SENSE OF WONDER
TOKYO

Preface: Design and branding firm Wonderwall is responsible for some of your favourite shop interiors. The company's Tokyo HQ, designed by founder Masamichi Katayama, reflects the inspiring environments he is famous for creating worldwide.

Company: Wonderwall
Location: Tokyo
Founded: 2000
Number of employees when founded: 5
Number of employees now: 22
Number of premises: 1

On a quiet side street in the Tokyo neighbourhood of Sendagaya a cool, concrete structure has become an unlikely shrine for frustrated retailers, visionary entrepreneurs, students of fashion merchandising and architecture groupies. Branding specialist Masamichi Katayama's design firm Wonderwall took up residence in its handsome HQ in 2009.

Having come up with the design language for the A Bathing Ape clothing empire, the elegant shop interiors for Mackintosh, global flagship stores for Uniqlo and a host of hidden speciality boutiques all over Japan, Katayama knows how to excite clients, shoppers and the media alike.

"I'm always looking to create impact and generate a reaction," says Katayama, sitting at an impossibly long meeting table. "The analogue store has to excite and work harder than ever before."

His team of around 20 designers, project managers and miniature-model builders work long hours here and so the space – three levels above ground, two below, with an abundance of skylights and windows – is meant to be an inspirational haven from the bustle outside.

The rotating collection of art by Ryan Gander, Rieko Otake and others, along with knick-knacks from novelty and antique shops and thousands of books, give visitors the sense that, with such wide-ranging interests and a growing list of global clients, Katayama can easily attract top creative talent to build on the buzz surrounding Wonderwall's own brand. — (M)

Why it works:
The airy workspace offers would-be clients a fine example of the firm's design principles. Thanks to Katayama's obsession over every material used and each item on display, the office is an ideal environment for staff to spend long hours working on the unforgettable shop interiors for which global brands come to Wonderwall.

01

02

04
A three-storey
steel door leads
to the sloping
concrete entry
ramp inside
05
The conference
room table with
classic Charlotte
Perriand Indo-
chine chairs
06
Miniature store-
design mock-ups

04

05

06

07
Wonderwall's
design-team
work space
08
Katayama rotates
the art on display
and has cases
filled with
knick-knacks
and antiques

09
Katayama's
office on the top
floor is his per-
sonal workspace,
lounge and
music room

07

08

09

WHAT LIES BENEATH INNSBRUCK

Preface: Faced with a growing business and limited space, architect Daniel Fügenschuh came up with the ingenious solution of building an underground office in his garden. The sustainable, spacious studio also acts as a showcase for Fügenschuh's work.

Company: Daniel Fügenschuh
Location: Innsbruck
Founded: 2004
Number of employees when founded: 2
Number of employees now: 8
Best work: Austrian supermarket chain MPreis in Wiesing stands out for its unconventional design: the free-spanning timber-structure roof is folded diagonally, leading to a distortion of perspective inside and out

After working for Hopkins Architects in London, Daniel Fügenschuh set up his own studio in Innsbruck in 2004. At first he worked from home – a refurbished house built in 1914. When this no longer fitted his expanding business the architect looked at the huge garden behind the residence. Not wanting to sacrifice the greenery and the view, he came up with a rather surprising idea: to create a 300 sq m underground office beneath the garden.

The studio was finished in December 2008 and the architect used clever tactics to create a pleasant workplace that avoids feeling like a bunker. With the compound dropping seven metres towards street level, Fügenschuh could even install a huge glass window on one side of the office. An additional skylight – level with the grass – also provides natural light, so the illumination inside meets with official standards for offices in Austria. Inside the studio there's lots of fair-faced concrete, larch wood and steel that contrasts beautifully with Vitra furniture and the spectacular view through the frameless window.

Fügenschuh and his team have worked on projects as diverse as building a school extension adjacent to an old monastery and a supermarket for Tyrolean chain MPreis, known for commissioning re-nowned architects with unusual designs. His studio designed new headquarters for the UN in Podgorica, Montenegro, and a multi-purpose inner-urban complex in Kufstein, Tyrol's second-largest city.

Working in an unusual office space inspires new thinking and has also proved to be practical. By going underground, Fügen-schuh could create a completely new building without needing to adhere to problematic planning laws and regulations. It's sustainable, too: a heat exchanger produces the perfect room climate without the need for conventional heating, turning the office into a zero-energy and zero-emission building. — (M)

Why it works:
The space serves as an advert for the architect's imagination. Its extensive window facing the street attracts curious onlookers. Fügenschuh admits that most people experience an "Aha!" moment when they first see the ingenious architectural solution. On the very first day in the office a passer-by stopped and asked Fügenschuh to design a house for him.

01
Spacious interior inside the 300 sq m Fügenschuh office
02
Architectural plans held on the wall by magnets

01

02

03

04

05

06

07

01

EASY
DOES IT
MUNICH

Preface: The office of graphic-design agency Bureau Mirko Borsche, which has clients ranging from major newspapers to theatres, is a relaxed space that also serves as a home. That easygoing charm also reflects its founder's adaptable approach to business.

Company: Bureau Mirko Borsche
Location: Munich
Founded: 2007
Number of employees when founded: 1
Number of employees now: 8 at the office, plus freelancers

Award-winning graphic designer Mirko Borsche believes in fast, flexible companies – not least his own. The three members at the core of his team are based at his studio, the rest he has placed temporarily at his clients. Those include weekly quality newspaper *Die Zeit* – for which Borsche acts as a remote creative director, looking at layouts on his laptop and visiting the headquarters only every few weeks – as well as the renowned Thalia theatre in Hamburg, fashion designer Kostas Murkudis and industrial designer Stefan Diez. Other clients include the Bavarian State Opera, *Super Paper* magazine and record label Gomma.

Borsche has worked as art director for high-profile magazines such as *Jetzt*, *Neon* and *SZ-Magazin* after spending his early years in advertising. He started his firm with only two old computers and some Ikea furniture in a small wooden kiosk that cost him €450 rent a month. Soon Borsche moved to his 210 sq m office space with attached apartment and a terrace, on which he grows vegetables and frequently hosts barbecues for collaborators. Although technology often makes it possible for people to work from wherever they want, Borsche has created a pleasant home for those that stay a while. His bureau is a great example of the contemporary structure

of today's creative companies: based on a loose network of professionals, a non-hierarchical structure and mobile, flexible work schedules.

Sitting on his terrace stroking Felipe the cat, he admits he is regularly approached by big advertising agencies asking to acquire his business but he always turns them down, preferring to do things his own way.

Borsche has learned to only do what he loves. He cooks for staff and provides a relaxed atmosphere in the office. "I want to grow old with what I do. In my business this cannot be taken for granted. I want to decide where my career goes and not have other people decide." — (M)

Why it works:
A design practice should interpret the successful portfolio of the team working there as well as its founder's personality – happily, Bureau Mirko Borsche achieves both.

01
Mirko Borsche's
workers enjoying
natural light
from the terrace
02
The team's work
stations and
shift patterns
are flexible
03
Storage boxes –
and the way to
reach them
04
Quiet area with
inspiration close
at hand

03   04

01
Main office
space
02
Inner courtyard
03
Partners Peter
Dinesen (facing
camera) and
Andrew Smart
on the rooftop
terrace

04
Entrance to inner
courtyard
05
One of Mensch's
two meeting
rooms
06
Andrew Smart in
a side office off
the main space
07
Main office and
reception area

01

02

03

04

05

06

IN PLAIN SIGHT
COPENHAGEN

Preface: Renovating a century-old building while respecting the original features has created a light, spacious environment that is the antithesis of the dull, drab office block. It makes working at communications and marketing consultant Mensch a pleasure.

Company: Mensch
Location: Copenhagen
Founded: 2009
Number of employees when founded: 11
Number of employees now: 17
Number of premises: 1
Bestselling service: business and communication consultancy

Architects make a special trip to admire the offices of communications and marketing consultant Mensch. Built in 1905 by Copenhagen's public telephone company Kjøbenhavns Telefon Aktieselskab, they were redesigned by Mensch in 2010. During the renovation the team was conscious of respecting what was left of the original features.

The three-storey building is situated in the St Petri Passage, a quiet backstreet off the main thoroughfare of Nørre Voldgade. The exterior is in the early 20th-century *skønvirke* style (the Nordic equivalent of art nouveau) and built from red brick and granite. Inside, ceilings are five and a half metres high,

giving the large rooms a luxuriously spacious feel.

The building was once the workplace of around 1,000 people; Mensch employs 17 people in its vast 1,200 sq m third-floor office. The space is open-plan with separate glass offices for the partners, meaning they can have privacy for meetings and phone calls. The rest of the team shares the larger and completely open-plan workspace that takes up the majority of the floor.

Mensch designed the interior themselves. One of the most striking features is the quality of the furniture and furnishings. The boardroom, for instance, is home to some classic Danish designs, including Hans J Wegner Wishbone chairs and Poul Henningsen lampshades.

Renovating the century-old building was not cheap but the office that Mensch has created is definitely worth the investment. — (M)

Why it works:
Good lights (but not fluorescent strips) and simple whitewashed walls make for an airy and light space. The open-plan format makes a huge difference to everything from energy levels to ease of communication.

07

HOME MAKER SAITAMA

Preface: Combining work and pleasure is a lifestyle open to those doing jobs they are truly passionate about. Furniture maker Yoshiaki Tanaka has built his workshop into his home in Saitama to create an inviting base for his company, Mokkoku.

Company: Mokkoku
Location: Saitama, Japan
Founded: 2002
Number of employees when founded: 1
Number of employees now: 2
Number of premises: 1
Original start-up costs: about ¥5m
Time to make a table: 1 week to 10 days

Combining a house, workshop and showroom in one space isn't for everyone. It requires a well-ordered studio, an even tidier home and an unselfconsciousness about revealing both to passing customers.

Furniture maker Yoshiaki Tanaka has made a virtue of blurring the line between his life and work ever since he started his business Mokkoku in Saitama in 2002. He works from a studio in a residential neighbourhood and uses the home he shares with his wife upstairs as the showroom for the bespoke furniture that he builds.

Tanaka is a self-taught carpenter who learnt on the job rather than in college. Inspired by the work of Hans J Wegner and good with his hands, he joined a small furniture company in 1995 to acquire skills. A few years later he launched his own business.

The Mokkoku premises are striking in their simplicity, with only the smallest of signs announcing the business within.

The workshop on the ground floor is clean and uncluttered, even though it is stacked with timber and power tools.

Upstairs, the living room provides a comfortable setting for Tanaka's work, much of which is destined for customers' homes. Natural light pours in and there are plenty of concealed cupboards to store the essentials of daily life. There is no sign of the futons that are rolled out each night for sleeping on and no television either. It's a tidy arrangement for an entrepreneur at home with his business model. — (M)

Why it works:
Customers can try the chairs, tables and sofas in a real domestic interior to get a feel for the pieces and how they function in a home. There's a sense of honesty to Tanaka's set-up that people appreciate, both in the products and in the man who makes them. Seeing the workshop is inspiring, reinforcing the fact that these pieces are skilfully made from raw timber.

01

02

03

04

05

06

07

PAST
MODERN
BOLZANO

Preface: Vudafieri Saverino Partners combined tradition and modernity for the offices of accountancy firm Hager & Partners. Over two floors of an 18th-century baroque building, original and contemporary features are mixed to create a welcoming space.

Company: Hager & Partners
Location: Bolzano
Founded: 1995
Number of employees when founded: 10
Number of employees now: 100
Number of premises: 3 (Bolzano, Milan and Rome)

When the Bolzano office of accounting firm Hager & Partners decided it was time to upgrade to a roomier workspace they sought out expert advice.

Completed in 2008 by Milan studio Vudafieri Saverino Partners, the brief was to house the staff on two floors of an 18th-century palazzo in the historic centre of the South Tyrolean capital. The baroque building had beautiful original details – stucco ceilings and parquet flooring – that were refurbished. Architect Tiziano Vudafieri looked to incorporate the building's pre-existing interiors with modern elements to create a dialogue between the contemporary and the historical.

His practice added a collection of sculptural lighting to the 1,000 sq m space – several designed in-house by Vudafieri – and a conference table in gold-leaf finish with curvy legs. Through the use of bespoke lamps the setting is given a warmth not often associated with the offices of accountancy firms. It communicates to prospective clients that while the firm is rooted in tradition it is also imaginative enough to come up with solutions to assist them.

While walls are a sober white, the architects have punctuated the space with contemporary artwork. Slightly more austere is the owner's corner office, which includes a side table with fold-out chairs in velvet, similar to that used at the Opéra de Paris.

A lone Tolomeo lamp is the only desk accessory, while two provocative paintings hang opposite each other. The architects believed that the head of the company should reside in a space that projected transparency to better set the clients' minds at ease. — (M)

Why it works:
The original parquet flooring throughout most of the office keeps staff grounded. Modern art stimulates creative minds and shows off good taste to clients. The handcrafted wooden accents dotted around recall the area's local carpentry heritage.

01

02

01
Office with stucco ceiling
02
Sculptural lighting

03
The office space
04
Internal staircase in palazzo where Hager & Partners is based

03

05

05
Offices feature
Aldo Rossi
leather chairs
06
Original parquet
flooring features
throughout the
building
07
Modern
artwork outside
conference room

06

08
Main entrance
to office
09
Natural light fills
a meeting room
10
Exterior of
the palazzo

07

08   09

10

01

02

01
The Rochelle
School from
neighbouring
Arnold Circus
02
Workers in the
Frieze office
03
Enjoying Frieze's
rooftop garden

04
The Rochelle
Canteen
05
Shared lunch
provided by
the Rochelle
Canteen at the
Frieze office

03

04

05

THE ART OF WORK LONDON

Preface: A converted London schoolhouse is home to Frieze, the organisation famous for two annual art fairs. But the Rochelle School's communal atmosphere is not down to just one company – the building's other tenants add to the creative mix.

Company: Frieze
Location: London
Founded: 1991
Number of employees when founded: 3
Number of employees now: 50

Frieze, the company for which life is a show of agenda-setting art fairs in New York and London and eight issues of its immaculate magazine a year, occupies the top floor of a former Victorian schoolhouse in east London. Fellow occupants of the Rochelle School include creatives such as accessories designer Katie Hillier, Turner Prize-nominated artist Goshka Macuga and celebrated caterers Arnold & Henderson whose restaurant, the Rochelle Canteen, is a converted bike shed on the ground floor. "I think we benefit from the creative community here." says Frieze's deputy director Joanna Stella-Sawicka.

The 50 or so employees at the Frieze office enjoy a rooftop garden bounded by four purpose-built marquees. Its Iroko timber flooring is the choice of local designers (very local: they're on the floor below) Quinn Architects, borrowing from the reddish browns of the 19th-century buildings in the surrounding Boundary estate.

In an industry dominated by single-minded ambition, Frieze is proving it doesn't hurt to make a few friends. And if they're your neighbours too? Even better. — (M)

Why it works:
Traditional space filled with a broad mix of exciting companies creates a natural environment for good ideas.

SPACE TO BREATHE
PARIS

Preface: Shared space for multiple companies is tricky – it requires enough division to keep business straightforward and yet the kind of openness that helps firms share useful ideas. Paris design firm Cigüe knows how to get the balance right.

Company: Cigüe
Location: Paris
Founded: 2003
Number of employees when founded: 6
Number of employees now: 18
Start-up cost: €7,500
Best work: with clients ranging from Aesop to Dover Street Market, Cigüe is known for making the most out of design within limited spaces

When Paris-based studio Cigüe was asked to create a shared office space for three companies in the heart of the city, it was confronted with restoring architectural harmony to a once glorious classical building hacked apart by overzealous 1970s developers.

The main question for Cigüe's team of architects, designers and carpenters was how to preserve the boundaries between the private and public space without hiding the businesses away. The answer? Taking inspiration from doorways in traditional Chinese houses. The shapes appealed to Cigüe co-founder Hugo Haas and his colleagues as a means of creating sensitive divisions. Drop ceilings were removed and 100 sq m of pale-oak parquet flooring was added, chosen for its classic Haussmannian feel.

White walls and scant furnishings make for a cool, calm look around decorative touches such as soft leather handles on overhead cupboards and elegant Habitat lamps. The oak doors and benches running around the sides of rooms were crafted, of course, by Cigüe themselves. — (M)

Why it works:
Privacy is maintained in this small shared space by the clever use of partitions, while communal areas help bring all the employees together.

01

02

01
Doors and tables were made by hand by Cigüe
02
Oak door
03
Small corner kitchen with black-stained oak surfaces
04
Translucent panelling lets light through
05
Each office enjoys privacy behind closed doors

03

04

05

04/04

A desk of one's own
Why we all need a homely workspace
by Tom Morris

PREFACE: The idea of having a permanent desk at work is giving way to laptop culture and the buzzwords of flexibility and movement, leaving many workers homeless. But we still spend a large portion of our life at a desk and it's important for the office to be a familiar place. That's why some designers and architects have reacted to this new environment by putting the worker at the centre of the working world.

On those odd Sunday afternoons or public holidays when I find myself at home with work to catch up on, I have a routine procedure. I sit at the same chair at my dining table facing towards the window, Kate Bush's *Aerial* record goes on, I open up the Google Chrome browser (the one I reserve for work) on my laptop and quit Safari (that's personal). My notepad is placed to my left on the table, just as it is when I'm in the office. Then I get down to business for an hour or two. Try as I might, it's only once this little set-up is in place – my mock-up desk space – that I can properly get into gear.

Work needs routine and regularity. It needs a system. That is why hot-desking is the most catastrophic thing to assault offices since dress-down Friday. The phenomenon of making staff members essentially homeless is a mystery. Even in my own home, I can't hot-desk. Creating a proper and familiar workstation in my own apartment is the only way I can get things done.

If you've had a browse through the offices in the pages leading up to this essay you'll notice one combining trait: they aren't stark, impersonal spaces. They are warm environments; pleasant places to pass the day productively and comfortably. These offices all provide a familiar and pleasant home for the day, which is logical; most of us spend more time desk-bound than in bed. But essentially they still stick to the standard tenets of what an office should be: a place where people sit at their desk and get things done. They show that even above nice bonuses such as communal lunches or a beautifully designed environment, the one thing that really matters is honouring staff with their own space. It is as important as giving them a business card: it's welcoming them to the fold.

Imagine you went to work tomorrow and all the desks had been cleared of their paraphernalia. Go take a seat, sit where you want. Now, imagine it's the next day and once again the desks are free of all belongings. Where would you set up shop for the day? My money's on the same place as yesterday, and you'd probably plop your glass of water and notepad in the same place too. Tomorrow you'd do the same. We are creatures of habit and for the majority of us nothing is more habitual than work. The workplace should respect this.

And yet offices are increasingly environments where homing pigeons are forced to flutter about the sky. Flexibility and movement are the buzzwords of the moment. Desks are confused with sun-loungers around the pool. The only difference is that towels have been replaced by MacBooks: they are the things to bag first in the morning. Fingers crossed you can get it again tomorrow; fingers crossed it's still yours when you come back from lunch. Laptop culture has undoubtedly and irreversibly altered the way the world works. These mobile, self-sufficient units have effectively turned everything into a workstation and made so many workers homeless in the process.

Think back to the office of the 1950s or 1960s. Perhaps take a *Mad Men* box set for a spin. The average corporate office was clearly divided up by occupational hierarchy. Top-level management were sectioned off in their own private rooms; the top CEOs had corner offices with the best views and their own furniture. The majority of white-collar workers had their own cubicles in an otherwise open-plan space. Secretaries had their own desks, most usually with their name on a sign. Everyone had their own phone, Rolodex and, perhaps rather naffly, their own mug for a morning coffee. This model lasted for decades, especially in the US. And although cubicles can alienate workers from one another, and as classist as this system may be, at least it provided a context for everyone. Nowadays it's seen as the norm – it's actually seen as a positive – for chief executives to be flitting and floating around as and where the mood takes them. A chat with your PA over here; a Skype meeting with your New York team while sat in a corner over there. It's all gone so Wagamama.

Getting it right

1 Flexible approach
Although there may be a fashion for furniture that changes purpose at the kick of a pedal, we firmly believe that if you provide your employees with large enough desks they can be multi-purpose, too. Just have some stools to hand.

2 Here to stay
Hot-desking's most apparent by-product is making everything feel so temporary. Invest in good-quality office furniture to create a sense of permanence, letting everyone know you and your employees aren't going anywhere.

3 In the zone
If space is a problem or your company is one that relies on shift work, use clever zoning to allow employees to at least have a larger section of the office they can call their own.

4 Nice touch
There are few offices in the world that aren't dependent on computer screens. Counteract this hi-tech world with low-tech materials: furnish your space with wood-topped desks and upholstered chairs.

5 Clean start
We could all do with stiffening up a bit. Just like a shirt and tie makes you feel prepared for a meeting, nothing makes you feel more ready to work than a tidy desk.

It's hard not to be cynical when office systems such as "ABW" (action-based work) seem to be a way for companies to keep floor rents low by encouraging staffers to flap about, laptop and coffee in hand, and lay their hat down wherever they feel like. It may be good for internal office relations but so is an after-work drink – and that is far less confusing.

But this trend isn't limited to design studios or quirky Silicon Valley start-ups as it was in the 1990s and early 2000s. Everyone these days is encouraged to have short attention spans when it comes to their placement. Many corporate work environments are even getting in on the act, devoting entire floors to "ABW" (I'm unable to take the term out of quotation marks). What on earth would Don Draper have made of that? Yet designers of the world have fought back – or, more accurately, reacted to – this modern-day dilemma. They understand that good design has a part to play in helping to shape this new work environment.

Sam Hecht and Kim Colin, the designers behind the UK studio Industrial Facility, conceived the Locale concept for US office-furniture manufacturer Herman Miller. Locale is a range of furniture that tries to honour the worker in a hot-desking world. Noting how laptops have made desk spaces more compressed than ever, Hecht and Colin's desks are marginally bigger than what has become the norm. Crucially, they are also softer, thinner, rounder and can be raised, equipping them for more flexible use. They have no obtrusive table legs (they are supported by a cantilevered structure) so can quickly transform from a desk into a meeting table. Each of these desks has a shield curving around it, allowing privacy if needs be. It reinforces the idea that work is about more than just you and a computer; it's about you in a space that is connected – physically, not virtually – to others in other spaces. More to the point, it still feels proper and looks good. It values the worker.

Architects are also trying to cope with hot-desking culture. Zürich-based Mach Architektur is a studio that has master-planned office spaces for the likes of Novartis, Bally and Toto. In the work they do, they understand how a successful office should be zoned off into sections, much like a city is broken up into neighbourhoods. Each one acts as a home for between eight to 12 people. They are spaces of understandable sizes creating areas on a human scale, regardless of how big the company is. This model can be multiplied so that there are a couple of areas per floor, a couple of floors per building and a couple of buildings per campus. While this allows for flexibility, for people to move around as each chore requires,

it also provides an anchor for each staff member; a home for homing pigeons to land. It's a fluid space but people know where they belong.

The digital world is what has forced this change on the way we work. We can work anywhere. Hot-desking is not limited to the four walls of an office: people can now ostensibly hot-desk between countries, even continents. We don't need to visit an HQ for a job interview these days: they can be done on Skype. We don't need to go to work to use the photocopier or fax machine and who really uses those anyway? Stationery cupboards are obsolete; we have iPads to scribble on. You don't have broadband at home? There's always Starbucks. In the eyes of many, offices are pointless.

And yet what do you think has led to the trend of the shared office, places like The Exchange in London or Creative Lounge MOV in Tokyo? People like people, and people like working with other people. But more importantly, people like having a place to do work. Even after the work-from-home boom that has occurred over the past two decades, freelancers have turned back to wanting to go to a place dedicated to work; a place that helps them work surrounded by other workers. And to me, being in an office without your own desk is like living in a house without a bed.

That is why, even when I need to work away from my desk, I like to create some sort of familiarity. A regulated system in a regular spot that puts me in the work frame of mind. Even sat here at my dining table, with Kate singing away. — (M)

PLAN ORGANISE CREATE FURNISH & PERFECT

1 *Lessons in first impressions – from lobby protocol to the sweet smell of success*

2 *Sometimes you need more than a keyboard to say your piece: a stationery cupboard stock list*

3 *Essential items for making the office work*

4 *The kit you need to build an office from scratch*

→

Soaps, staplers, shoe trees, scalpels, sharpeners, shredders, stools and sofas – all of this and more can be found over the next 19 pages for you to create your perfect office

FINISHING TOUCHES GLOBAL

Preface: A good first impression starts with how you and your office look. From shiny shoes to sweet treats for visitors, here are some oft-overlooked details that will help you get your business relationships off on the right foot.

01
Flowers
By Appointment Only Design

Discreet, unfussy flower arrangements add to your reception's allure. Stick to leafy branches or same-colour blooms.
byappointmentonlydesign.com

02
Eau de toilette
Comme des Garçons

Opt for an unintrusive unisex scent – applied in moderation – like this offering from Rei Kawakubo's Comme des Garçons line.
comme-des-garcons.com

03
Brushes
Redecker

The natural fibres of these Redecker brushes will keep your office's nooks polished and its crannies clean.
redecker.de

04
Wooden bowl
Muji

Greet your guests with sweets perched in one of these handy holdalls on your front desk.
muji.net

05
Soap
Izola

Many varieties of soap dry out your hands so stock up on some of these all-natural oatmeal bars for the guest loos.
izola.com

06
Balsam fir incense
Paine Products

Comforting smells stay in our memory so it's a wonder that many businesses neglect our keenest sense.
paineproducts.com

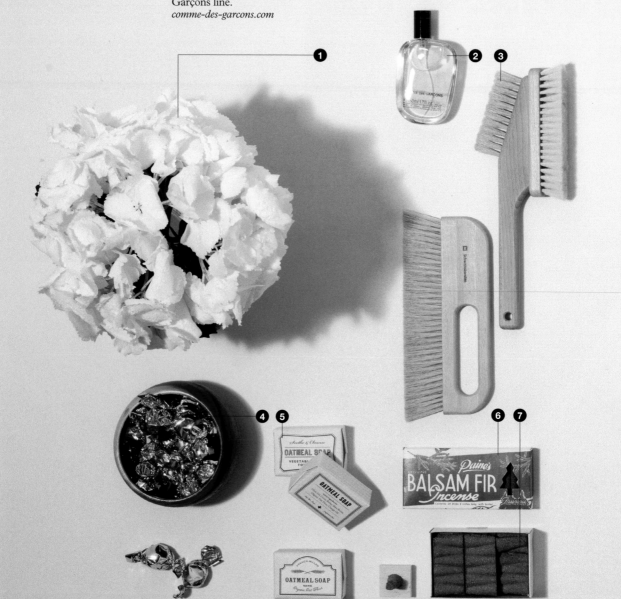

07
Red cedar incense
Paine Products

Established in Auburn, Maine, Paine Products has manufactured incense from local wood since 1931.
paineproducts.com

08
Shoe tree
Alden

Put your best foot forward with Alden's shoe tree, made from a fragrant, moisture-absorbent red cedar.
aldenshoe.com

09
Shoe-cleaning kit
Alden

This handy kit contains wax, a horse-hair brush and a chamois buffing cloth.
aldenshoe.com

10
Apron
Ichizawa Shinzaburo Hanpu

An apron isn't something you buy often so be sure to invest in a durable one.
ichizawa.co.jp

11
Room spray
Aomori Hiba

Keep the building fresh with this chemical-free fragrance,

made of cypress wood from Japan's forest-rich Aomori prefecture.
d2.dion.ne.jp/~pinsta

12
Toothbrush
Okina

Whether you've rolled into the office from an early flight or are back from a business lunch, disposable toothbrushes are always a welcome touch at work.
okina.jp

13
Mouthwash
Aitec

These breath-freshening capsules from Japanese firm Aitec will leave a good taste in your mouth.
aitec-dc.com

TAKING STOCK GLOBAL

Preface: Technology means that a thousand files can sit on a computer's desktop and occupy less room than this book. As such, you might imagine that stationery – that old schoolroom stalwart – has no place in today's tech-savvy workspaces. However, stationery is about more than simply keeping store cupboards stocked – these are the tools that your team will be using day in, day out. Essentials need to be built to last and should look and feel appealing to use, too. Whether yours is a company large or small, a good office begins with getting these small things right. And fortunately, there will always be a place in pen pots for office necessities that are made with quality in mind. Here are a few top-drawer ideas to get your own workplace collection started.

1   Craft Paper hang tag, *rsvp-berlin.de*
2   Rivoli envelope, *rsvp-berlin.de*
3   Pencil, *staedtler.de*
4   Pencil sharpener, *moebius-ruppert.com*
5   Erasable pen, *muji.net*
6   Scalpel, *swann-morton.com*
7   Clutch pencil, *faber-castell.com*
8   Graphite stick, *koh-i-noor.cz*
9   Butterfly clips, *stationery.sdi.com.tw*
10   Bulldog clip, *modulor.de*
11   Magnifying loupe, *modulor.de*
12   MT tape, *masking-tape.jp*
13   Eraser, *koh-i-noor.cz*
14   Two-metre tape measure, *stanleytools.com*
15   Page markers, *muji.net*
16   Neon tape, *modulor.de*
17   Tape dispenser, *jglinert.com*

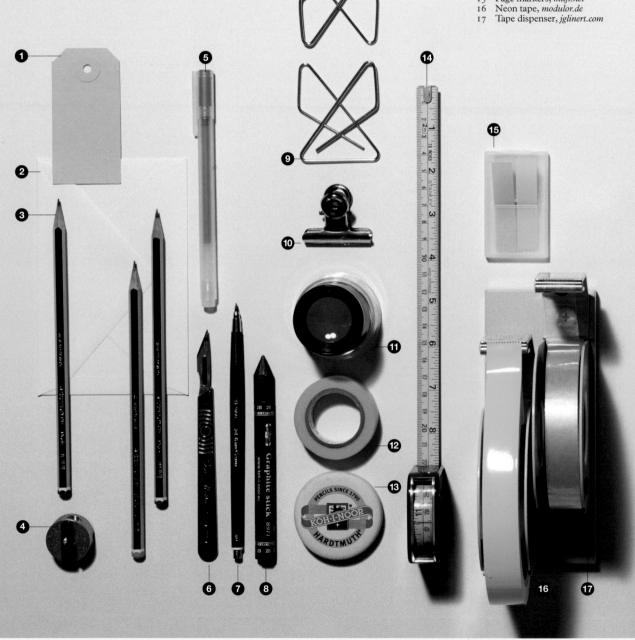

18 A4 pad, *stalogy.jp*
19 Mark's W-Note pen, *marks.jp*
20 A4 file, *rsvp-berlin.de*
21 Pencil, *viarco.pt*
22 Läufer rubber X-band,
    modulor.de
23 A5 notebook, *muji.net*
24 Rumo Duo ruler, *rumold.de*
25 Burnishing Bone paper folder,
    rsvp-berlin.de
26 Gachuck paper clipper,
    ohto.jpn.org
27 Penholder, *rsvp-berlin.de*
28 Single-sheet paper cutter,
    olfa.com
29 Erasable pen, *muji.net*
30 Cotton twine, *modulor.de*
31 Bulldog clip, *modulor.de*
32 Chalk, *jglinert.com*
33 Pastel crayon, *jglinert.com*

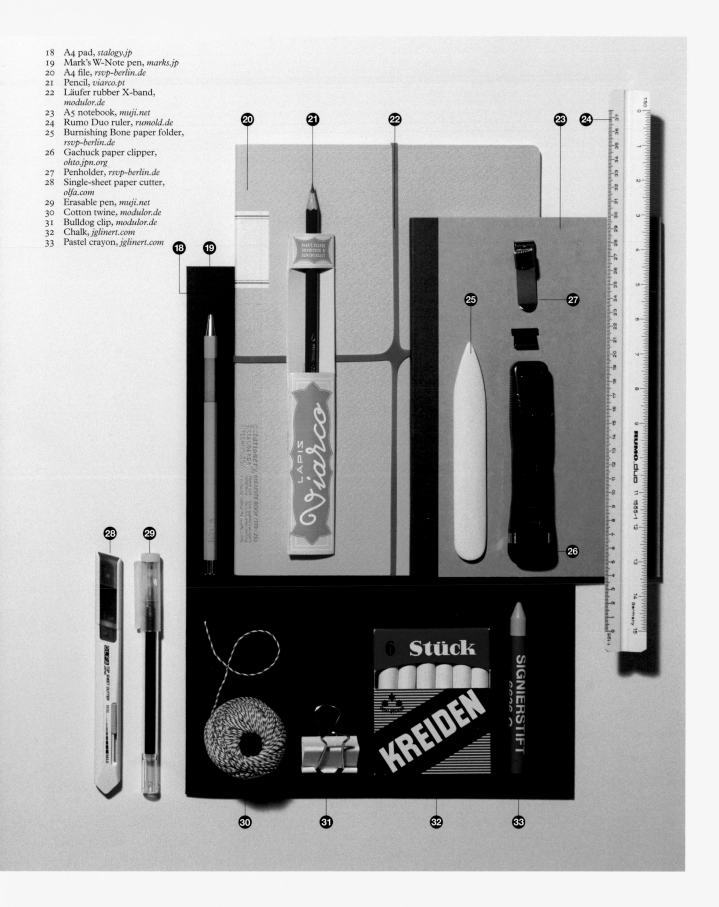

259

ALL IN THE DETAIL
GLOBAL

Preface: You've found a site for your business, established your brand and kitted out your workspace. Now that your office is up and running here are 10 simple additions to set the day-to-day tone of how your business really works.

OI
See the light
Artemide Tolomeo desk lamp

Sticking to a single style throughout an office can create continuity. As you're likely to spend a great deal of time working with it, pick a time-tested desk lamp that won't waver in its appeal as your company grows. The Tolomeo series by Italian manufacturer Artemide has a cantilevered aluminium body and adjustable reflector that can be moved to create an intimate setting or cast its light across a larger area.

02
Daily grind
De'Longhi coffee machine

Whether it's a state-of-the-art machine or a favoured French press, a cup of
the black stuff is a morning ritual that should be encouraged. Steer clear of
instant gratification (and coffee) and invest in a machine that will be adored
and appreciated for years to come. It's also the first thing your guests will taste
when they arrive.

03
Green fingers
Paul Loebach watering can

Take a leaf out of Japan's affinity with greenery and invest in an office garden – and if you haven't got an outdoor plot then bring the plants indoors. They are proven stress reducers, plus the act of watering and caring for them helps to cultivate positive practices that will stand your business in good stead and go towards creating a pleasant environment for everyone to work in.

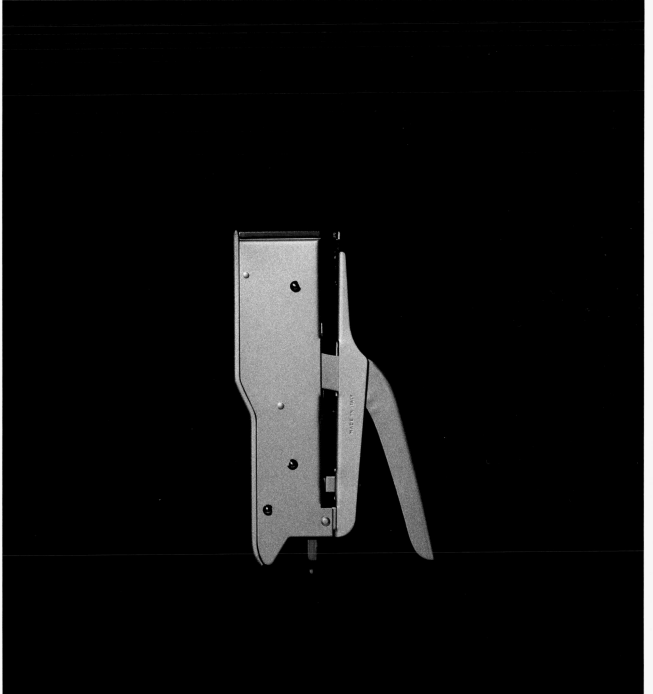

04
Innovative stationery
Zenith stapler

Be ambitious about what you surround yourself with: if you're going to be using a
stapler every day then make sure it's the nicest one you can find. Attention to detail
shows itself in many ways and if you're willing to settle for less it will be obvious to
others. Keep it together with this Italian-made offering.

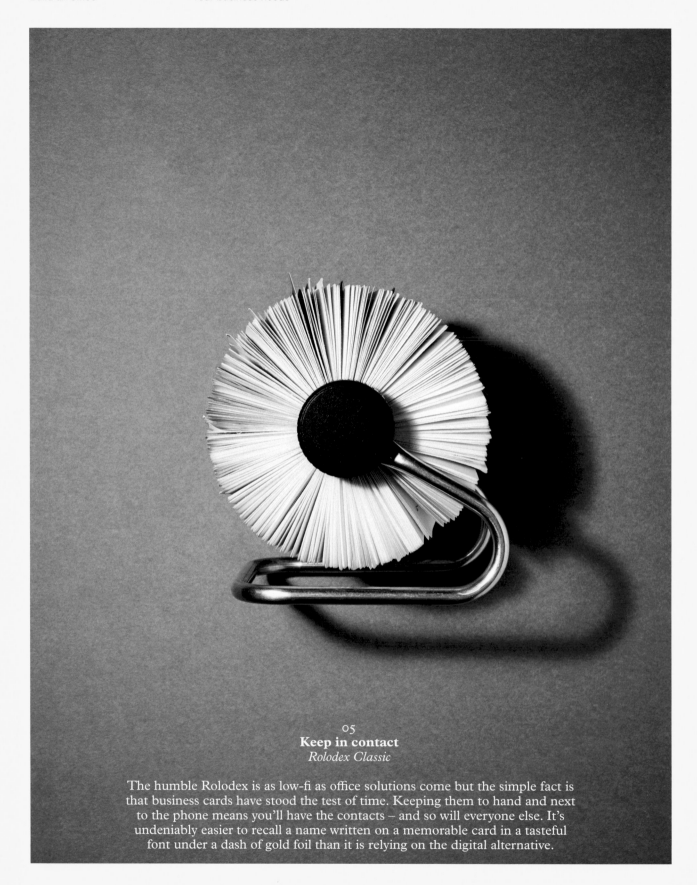

05
Keep in contact
Rolodex Classic

The humble Rolodex is as low-fi as office solutions come but the simple fact is
that business cards have stood the test of time. Keeping them to hand and next
to the phone means you'll have the contacts – and so will everyone else. It's
undeniably easier to recall a name written on a memorable card in a tasteful
font under a dash of gold foil than it is relying on the digital alternative.

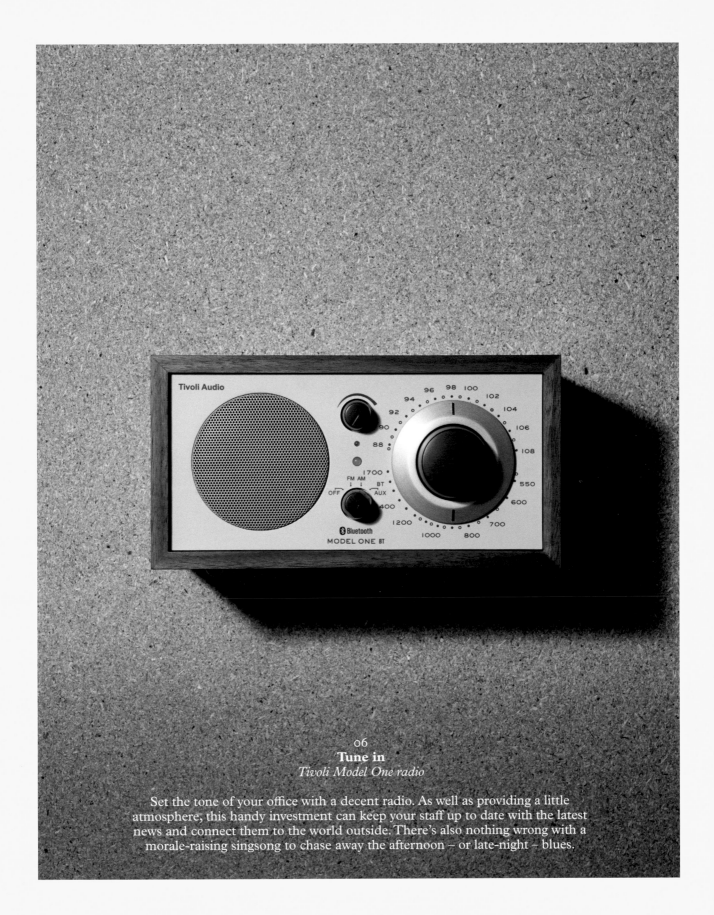

06
Tune in
Tivoli Model One radio

Set the tone of your office with a decent radio. As well as providing a little atmosphere, this handy investment can keep your staff up to date with the latest news and connect them to the world outside. There's also nothing wrong with a morale-raising singsong to chase away the afternoon – or late-night – blues.

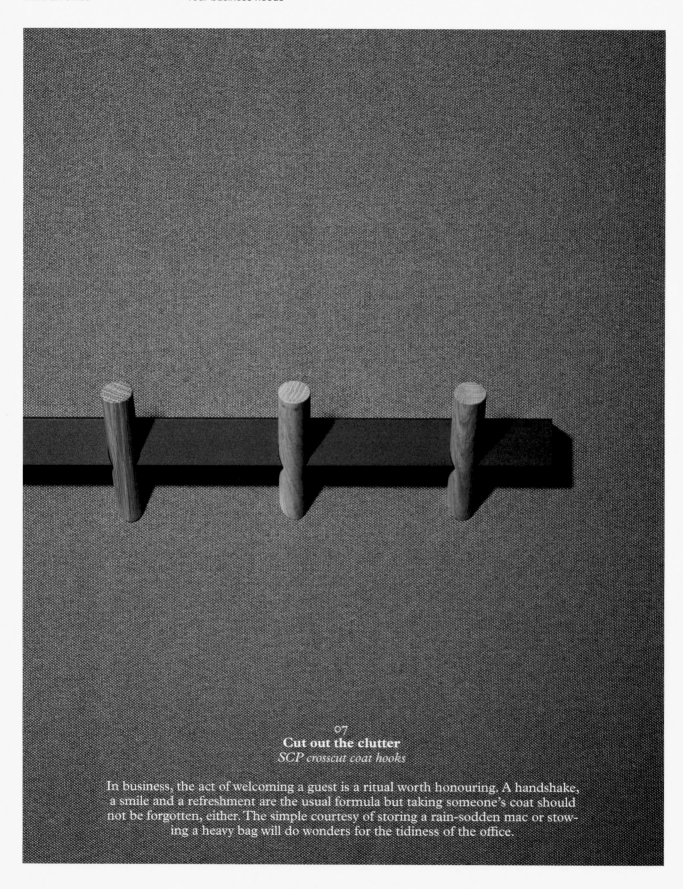

○7
Cut out the clutter
SCP crosscut coat hooks

In business, the act of welcoming a guest is a ritual worth honouring. A handshake,
a smile and a refreshment are the usual formula but taking someone's coat should
not be forgotten, either. The simple courtesy of storing a rain-sodden mac or stow-
ing a heavy bag will do wonders for the tidiness of the office.

08
Drink cans be gone
Menu carafe

A small investment can go a long way to keeping the office spick and span and a carafe is an all-too-often overlooked weapon in the battle against clutter. Unwanted drink cans and giant plastic bottles on desks can be banished to the bins where they belong, in favour of an understated vessel that can be shared around, reused and refilled.

09
Power trip
Fujifilm WorldTrip dual USB charger

Adapting is everything and savvy business sorts should be ready to seize
opportunities at the drop of a hat, whether this means getting around town or
criss-crossing continents to meet a client or shake hands on a deal. You'll also know
that to avoid the nuisance of a last-minute scramble, a well-stocked office should
always carry a handy supply of global plug adaptors.

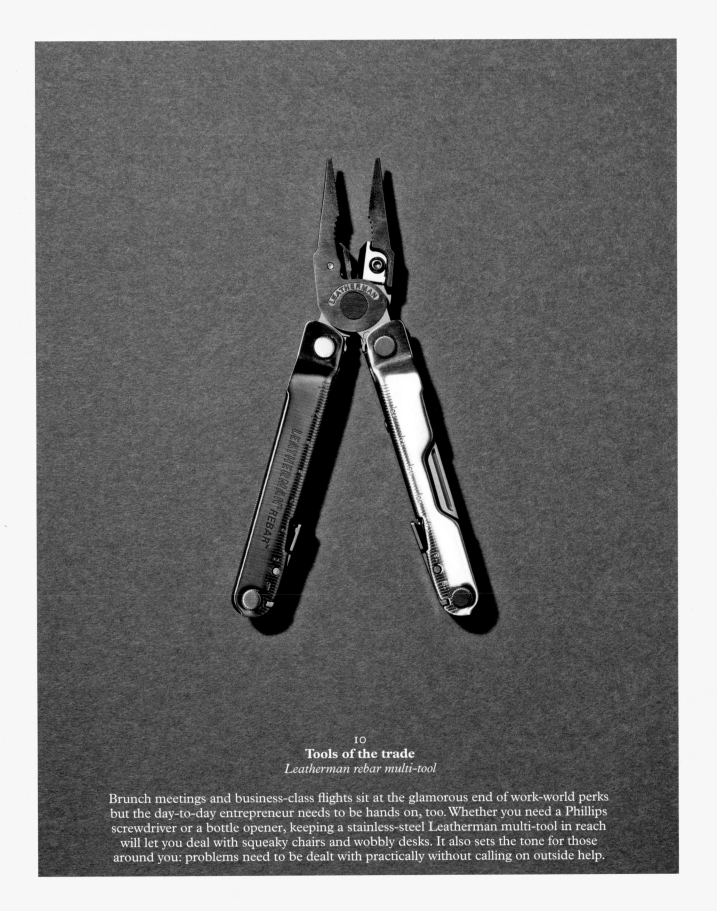

10
Tools of the trade
Leatherman rebar multi-tool

Brunch meetings and business-class flights sit at the glamorous end of work-world perks but the day-to-day entrepreneur needs to be hands on, too. Whether you need a Phillips screwdriver or a bottle opener, keeping a stainless-steel Leatherman multi-tool in reach will let you deal with squeaky chairs and wobbly desks. It also sets the tone for those around you: problems need to be dealt with practically without calling on outside help.

WORKING BRIEF GLOBAL

Preface: Having chosen your sector and city, it's time to settle on an interior that's both accommodating and easy on the eye. This hand-picked spread of design-minded goodies covers a number of bases – from tableware to seating and locks to lights – that will help turn the office from a nine-to-five into a space you are happy to linger in. Your company's HQ should be a palpable representation of the values you promote. As such, the furniture that adorns your workspace should suggest that provenance and good design are priorities that your firm invests in.

01
Mug
Hasami

It might well be the very first thing a guest in the office handles so it's reassuring to know that a company's priorities extend all the way to the coffee cups it stocks. Having helped change the fate of his ailing family firm in southern Japan (*see page 031*), Kyohei Baba worked with ceramicists to design this simple but effective stacking mug.
hasamiyaki.jp

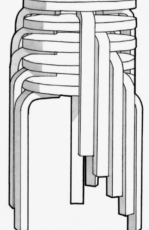

03
Stools
Artek

Keep your workspace lively with a tactically placed stack of Alvar Aalto-designed 60 stools. Perfect for a perch at a colleague's desk – or to bolster a meeting room when your New York team is in town – the birch stools include limited-edition collaborations in a choice of colours or upholsteries. For a touch of real character, beautifully battered versions are available through Artek's 2nd Cycle retail venture, which sells pre-owned stools.
artek.fi

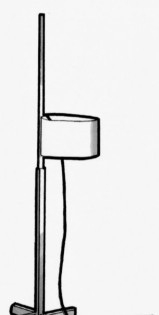

02
Paper shredder
Conof

Finding a paper shredder that's built to last *and* attractive is harder than you'd hope – so thank goodness for Japanese brand Conof. Available in white, green or brown, the device transforms confidential documents into confetti-sized pieces and can dispose of around six leaves of paper per feed. The machine is refreshingly quiet and can also shred CDs and DVDs.
color-81.com

05
Rugs
Kasthall

Sweden's first industrial rug factory still combines the country's age-old weaving traditions while rolling out forward-thinking design. Kasthall's rugs honour its legacy and each one is made to order and durable. You can choose from 10 patterns in 160 colours when it comes to the woollen rugs in the Arkad collection; the fine yarns are biodegradable, too. If you want something unique, look into Kasthall's collaborations with designers such as Ingrid Dessau and Viola Gråsten.
kasthall.com

04
Lamp
Santa & Cole

Barcelona-based manufacturer Santa & Cole has forged a strong reputation with its designs since setting out in 1985. This signature TMM lamp is no exception, as well as being a welcome addition to any contemporary office space. Its sculpture-like form balances on a cross-shaped base while its circular centre piece allows the height of the light-softening shade to be adjusted effortlessly.
santacole.com

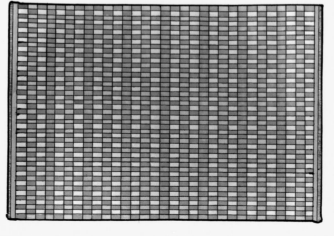

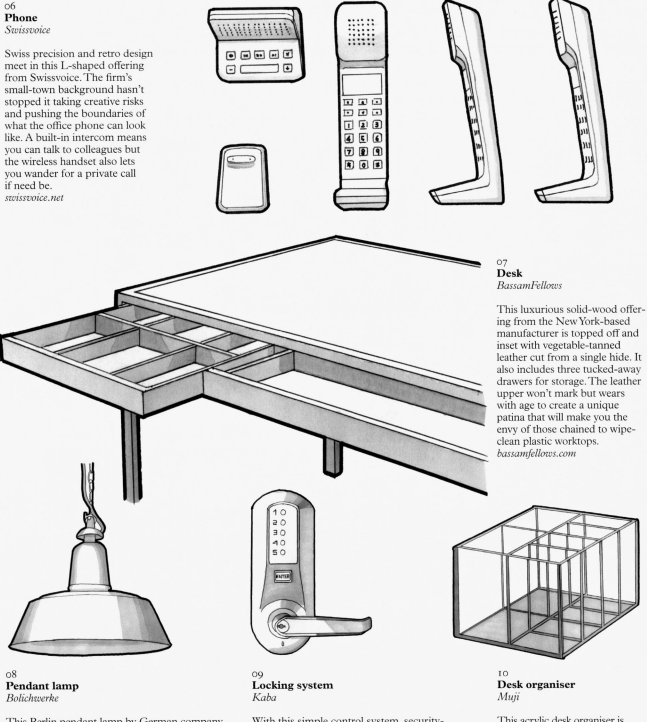

o6
Phone
Swissvoice

Swiss precision and retro design meet in this L-shaped offering from Swissvoice. The firm's small-town background hasn't stopped it taking creative risks and pushing the boundaries of what the office phone can look like. A built-in intercom means you can talk to colleagues but the wireless handset also lets you wander for a private call if need be.
swissvoice.net

o7
Desk
BassamFellows

This luxurious solid-wood offering from the New York-based manufacturer is topped off and inset with vegetable-tanned leather cut from a single hide. It also includes three tucked-away drawers for storage. The leather upper won't mark but wears with age to create a unique patina that will make you the envy of those chained to wipe-clean plastic worktops.
bassamfellows.com

o8
Pendant lamp
Bolichwerke

This Berlin pendant lamp by German company Bolichwerke is great for retail spaces and restaurants and will suit almost any office. Its reflector is a flattened cone made from cast iron and finished with elements in porcelain. Time-tested and reliable, this model has been part of the Ebolicht collection since 1911. The lamp is hung by an aluminium-cast suspension with a nickel-plated chain and the height is easily adjusted.
bolichwerke.de

o9
Locking system
Kaba

With this simple control system, security-conscious users can programme and change an access code of up to five digits on the keypad, removing the hassle of duplicating keys for colleagues or replacing locks. Fully mechanical, this model does not require any wiring or batteries – proof that despite the prominence of electronic gizmos, there's still room in the market for a sturdy analogue locking system.
kaba-ilco.com

10
Desk organiser
Muji

This acrylic desk organiser is simple but effective when it comes to keeping clutter to a minimum. Divided into six compartments, the versatile piece can hold pens and pencils in the smaller sections, while the larger sections can accommodate cards and Post-its.
muji.net

11
Shelving
USM

Swiss manufacturer USM was founded in 1885 and has become synonymous with its modular designs, first created in 1961, that have since made it into the permanent collection of the Museum of Modern Art in New York. Functional design is at the heart of this customisable Haller shelving that will organise your office space and help brighten it up (they come in various colours). Chrome ball joints combine various modules, making each USM piece a unique and timeless storage and archiving solution. As your business grows, so can your shelves.
usm.com

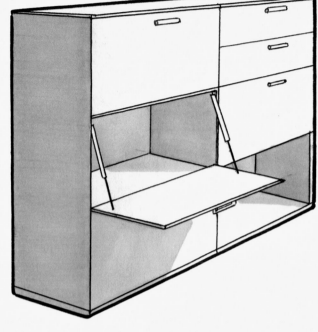

12
Track lighting
Erco

Whether you're spotlighting a bestseller in your retail space or working into the wee small hours at your desk, having adjustable lighting options is vital to setting the tone. German brand Erco has been producing sharp lighting solutions from its factory in Lüdenscheid since 1934. Its Parscan track lights are as polished and unobtrusive as they come, with the option of warm hues, neutral LED lights or spotlights. With a flexible track system, the easily adjusted units can be redirected, moved or replaced to add light and shade to the office floor.
erco.com

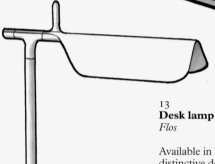

13
Desk lamp
Flos

Available in black or white, this distinctive desk lamp from Italian luminary Flos was designed by London-based duo Edward Barber and Jay Osgerby. The tapering body, circular base and angular reflector are folded from painted aluminium and the lamp's adjustable head allows it to project its light downward or sideways.
flos.com

14
Sofa
Maruni

Naoto Fukasawa has partnered with Japanese furniture firm Maruni to create the Hiroshima sofa, available in beech, oak and walnut. It is made to order in Japan and upholstered in fabrics including Italian linen and Danish wool felt. Marrying traditional Japanese methods with contemporary minimalist design, Fukasawa has created a piece that will sit well in any office.
maruni.com

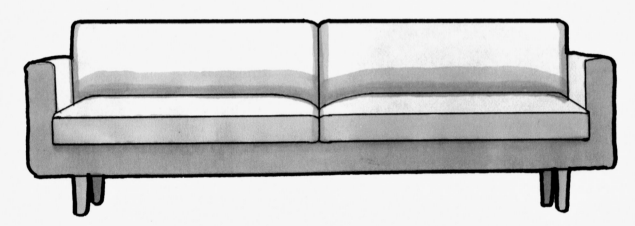

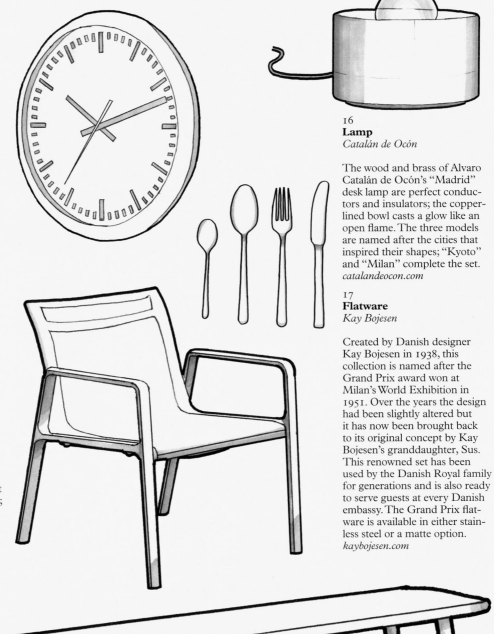

15
Clock
Bodet

Since its start making elaborate tower clocks in 1868, Bodet has manufactured trusty timepieces. In recent years the company has become known as the brand that tells travellers the time on French train platforms. Continuing its family-owned tradition, Bodet's analogue clocks are still manufactured in the company's factory in the commune of Trémentines, western France. With quartz technology enclosed within an aluminium casing, the clean design makes the analogue series a simple aid for keeping the office ticking over.
bodet-time.com

16
Lamp
Catalán de Ocón

The wood and brass of Alvaro Catalán de Ocón's "Madrid" desk lamp are perfect conductors and insulators; the copper-lined bowl casts a glow like an open flame. The three models are named after the cities that inspired their shapes; "Kyoto" and "Milan" complete the set.
catalandeocon.com

17
Flatware
Kay Bojesen

Created by Danish designer Kay Bojesen in 1938, this collection is named after the Grand Prix award won at Milan's World Exhibition in 1951. Over the years the design had been slightly altered but it has now been brought back to its original concept by Kay Bojesen's granddaughter, Sus. This renowned set has been used by the Danish Royal family for generations and is also ready to serve guests at every Danish embassy. The Grand Prix flatware is available in either stainless steel or a matte option.
kaybojesen.com

18
Outdoor furniture
Kettal

London-born designer Jasper Morrison's Park Life series for Spanish manufacturer Kettal can be used indoors, outdoors and almost anywhere else. The simple silhouette of this lightweight aluminium chair makes it ideal for moving between rooms; it can also be easily stacked for storage and transportation. In keeping with its no-nonsense design, the pared-down chair is available in a choice of black or white.
kettal.com

19
Bench
Another Country

Don't overlook the simple pleasures of a low-slung bench to transform outdoor spaces into places to linger. This neatly hewn offering from UK brand Another Country (*see page 30*) is part of its debut collection created in 2010. Available in natural oak or a darker lacquer-finished chestnut, the Portuguese-made piece features a screw-on leg system and comes flat-packed for easy haulage.
anothercountry.com

20
Trolley
SP Tools

Designed for the daily rhythm of a professional trade floor, Nagano-based SP's Japanese tool trolleys have combined brains with brawn since the company started in 1973. The seven-drawer heavy-duty roller has an internal locking system and is finished with double powder coating for scratch resistance. Featuring 28 extendable drawers for storage, this mobile four-wheeled workhorse is a worthwhile investment.
sptools.com

21
Glasses
Sasaki

These stacking tumblers are a welcome space-saving addition to any office kitchen. Magoichi Shimada, a glassmaking pioneer and one of the first artisans to bring European techniques back to Japan, began his craft in 1878. The company has maintained its founder's innovative urges: each glass undergoes a strengthening process that was developed in-house in 1967.
sasaki.co.jp

22
Tableware
Figgjo

Norwegian tableware firm Figgjo's Felt collection was created in collaboration with chefs from Spiseriet, the restaurant at Stavanger concert hall. The plates and bowls have multi-level rims but are otherwise uniformly minimal. This allows for efficient stacking and also enables ingredients to be presented on different levels, a design cue taken from Stavanger's stepped outdoor theatre.
figgjo.com

24
Chair
Vitra

Back in 1958, designers Charles and Ray Eames changed work seating forever by doing away with the design conventions of the day. The pair stretched a ribbed panel of upholstery over an aluminium frame to create a supportive and comfortable chair that gradually takes on the shape of its user. That chair is now available in a wide range of options: with or without arms; leather or upholstery; on wheels or static.
vitra.com

23
Bin
Brabantia

Family-run firm Brabantia has almost a century of homeware manufacturing under its belt; this bin is testament to the Dutch firm's commitment to avoiding the scrap heap marked "old-fashioned". The hallmark of the corrosion-resistant steel receptacle's design is its Soft-Touch technology, allowing users to open or close the lid quietly with a tap. This model holds a ventilated 45-litre plastic bucket that can be easily cleaned and removed. The bin also sports a sturdy handle and the base has a protective rim that is in contact with the floor to prevent scuffing.
brabantia.com

Preface

You need to be hitting the road and the sea lanes in search of new markets, refreshing ideas and good contacts. Businesses blossom by engaging with the world, making the most of looking people in the eye and shaking hands on newly minted deals. And as you travel you need to make sure that the people you meet get a hint of your belief in taking care of things properly. That's where that old concept of corporate hospitality comes in.

Be prepared (ie, know where you're going) to meet clients for a snappy breakfast (avoid the kippers), know a café where you can do some job interviews on the run and a bar where the tone is right for an honest conversation about how you see your company developing.

No one remembers a great video conference – ever. But they do remember the company owner who took them for lunch and, over two courses, delivered a masterful run-through of all that they could offer.

It's never good when you hear about companies that impose travel bans because it always sounds like a recipe for shrivelled ambitions. So be wise with how you use your resources but never believe that staying at home and waiting for business to come to you is ever going to be a good idea. Go on: jump on a bus, a tram, a train or a plane and make today count.

Contents

7

BUSINESS TRAVEL & ENTERTAINMENT

Corporate hospitality – plus where to eat, drink and sleep when you're on the move

FULLY BOOKED GLOBAL

Preface: Whether stepping out for coffee in Singapore or putting on a culinary show in New York, dining with clients and colleagues should be fun and ensure new and lasting connections are made. Take a global tour of some spots guaranteed to make the right impression, from breakfast hangouts to cocktail bars that are great shakes.

①

Chye Seng Huat Hardware, Singapore
Right blend

Leon Foo founded coffee roastery Papa Palheta in 2009, later adding a flagship café, Chye Seng Huat Hardware, housed in a restored art deco hardware shop. The setting showcases the company's coffees and meticulous brewing techniques. It's the sort of place where you can find a quiet table and pull out your plans to show investors but it's also cool enough to quietly impress them with your taste. Not to mention the fact that it serves the best anti-jet lag coffee in the city.
cshhcoffee.com

②

Ortolana, Auckland
Bright idea

Ortolana in Auckland is part of the Hip Group of cafés and hospitality outposts – all owned by Jackie Grant and Scott Brown. Grant and Brown previously worked in the hotel business internationally before returning home; Ortolana is the company's flagship bistro, found in downtown Auckland's Britomart development. The restaurant's sunlit conservatory is an ideal location to enjoy a delicious light breakfast or lunch. It's a setting that should make even the most tiresome adversary give in and sign the contract.
britomart.org/ortolana

③

Mellqvist Kaffebar, Stockholm
Morning pick-me-up

If you find yourself in Stockholm needing a breakfast catch-up with a client and want to keep it casual, this is where you should head. Every day, a substantial number of Södermalm's residents pass through Mellqvist Kaffebar for the perfect espresso, a quick lunch or simply a chat with owners Erik Mellqvist and Patrik Asplund, who founded a sister outlet in Birkastan in 2001. Since then the cafés have firmly established themselves as neighbourhood hubs. "For us, this place is about so much more than just the coffee," says Mellqvist. "Coming here should feel like coming home. That's the welcome you should get."

+46 7 6875 2992

④

Granger & Co, London
Home from home

After looking for a site all over London, Australian chef Bill Granger decided to set up restaurant Granger & Co in a corner on Westbourne Grove close to where he lives. It's a typically no-nonsense location for the self-trained chef, restaurateur and author, who has become famous for his easy-to-do recipes and scrumptious scrambled eggs (made with cream). Granger's London joint has been designed by Australia's Meacham Nockles McQualter studio and is open from early morning until late. "Australian breakfasts are very popular here," says Granger. It's also got a great background buzz for any early starts.

grangerandco.com

①

Loeb Boathouse, New York
Timeless classic

The Loeb Boathouse in New York's Central Park overlooks the lake in the heart of Manhattan. Originally designed in 1872 by Calvert Vaux, one of the park's architects, the boathouse fell into disrepair but was rebuilt in the 1950s. Among its quirks: keeping a handwritten "bird register" of visitors' avian sightings.
thecentralparkboathouse.com

②

Marinehof, Hamburg
Easy does it

Hamburg's Marinehof has been serving the city since 1990. Owner Astrid Wettstein had the idea for the restaurant in 1984; her menu is an unfussy selection of German standards and modern takes on *Muttis Küche* ("mum's comfort food"). Casual enough to relax in but proper enough to talk business over lunch, too.
marinehof.de

③
Trattoria Masuelli
S Marco, Milan
Family tradition

Opened in 1921, this Milan
trattoria delivers familiar
favourites from Pino Masuelli,
his wife Tina and their son Max
(*pictured*). It's the perfect setting
for a break between meetings.
masuellitrattoria.com

④
Taverna Brillo, Stockholm
Keep your options open

Taverna Brillo in the well-heeled
neighbourhood of Östermalm is
a multi-purpose space seeking
to elevate Swedish ideas about
food – with everything from a
gelateria to a great dining room.
tavernabrillo.se

⑤
Life Son, Tokyo
Local favourite

Life Son is the creation of
owner-chef Shoichiro Aiba,
whose time working in Florence
taught him to appreciate the
charm of a local neighbourhood
restaurant. At Life Son he serves
delicious, hearty food with an
Italian twist; a couple of highlights are his chunky minestrone
soup and perfect roast.
s-life.jp

1

Tadich, San Francisco
All-American dining

The oldest restaurant in San Francisco, Tadich is a classic US dining room with mahogany booths where solicitous waiters in white jackets serve seafood dishes. A smart place to entertain a client.
tadichgrill.com

2

Cole's, New York
Local hot spot

Cole's caters to Greenwich Village's well-fed and knowledgeable patrons. It offers a new spin on classic New York cocktails as well as traditional dishes, all prepared with local ingredients in a 1950s-inspired diner.
colesgreenwichvillage.com

3

Oslo Court, London
Familiar surroundings

The décor is a bit retro but this is actually a casual affair; everyone at this London institution is made to feel at home (*see page 203*). It's a bit like stepping back into the 1980s (in a good way).
+44 20 7722 8795

4

Vivant Table, Paris
Natural winner

A bistro located in what was once a bird-seller's shop. It has built a reputation for a love of organic products – as well as unwavering support for those who make them.
vivantparis.com

5

Roberto, Geneva
Years of practice

This classic Italian restaurant has been the place to come in Geneva since 1945. Most of the waiters have worked here for decades and you will feel in safe hands when you dine with any associates.
restaurantroberto.ch

6

Bar Numero, São Paulo
Designer dining

Located in the Jardins district of São Paulo, this nightspot was designed by Isay Weinfeld and serves drinks and food in a seductive setting. Good for after-dinner entertaining.
barnumero.com.br

7

Meinl, Vienna
Fine drop

Oenophiles head to this wine Mecca in the basement of Julius Meinl's vast gourmet supermarket. It stocks over 2,000 wines, an impressive 500 of which are of Austrian origin; the cheese selection is impressive, too. Enjoy a glass of Bründlmayer's Gruner Veltliner with a plate of *Beinschinken Mit Kren* (ham with grated horseradish) to keep you going until dinner time.
meinlamgraben.at

8

Y&M Bar Kisling, Tokyo
Quality assured

Tokyo's Ginza is where you will find Japan's top bartenders plying their trade and upholding tradition at so-called "authentic bars". Discerning drinkers head to Seiichi Serizawa's Y&M Bar Kisling. The ambience is a Japanese interpretation of an Old World bar with wood-panelled walls and white-jacketed waiting staff.
+81 3 3573 2071

9

Dry Martini, Barcelona
Spanish intuition

Need somewhere to take the Barcelona team for some classic drinks served by immaculately turned-out waiters? Try Javier de las Muelas's group of bars.
drymartinibcn.com

10

Pierluigi, Rome
Italians do it better

The go-to spot for a late cocktail when you're in the eternal city. A well-made negroni or rossini should help to seal the deal.
pierluigi.it

TOP TABLES
GLOBAL

Preface: Knowing a city well means having a list of locations immediately to hand for any type of gathering, be it an important business meeting, a last-minute client lunch or simply drinks with some good friends. The following directory is a global head start for opening up the city.

ZÜRICH

Transport runs smoothly, the view of the Alps from the lake is compelling, nights out are fun and the standard of living remains resolutely high. Business is also good in Zürich: the likes of Google and GM Europe have their European HQs here.

Population: 1.25 million
Locals are called: Züricher/
  Züricherin
Currency: Swiss franc
Annual sunshine hours: 1,480
Size: 938 sq km

1 Don't be late. Showing up five minutes early is the rule.
2 When expressing thanks, say *merci* rather than *danke schön*.
3 Impress locals by saying Züri instead of Zürich.
4 Install real-time public-transport app ZVV on your phone.
5 Don't drive: Zürich is a maze of one-way streets and easier on foot.

Dining

Fast breakfast
Confiserie Sprüngli
Bahnhofstrasse 21
+41 44 224 4646
spruengli.ch

Business breakfast
Terrasse Restaurant/Bar
Limmatquai 3
+41 44 251 1074

Mid-morning coffee
La Stanza
Bleicherweg 10
+41 43 817 6282
lastanza.ch

Working lunch with colleagues
Ristorante Italia
Zeughausstrasse 61
+41 43 233 8844
ristorante-italia.ch

Need-to-impress-clients lunch
Rico's Kunststuben
Seestrasse 160

+41 44 910 0715
kunststuben.com

Lunch on your own
Kindli at Rennweg
Pfalzgasse 1
+41 43 888 7678
kindli.ch

Afternoon tea/drink
Café des Amis
Nordstrasse 88
+41 43 536 9381
desamis.ch

Dinner on your own
Volkshaus
Stauffacherstrasse 60
+41 44 242 1155
restaurantvolkshaus.ch

Dinner with colleagues
Kronenhalle
Rämistrasse 4
+41 44 262 9900
kronenhalle.ch

Private dinner
Caduff's Wine Loft
Kanzleistrasse 126
+41 44 240 2255
wineloft.ch

Drink after dinner
Kronenhalle Bar
Rämistrasse 4
+41 44 262 9911
kronenhalle.com

Late drinks
Josef
Gasometerstrasse 24
+41 44 271 6595
josef.ch

On the tiles
Plaza
Badenerstrasse 109
+41 44 542 9090
plaza-zurich.ch

Where to stay

Independent and easy
Hotel Rössli
Rössligasse 7
+41 44 256 7050
hotelroessli.ch

Dependable chain
Park Hyatt
Beethovenstrasse 21
+41 43 883 1234
zurich.park.hyatt.com

Premium
Baur au Lac Hotel
Taltrasse 1
+41 44 220 5020
bauraulac.ch

HONG KONG

Hong Kong has never been so sure about its place at the top of the financial world and, increasingly, in the regional cultural game – the city is the biggest arts-auction hub in Asia. Not only has Hong Kong retained its distinct local character but the city has also embraced its new role as China's window on the West. From global cuisine and international brands to antique shops and *dai pai dongs* (the city's signature kerbside cafés), Hong Kong effortlessly mingles its business and cultural credentials.

Population: 7.2 million
Locals are called: Hong Kongers
Currency: Hong Kong dollar
Annual sunshine hours: 1,550
Size: 1,104 sq km

1 Hong Kong is known for its fast-paced business culture. Be on time for appointments; punctuality is expected.
2 Err on the side of formality. Do receive business cards with both hands and make a gesture to read it.
3 The MTR subway network is a comfortable and reliable way to get around. From the Hung Hom railway terminus you will also find services to major Chinese cities.
4 Sunday morning dim sum is a local tradition and a time for family. Try Lin Heung Tea House in Sheung Wan or the China Club in Central.
5 Visit one of Hong Kong's fishing villages such as Tai O or Lamma Island for some peace and quiet. Ferries run approximately every hour from Central.

Dining

Fast breakfast
Classified
Shop 1, 108 Hollywood Road
+852 2525 3454
classifiedfood.com

Mid-morning coffee
Amical
1F, 1 Sun Street
+852 5489 5330

Working lunch with colleagues
22 Ships
22 Ship Street
+852 2555 0722
22ships.hk

Need-to-impress-clients lunch
Duddell's
3F, Shanghai Tang Mansion,

1 Duddell Street
+852 2525 9191
duddells.co

Lunch on your own
The Herbivores
9F, Hysan Place, 500 Hennessy Road
+852 3419 6770
hp.leegardens.com.hk

Afternoon tea/drink
The Peninsula Lobby
Salisbury Road
+852 2920 2888
hongkong.peninsula.com

Dinner on your own
Olala Yat Wun Mien
2 Star Street
+852 2866 3381

Dinner with colleagues
Three Monkeys
151-155 Hollywood Road
+852 3151 7771

Big dinner with partner/clients
Sevva
Prince's Building, 25F,
10 Chater Road
+852 2537 1388
sevva.hk

Drink after dinner
001
Basement, 97 Wellington Street
+852 2810 6969

Late drinks
Salon 10
10 Arbuthnot Road
+852 2801 6768

On the tiles
Fly
24-30 Ice House Street
+852 2810 9902
clubfly.com.hk

Where to stay

Independent and easy
Lanson Place
133 Leighton Road
+852 3477 6888
hongkong.lansonplace.com

Dependable chain
Grand Hyatt
1 Harbour Road
+852 2588 1234
hongkong.grand.hyatt.com

Premium
Mandarin Oriental
5 Connaught Road
+852 2881 1288
mandarinoriental.com

NEW YORK

There's more than enough variety in New York to please those on a fleeting business visit. With developments such as the High Line and the Hudson River Park offering more landscaped green space than ever, you can take a break between meetings to sit back and take in one of the world's most impressive skylines. Or just head straight to your pick of the amazing bars on offer, of course.

Population: 8.4 million
Locals are called: New Yorkers
Currency: US dollar
Annual sunshine hours: 2,680
Size: 789 sq km

1. None of New York's three airports are efficient or user-friendly but JFK is the worst. Avoid the long immigration lines and the cab queues and pick Newark. There's a rail link into Manhattan's Penn Station.
2. Don't try to find a cab around 16.30: the drivers switch shifts between 16.00 and 17.00.
3. If you're staying for a while then rent a car. Within a couple of hours you can be on a beach in the Hamptons or hiking in the scenic Hudson Valley.
4. Get some air in the lungs with a morning jog or cycle in the newly landscaped parks. Head for the West Side along the Hudson or on the eastern edge of the East River.
5. Weekend brunch is one of New York's best traditions but turn up for a table before noon.

Dining

Fast breakfast
Smile To Go
22 Howard Street
+1 646 863 3893
smiletogonyc.com

Business breakfast
Balthazar
80 Spring Street
+1 212 965 1414
balthazarny.com

Mid-morning coffee
Bar Maialino
2 Lexington Avenue
+1 212 777 2410
maialinonyc.com

Working lunch with colleagues
John Dory Oyster Bar
1196 Broadway
+1 212 792 9000
thejohndory.com

Lunch on your own
Parm
248 Mulberry Street
+1 212 993 7189
parmnyc.com

Afternoon tea/drink
Crosby Street Hotel (bar)
79 Crosby Street
+1 212 226 6400
firmdalehotels.com

Dinner on your own
Perla
24 Minetta Lane
+1 212 933 1824
perlanyc.com

Dinner with friends
Il Buco
47 Bond Street
+1 212 533 1932
ilbuco.com

Intimate dinner
Blue Hill
75 Washington Place
+1 212 539 1776
bluehillfarm.com

Big dinner with partner/clients
Masa
10 Columbus Circle, 4F,
Time Warner Center
+1 212 823 9800
masanyc.com

Late drinks
Brandy Library
25 North Moore Street
+1 212 226 5545
brandylibrary.com

On the tiles
Acme
9 Great Jones Street
+1 212 203 2121
acmenyc.com

Where to stay

Independent and easy
The Crosby Street Hotel
79 Crosby Street
+1 212 226 6400
firmdalehotels.com

Dependable chain
Four Seasons
57 East 57th Street
+1 212 758 5700
fourseasons.com/newyork

Premium
St Regis
2 East 55th Street
+1 212 753 4500
stregisnewyork.com

04

MILAN

As Italy's financial capital, Milan is all about business from Monday to Friday so expect residents to dress the part (the city is arguably the world's fashion capital too, of course). Meetings often take place around the restaurant table or at the bar, when locals partake an evening aperitivo. Don't expect to do deals at weekends as the majority of residents uproot to the mountains or seaside to recharge their batteries.

Population: 1.3 million
Locals are called: Milanese
Currency: euro
Annual sunshine hours: 1,900
Size: 1,500sq km

1. Don't hail taxis on the street. Book through your concierge or head to a taxi rank. Alternatively, try hire-car service Autoservizi Mariani.
2. Banks and pharmacies often close at lunch so plan accordingly.
3. For expert grooming, Antica Barbieria Colla on Via Morone does haircuts and wet shaves.
4. For a full-service business hotel, reserve a room at Park Hyatt Milan.
5. Visit Eataly in Piazza XXV Aprile for edible gifts to take home.

Dining

Fast breakfast
Pasticceria Marchesi
11/A Via Santa Maria alla Porta
+39 02 876 730
pasticceriamarchesi.it

Business breakfast
Sant Ambroeus
7 Corso Matteotti
+39 02 7600 0540
santambroeusmilano.it

Mid-morning coffee
Fioraio Bianchi Caffè
7 Via Montebello
+39 02 2901 4390
fioraiobianchicaffe.it

Working lunch with colleagues
Pisacco
48 Via Solferino
+39 02 9176 5472
pisacco.it

Need-to-impress-clients lunch
Al Porto
Piazzale Antonio Cantore
+39 02 8940 7425
ristorantealportomilano.it

Lunch on your own
Obikà
1 Via Santa Radegonda
+39 02 8852 453
obika.com

Evening cocktails
N'ombra de Vin
2 Via San Marco
+39 02 6599 650
nombradevin.it

Dinner on your own
Pizzeria Spontini
60 Corso Buenos Aires
(entrance 4 Via Spontini)
+39 02 2047 444
pizzeriaspontini.it

Dinner with colleagues
Trattoria Masuelli
80 Viale Umbria
+39 02 5518 4138
masuellitrattoria.com

Private dinner
Il Faro
6 Via Marco D'Oggiono
+39 02 5810 4107
ilfarodimilano.com

Big dinner with partner/clients
Don Carlos
29 Via Manzoni
+39 02 7231 4604
ristorantedoncarlos.it

Drink after dinner
Dry
33 Via Solferino
+39 02 6379 3414
drymilano.it

Late drinks
Bar Basso
39 Via Plinio
+39 02 2940 0580
barbasso.com

Late bite
Princi
5 Piazza XXV Aprile
+39 02 2906 0832
princi.com

Where to stay

Independent and easy
Palazzo Segreti
8 Via San Tomaso
+39 02 4952 9250
palazzosegreti.com

Dependable chain
Park Hyatt Milan
1 Via Tommaso Grossi
+39 02 8821 1234
milan.park.hyatt.com

Premium
Four Seasons Hotel
6/8 Via Gesù
+39 02 77088
fourseasons.com/milan

PARIS

Chic, seductive, inimitable: Paris remains a beacon for the arts, fashion and gastronomy, luring more foreign visitors each year than any other city on Earth. Métro upgrades have been carried out, the tram network continues to grow and the pioneering bike and car-sharing schemes are expanding, which is helping to alleviate traffic. That said, bureaucracy, high rents and punitive taxation are taking away some of the City of Light's sparkle.

Population: 12.2 million
Locals are called: Parisians
Currency: euro
Annual sunshine hours: 1,780
Size: 1,500 sq km

1. Although Parisians might seem rude at times, a little *s'il vous plaît* and *merci* goes a long way.
2. Get a Navigo travel pass and explore to your heart's content.
3. Be vigilant and make life difficult for the city's bands of pickpockets.
4. Pick up a copy of the weekly *Pariscope* at any news kiosk for entertainment listings.
5. Listen to some comedy to keep spirits up when at the not-so-user-friendly Charles de Gaulle Airport and the gloomy Gare du Nord.

Dining

Fast breakfast
Du Pain et Des Idées
34 Rue Yves Toudic
+33 1 4240 4452
dupainetdesidees.com

Business breakfast
Camélia
Mandarin Oriental,
251 Rue Saint Honoré
+33 1 7098 7400
mandarinoriental.com/paris

Mid-morning coffee
Ten Belles
10 Rue de la Grange aux Belles
+33 1 4240 9078
tenbelles.com

Working lunch with colleagues
Septime
80 Rue de Charonne
+33 1 4367 3829
septime-charonne.fr

Need-to-impress-clients lunch
L'Agapé
51 Rue Jouffroy-d'Abbans
+33 1 4227 2018
agape-paris.fr

Lunch on your own
Restaurant Abri
92 Rue du Faubourg Poissonnière
+33 1 8397 0000

Afternoon tea/drink
KB Cafeshop
62 Rue des Martyrs
+33 1 5692 1241

Dinner on your own
L'Atelier de Joël Robuchon
5 Rue de Montalembert
+33 1 4222 5656
atelier-robuchon.com

Dinner with colleagues
Vivant
43 Rue des Petites Écuries
+33 1 4246 4355
vivantparis.com

Private dinner
Kunitoraya Villedo
5 Rue Villedo
+33 1 4703 0774
kunitoraya.com

Big dinner with partner/clients
Passage 53
53 Passage des Panoramas
+33 1 4233 0435
passage53.com

Drink after dinner
The Ballroom du Beef Club
58 Rue Jean-Jacques Rousseau
+33 9 5437 1365
eccbeefclub.com

Late bite
La Maison de l'Aubrac
37 Rue Marbeuf
+33 1 4359 0514
maison-aubrac.com

On the tiles
L'Arc
12 Rue de Presbourg
+33 1 4500 7870
larc-paris.com

Where to stay

Dependable chain
Shangri-La Hotel
10 Avenue d'Iéna
+33 1 5367 1998
shangri-la.com/paris

Premium
Mandarin Oriental
251 Rue Saint-Honoré
+33 1 7098 7888
mandarinoriental.com/paris

Luxury
Le Royal Monceau Raffles Paris
37 Avenue Hoche
+33 1 4299 8800
leroyalmonceau.com

SEOUL

Seoul is home to the ancient and modern, where progressive architecture sits next to palaces that date back 600 years. The Han River divides the sprawling metropolis into two and each side has its own character. The pace of life and work in this vibrant city is hectic. Yet, in the middle of it all, there are areas where you can take leisurely strolls and hear the birds sing.

Population: 10.5 million
Locals are called: Koreans
Currency: Korean won
Annual sunshine hours: 2,430
Size: 605 sq km

1. Don't be offended when people bump into you and offer no apology. Korean culture pays little heed to personal space.
2. Virtually everything can be found 24 hours a day: food, drink, shopping, haircuts, massages – you name it.
3. After a meal, look out for the free breath-freshening gum. It's offered for a reason.
4. City traffic is unpredictable – allow plenty of time when meeting clients.
5. Drinking etiquette requires that you pour drinks with two hands. Accept the drink with two hands, too.

Dining

Fast breakfast
Wood & Brick Bakery
5-2 Jae-dong
+82 2 747 1134
woodnbrick.co.kr

Business breakfast
The Ninth Gate
Westin Chosun Hotel,
87 Sogong-dong
+82 2 317 0366
echosunhotel.com

Mid-morning coffee
Bloom and Goûté
545-24 Sinsa-dong
+82 2 545 6659

Working lunch with colleagues
Yum China
573 Guro-dong
+82 2 818 1414

Need-to-impress-clients lunch
Dugahun
109 Sagan-dong
+82 2 3210 2100
dugahun.com/sagan

Lunch on your own
Bibigo
1F, Gwanghwamun Officia Building, Sinmunno 1-ga
+82 2 730 7423
bibigo.co.kr

Afternoon tea/drink
O'Sulloc Tea House
47-1 Myeongdong 1-ga
+82 2 774 5460

Dinner on your own
Homyeondang
4/F 82-9, Hawolgok-dong
+82 2 940 3040
homyeondang.com

Dinner with colleagues
Anzu (Jung Sik Dang)
649-7 Sinsa-dong
+82 2 517 4654
jungsik.kr

Private dinner
Poom Seoul
(Book at least a day in advance)
3/F, Daewon-jeongsa, B/D 358-17
+82 2 777 9007
poomseoul.com

Drink after dinner
Malt Bar Off
9-7 Samseong-dong, Gangnam-gu
+82 2 516 6201

Late drinks
Seoul Ludens
B1, 5-12 Itaewon-dong
+82 2 795 4151

Late bite
Bangbeom Pocha
260-100 Itaewon
+82 70 8151 5587

On the tiles
Coffee Bar K
89-20 Cheongdam-dong
+82 2 516 1970

Where to stay

Independent and easy
Metro Hotel
14 Myeongdong 9ga-gil
+82 2 752 1112
metrohotel.co.kr

Dependable chain
Park Hyatt
606 Teheran-ro
+82 2 2016 1234
seoul.park.hyatt.com

Premium
The Shilla
249 Dongho-ro
+82 2 2233 3131
shilla.net/seoul

The inevitable Sydney versus Melbourne debate can be summarised thus: Sydney is the beautiful, popular captain of the athletics team; Melbourne the smart girl on the debating squad. Whatever your preference, Sydney will win you over with its seemingly perennial blue skies and its sparkling geography that sees locals mix business and pleasure at every opportunity. Deals are frequently done harbourside over a beer or wine.

Population: 4.6 million
Locals are called: Sydneysiders
Currency: Australian dollar
Annual sunshine hours: 2,600
Size: 12,368 sq km

1. Don't be aghast if your Sydney-side client or colleague arrives to your meeting in shorts. Work attire, especially in summer, can be casual but don't be fooled – informal workwear still means business in the city.
2. Lunch is usually early, by 13.00, and over quickly; an hour or hour-and-a-half lunch meeting is about as long as it gets.
3. The taxi changeover time is 15.00 so if you need to get to, or exit, a meeting quickly around that hour, make a reservation with *silverservice.com.au* or *uber.com/cities/sydney*, which offer a prepay service.
4. In summer the sun doesn't go down until 20.00 so ensure that late meetings are held outside – with a drink in everyone's hand where possible.
5. Tipping is not essential but warmly appreciated. Locals tend to tip at least 10 per cent on a restaurant or bar bill and more if service was exemplary.

Dining

Fast breakfast
Bills
359 Crown Street
+61 2 9360 4762
bills.com.au

Business breakfast
Bambini Trust Café
185 Elizabeth Street
+61 2 9283 7098
bambinitrust.com.au

Mid-morning coffee
Koko Espresso Bar
118 Devonshire Street
+61 2 8399 0100

Working lunch with colleagues
The Restaurant Pendolino
The Strand Arcade,
412-414 George Street
+61 2 9231 6117
pendolino.com.au

Need-to-impress-clients lunch
Flying Fish
Jones Bay Wharf Lower Deck,
19-21 Pirrama Road
+61 2 9518 6677
flyingfish.com.au

Lunch on your own
Sosumi Sushi
GPO Building, 1 Martin Place
+61 2 9229 7710
gposydney.com

Afternoon tea/drink
The Tea Room
Level 3, Queen Victoria Building
455 George Street
+61 2 9283 7279
thetearoom.com.au

Dinner with colleagues
Mr Moustache
75-79 Hall Street
+61 2 9300 8892
mr-moustache.com.au

Big dinner with partner/clients
Tetsuya's
529 Kent Street
+61 2 9267 2900
tetsuyas.com

Drink after dinner
Bambini Wine Room
185 Elizabeth Street
+61 2 9283 7098
bambinitrust.com.au

On the tiles
The Baxter Inn
152-156 Clarence Street
thebaxterinn.com

Where to stay

Independent and easy
The Russell Hotel
143A George Street
+612 9241 3543
therussell.com.au

Dependable chain
Sheraton on the Park Sydney
161 Elizabeth Street
+61 2 9286 6000
sheratonontheparksydney.com

Premium
Park Hyatt Sydney
7 Hickson Road
+61 2 9256 1234
sydney.park.hyatt.com

For such a densely populated metropolis, Tokyo is a surprisingly liveable place. It's not all skyscrapers and neon lights as you might expect, although that does exist. Wander a bit and you'll find narrow back streets, abundant greenery, hidden cafes, top-notch restaurants, artisanal workshops and speciality retailers that set a standard few cities can match.

Population: 13.2 million
Locals are called: Tokyoites
Currency: yen
Annual sunshine hours: 2,190
Size: 2,188 sq km

1. Carry more business cards than you know what to do with because you will find that you run through a stack very quickly.
2. Always use two hands when exchanging business cards. Your own name should be right side up for the person receiving your card.
3. Prepare for numerous meetings with low-ranking staff before you reach anyone with decision-making authority.
4. Bowing is an art form. It will feel awkward if you're not used to it but will leave a good impression.
5. Lunch is a bargain in Tokyo. Even the best restaurants offer a good-value set meal.

Dining

Fast breakfast
Royal Host
All over Tokyo
royal.co.jp

Business breakfast
French Kitchen
Grand Hyatt Hotel,
6-10-3 Roppongi
+81 3 4333 8781
tokyo.grand.hyatt.com

Mid-morning coffee
Omotesando Koffee
4-15-3 Jingumae
+81 3 5413 9422
ooo-koffee.com

The Monocle Café
B1F Hankyu Men's Tokyo,
2-5-1 Yurakucho
+81 3 6252 5285

Working lunch with colleagues
Mus Mus
Shin-Marunouchi Building 7F,
1-5-1 Marunouchi
+81 3 5218 5200
musmus.jp

Need-to-impress-clients lunch
Yakumo Saryo
3-4-7 Yakumo, Meguro-ku
+81 3 5731 1620
yakumosaryo.jp

Lunch on your own
Maru Ginza
2F, Ichigo Ginza 612 Building,
6-12-15 Ginza
+81 3 5537 7420
maru-mayfont.jp

Dinner with colleagues
Cujorl
22-8 Sakuragaoka-cho
+81 3 5784 5818
cujorl.jp

Private Dinner
Beard
1-17-22 Meguro
+81 3 5496 0567
b-e-a-r-d.com

Big dinner with partner/clients
New York Grill
Park Hyatt, 3-7-1-2 Nishi Shinjuku
+81 3 5323 3458
tokyo.park.hyatt.com

Drink after dinner
Bluestone
6-4-14 Minami-Aoyama
+81 3 5485 0818
bluestone-omotesando.jimdo.com

On the tiles
Le Baron de Paris and Amour Karaoke
1F/B1F, Aoyama Center,
3-8-40 Minami-Aoyama
+81 3 3408 3665
lebaron.jp

Where to stay

Independent and easy
Marunouchi Hotel
1-6-3 Marunouchi
+81 3 3217 1111
marunouchi-hotel.co.jp

Dependable chain
Grand Hyatt Tokyo
6-10-3 Roppongi, Minato-Ku
+81 3 4333 1234
tokyo.grand.hyatt.jp

Premium
The Peninsula Tokyo
1-8-1 Yurakucho, Chiyoda-ku
+81 3 6270 2888
tokyo.peninsula.com

09
SÃO PAULO

São Paulo is South America's melting pot and financial powerhouse. It has the second biggest GDP per capita in the country after Brasilia (the seat of the government but little else). The city is defined by its enormity: the traffic jams, the numerous bars and restaurants, the number of helicopters in the air and homes with bodyguards – and the scale of the cultural divide.

Population: 20 million
Locals are called: Paulistano/ Paulistana
Currency: real
Annual sunshine hours: 1,950
Size: 7,951 sq km

1 Avoid the roads between 07.30 to 10.00 and from 17.00 to 20.00 – São Paulo redefines rush hour.
2 Most cab drivers speak little or no English; always carry your address.
3 Check the weather forecast. It often pours down in the afternoon and when it does the traffic stops.
4 Carry identification with you at all times. Most buildings won't let you in without it.
5 Enjoy the nightlife. Other cities pretend that you can go out every night of the week but in São Paulo you actually can – and it's the best way to celebrate sealing a deal.

Dining

Fast breakfast
Galeria dos Pães
Rua Estados Unidos 1645
+55 11 3064 5900
galeriadospaes.com.br

Business breakfast
Octavio Café
Avenida Brigadeiro Faria Lima 2996
+55 11 3074 0110
octaviocafe.com

Mid-morning coffee
Padaria Benjamin Abrahão
Rua José Maria Lisboa 1397
+55 11 3061 4004
benjaminabrahao.com.br

Weekend brunch
Casa Tavares
Rua da Consolação 3212
+55 11 3062 6026

Working lunch with colleagues
Rodeio
Rua Haddock Lobo 1498
+55 11 3474 1333
rodeiosp.com.br

Need-to-impress-clients lunch
A Figueira Rubaiyat
Rua Haddock Lobo 1738
+55 11 3087 1399
rubaiyat.com.br

Lunch on your own
La Frontera
Rua Cel. José Eusébio 105
+55 11 3159 1197
restaurantelafrontera.com.br

Afternoon tea/drink
The Gourmet Tea
Rua Mateus Grou 89
+55 11 2691 2755
thegourmettea.com.br

Dinner with colleagues
Maní
Rua Joaquim Antunes 210
+55 11 3085 4148
manimanioca.com.br

Private dinner
D.O.M.
Rua Barão de Capanema 549
+55 11 3088 0761
domrestaurante.com.br

Drink after dinner
Número
Rua da Consolação 3585
+55 11 3061 3995
barnumero.com.br

Late drinks
Balcão
Rua Dr. Melo Alves 150
+55 11 3063 6091

Late bite
Spot
Alameda Ministro Rocha Azevedo 72
+55 11 3283 0946
restaurantespot.com.br

On the tiles
Lions
Avenida Brigadeiro Luís Antônio 277
+55 11 3104 7157
lionsnightclub.com.br

Where to stay

Independent and easy
Hotel Emiliano
Rua Oscar Freire 384
+55 11 3068 4399
emiliano.com.br

Dependable chain
Grand Hyatt São Paulo
Avenida das Nações Unidas 13301
+55 11 2838 1234
saopaulo.grand.hyatt.com.br

Premium
Fasano Hotel
Rua Vittorio Fasano 88
+55 11 3896 4000
fasano.com.br

10
LONDON

London has been a global financial centre for many years but recent times have seen a blossoming of other industries in the English capital, particularly in more creative fields. Nowadays you're just as likely to spot trendy web designers commuting to Old Street – London's Silicon Roundabout – as you are traditional businessmen in suits and ties.

Population: 8.3 million
Locals are called: Londoners
Currency: British pound
Annual sunshine hours: 1,460
Size: 1,582 sq km

1 Public transport is generally good but getting across town can take an age. Investing in an Oyster card is a sensible bet if you're planning more than one journey.
2 The stereotype is true: English people do indulge in small talk. Don't be put off if your business partners start by talking about the weather. Humour them; the important stuff will come eventually.
3 Depending on the type of business you are involved with, it's better to be overdressed than scruffy.
4 It is a perplexing myth that British cuisine is terrible. Some of the best restaurants in the world are to be found in the capital so expect to be pleasantly surprised.
5 With so many new companies cropping up there is an amazingly vibrant and creative atmosphere in parts of London. Embrace it and don't be insular.

Dining

Fast breakfast
Any early-opening café on Borough High Street

Business breakfast
The Wolseley
160 Piccadilly
+44 20 7499 6996
thewolseley.com

Brunch
Kopapa
32-34 Monmouth Street
+44 20 7240 6076
kopapa.co.uk

Mid-morning coffee
The Monocle Café
18 Chiltern Street
+44 20 7135 2040
monocle.com/about/contacts

Working lunch with colleagues
Balthazar
4-6 Russell Street
+44 20 3301 1155
balthazarlondon.com

Need-to-impress-clients lunch
River Café
Thames Wharf, Rainville Road
+44 20 7386 4200
rivercafe.co.uk

Afternoon tea/drink
Tate Modern
Bankside
+44 20 7887 8888
tate.org.uk/modern

Dinner on your own
Providores
109 Marylebone High Street
+44 20 7935 6175
theprovidores.co.uk

Dinner with colleagues
La Famiglia
7 Langton Street, Worlds End
+44 20 7351 0761
lafamiglia.co.uk

Big dinner with partner/clients
La Bodega Negra
9 Old Compton Street
+44 20 7758 4100
labodeganegra.com

Drink after dinner
Claridge's Bar
49-55 Brook Street
+44 20 7629 8860
claridges.co.uk

Late drinks
Experimental Cocktail Club
13a Gerrard Street
+44 20 7434 3559
chinatownecc.com

Where to stay

Independent and easy
The Grazing Goat
6 New Quebec Street
+44 20 7724 7243
thegrazinggoat.co.uk

Dependable chain
Charlotte Street Hotel
15-17 Charlotte Street
+44 20 7806 2000
firmdalehotels.com

Premium
The Connaught
Carlos Place
+44 20 7499 7070
the-connaught.co.uk

II

ISTANBUL

Doing business in Turkey can be riddled with bureaucracy but a burgeoning economy and increasingly nimble transport links have made Istanbul an important hub for East/West deals. Istanbul also remains the imperial capital built on Seven Hills – so pack some sensible shoes if you're walking between appointments. After work, treat yourself to a cold Efes beer in the Tunel neighbourhood of Beyoglu.

Population: 14.1 million
Locals are called: Istanbullu
Currency: Turkish lira
Annual sunshine hours: 2,420
Size: 5,398 sq km

1 Be sure to drink a thick, dark Turkish coffee by the glistening waters of the Bosphorus.
2 On each weekday a different neighbourhood features its fresh produce in the open markets.
3 Take a ferry ride to the Asian shores past the breathtaking Haydarpasa Station, then on to Kadikoy.
4 Take a walk along the ancient city walls at the Yedikule Fortress Museum.
5 Try a fresh mackerel sandwich from the boats in Eminonu.

Dining

Fast breakfast
Café Setup
Ömer Avni Mahallesi Inebolu
Sokak No 9/15
istanbulsetup.com

Business breakfast
Mangerie
Cevdetpasa Caddesi 69
+90 212 263 5199
mangeriebebek.com

Mid-morning coffee
Asskkahve
Muallim Naci Caddesi 64
+90 212 265 4734
asskkahve.com

Working lunch with colleagues
Karakoy Lokantasi
Kemankes Caddesi 37
+90 212 292 4455
karakoylokantasi.com

Need-to-impress-clients lunch
Muzedechanga
Sakip Sabanci Caddesi 42
+90 212 323 0901
changa-istanbul.com

Lunch on your own
Kantin
Akkavak Sokak 30
+90 212 219 3114
kantin.biz

Afternoon tea/drink
Leb-i Derya
Kumbaraci Yokusu 57/6
+90 212 293 4989
lebiderya.com

Dinner with colleagues
Asmali Cavit
Asmalimescit Caddesi 16/D
+90 212 292 4950

Private dinner
Munferit
Yeni Carsi Caddesi 19
+90 212 252 5067
munferit.com.tr

Big dinner with partner/clients
Mikla
The Marmara Pera, Mesrutiyet
Caddesi 15
miklarestaurant.com

Drink after dinner
Lucca
Cevdet Pasa Caddesi 51
190 212 257 1255
luccastyle.com

Late drinks
The Alchemist
Gönül Sokak 7A

Late bite
Lucca, Bebek
Cevdet Pasa Caddesi 51
+90 212 257 1255
luccastyle.com

On the tiles
NuTeras
Mesrutiyet Caddesi 67
nupera.com.tr

Where to stay

Independent and easy
The House Hotel
Nisantasi Abdi Ipekci Caddesi 34
+90 212 224 5999
thehousehotel.com

Dependable chain
Park Hyatt
Macka Palas Tesvikiye, Bronz Sokak 4
+90 212 315 1234
istanbul.park.hyatt.com

Premium
Sumahan on the Water
Kuleli Caddesi 43
+90 216 422 8000
sumahan.com

I2

SAN FRANCISCO

Preface: A vibrant tech scene has breathed new life into the city by the bay. A paradise for food lovers, this hilly metropolis also has a spectacular setting, with water on three sides. Skip the touristy Fisherman's Wharf to feel the authentic multicultural pulse.

Population: 805, 235
Locals are called: San Franciscans
Currency: US dollar
Annual sunshine hours: 2,950
Size: 121 sq km

1 Even the sunniest days can end in chilling fog so don't forget a jacket, especially after 16.00.
2 The trendiest areas are ground zero for tech start-ups: the Mission district, SoMa and the Dogpatch.
3 A new city bike-share scheme offers a convenient way to get around town. Street gradients should always be considered and are available online.
4 Take a stroll through Golden Gate Park or drive across the Golden Gate Bridge if you have time.
5 Plan a meeting across the new Bay Bridge in Oakland.

Dining

Fast breakfast
Ferry Building Marketplace
1 Ferry Building
+1 415 983 8030
ferrybuildingmarketplace.com

Business breakfast
Vitrine
4F, St Regis Hotel, 125 Third Street
+1 415 284 4049
stregis.com/sanfrancisco

Mid-morning coffee
Four Barrel Coffee
375 Valencia Street
+1 415 896 4289
fourbarrelcoffee.com

Working lunch with colleagues
The Slanted Door
1 Ferry Building #3
+1 415 861 8032
slanteddoor.com

Need-to-impress-clients lunch
Ame
689 Mission Street
+1 415 284 4040
amerestaurant.com

Lunch on your own
Tadich Grill
240 California Street
+1 415 391 1849
tadichgrill.com

Afternoon tea/drink
Tartine Bakery
600 Guerrero Street
+1 415 487 2600
tartinebakery.com

Dinner on your own
Beretta
1199 Valencia Street
+1 415 695 1199
berettasf.com

Dinner with colleagues
Frances
3870 17th Street
+1 415 621 3870
frances-sf.com

Private dinner
Atelier Crenn
3127 Fillmore Street
+1 415 440 0460
ateliercrenn.com

Big dinner with partner/clients
Spruce
3640 Sacramento Street
+1 415 931 5100
sprucesf.com

Drink after dinner
Comstock Saloon
155 Columbus Avenue
+1 415 617 0071
comstocksaloon.com

Late drinks
Smuggler's Cove
650 Gough Street
+1 415 869 1900
smugglerscovesf.com

On the tiles
Bourbon & Branch
501 Jones Street
+1 415 346 1735
bourbonandbranch.com

Where to stay

Independent and easy
Hotel Vitale
8 Mission Street
+1 415 278 3700
hotelvitale.com

Dependable chain
The Ritz-Carlton
600 Stockton Street
+1 415 296 7465
ritzcarlton.com

Premium
Mandarin Oriental
222 Sansome Street
+1 415 276 9888
mandarinoriental.com/sanfrancisco

GOOD
LUCK

Acknowledgements

Writers
Matt Alagiah
Markus Albers
Liam Aldous
Barrett Austin
Michael Booth
Tyler Brûlé
Ivan Carvalho
Adrian Craddock
Ornella D'Alessio
Lizzy Davies
Jonathan Durbin
Linda Dyett
Josh Fehnert
Christopher Frey
Alastair Gee
Nelly Gocheva
Sophie Grove
Kenji Hall
Tom Hall
Isabel Käser
Alicia Kirby
Jason Li
Vivien Lu
Gaia Lutz
Tristan McAllister
Hugo Macdonald
Tom Morris
Elna Nykänen Andersson
Jonathan Openshaw
Giorgia Orlandi
Patrick Pittman
David Plaisant
Carli Ratcliff
Mark Robinson
Marie-Sophie Schwarzer
Aisha Speirs
Andrew Tuck
Ben Williams
Fiona Wilson

Photographers
Terumasa Akasaki
Peter Ash Lee
Simon Bajada
Aurélien Bergot
Jeremy Bierer
Peter Bohler
Aya Brackett
Laurent Burst
Santi Caleca
Gaia Cambiaggi
Jon Cardwell
Guido Castagnoli
François Cavelier
Tom Cockram
Emanuele Cremaschi
Ana Cuba
Thomas Dashuber
Simone Donati
Sean Fennessy
Luigi Fiano
Alex Fradkin
Daniel Gebhart de Koekkoek
Anthony Geernaert
Francesco Giusti
Adam Golfer
Fabien Gordon
Alexandre Guirkinger
Grant Harder
Tina Hillier
Véronique Hoegger
Kristian Holm
Enok Holsegaard
Dorothy Hong
Satoko Imazu
Malte Jäger
Drew Kelly
Dalia Khamissy
Rama Knight
Salva López
Lit Ma
Benjamin McMahon
Andreas Mader
Ross Mantle
Amanda Marsalis
Silvia Morara
Cary Norton
Felix Odell
Pietro Paolini
Isabel Pinto
Heiko Prigge
Benjamin Quinton
Johannes Romppanen
Rocco Rorandelli
Mattias Rudh
Nicky Ryan
Madoka Sakamoto
Mark Sanders
Seishi Shirakawa
Masahiro Shoda
Carrie Solomon
Jan Søndergaard
David Sykes
Kohei Take
Taro Terasawa
Peter Tillessen
Rebecca Toh
Jørn Tomter
Gianfranco Tripodo
Andrew Urwin
Mikkel Vang
André Vieira
Michael Wee
Elizabeth Weinberg
Cory White
Leslie Williamson
Simon Wilson
Andrea Wyner
Marvin Zilm
Motoko

Illustrators
Satoshi Hashimoto
Kaoru Ishikawa
Studio Tipi

Monocle
EDITOR IN CHIEF & CHAIRMAN:
Tyler Brûlé

**The Monocle Guide
to Good Business**
EDITOR:
Andrew Tuck

DESIGNERS:
Richard Spencer Powell
Emma Chiu
Jay Yeo

PHOTO EDITORS:
Poppy Shibamoto
Lois Wright
Ana Cuba

PRODUCTION:
Jackie Deacon
Dan Poole
Tom Hall
Beatrice Prokofiev

CHAPTER EDITING:

Get started
Josh Fehnert

Next steps
Sophie Grove
Aisha Speirs

Need to know
Sophie Grove

**Business cities
(and villages)**
Nelly Gocheva
Andrew Tuck

Observations
Sophie Grove

Build an office
Josh Fehnert
Nelly Gocheva
Sophie Grove
Tom Morris

⑦

**Business travel
& entertainment**
Josh Fehnert

Special thanks
Russell Bell
Henning Bock
Richard Dennis
Paul Fairclough
Natsumi Fujita
Akio Hasegawa
Lee Hickman
Martin Mörck
Gaku Nakagawa
Paul Noble
Ben Olsen
Rose Percy
Yoshitsugu Takagi
Kyoko Tamoto

Research
Mikaela Aitken
Megan Billings
Alexa Firmenich
Carlota Rebelo
Junichi Toyofuku

Colour reproduction
Tag

Fashion credits
Caruso
Drake's
Richard James

Product credits
The Conran Shop
Couverture and the Garbstore
David Penton & Son
Divertimenti
The Goodhood Store
J Glinert
SCP
Skandium
Trunk Clothiers

Index

More Monocle
Business coverage on the airwaves and in print

Monocle 24 is a round-the-clock radio station from the people who bring you MONOCLE magazine. Launched in 2011, it is run from our headquarters at Midori House in London's Marylebone and delivers four hours of news and comment every day.

Since the beginning we have followed the world of start-ups and people running successful businesses across every sector – and every corner of the world – on Monocle 24 with *The Entrepreneurs*. Our one-hour weekly show focuses on inspiring stories, fresh opportunities and people who do business in a way that we admire.

Our radio station also features specialist shows including *The Urbanist* (about the cities we live in), *Culture* with Robert Bound, *Section D* (about the world of design), *The Menu* (that's food and drink), *The Foreign Desk* (for in-depth global affairs), *The Stack* (the world of print media) and lots of great music.

Listen live (or download the shows as podcasts) from *monocle.com*. You can also find all Monocle 24 shows as podcasts on iTunes and SoundCloud, or live on any internet radio. It's the business.

Monocle 24 –
Keeping an ear on the world
monocle.com/radio

Sophie Grove: *The Entrepreneurs*

Robert Bound: *Culture*

Steve Bloomfield: *The Foreign Desk*

MONOCLE's Business section features new ventures, fresh-faced entrepreneurs, the lowdown on start-ups and more. Pick up the latest issue or subscribe at *monocle.com* for regular inspiration.

Tom Morris: *Section D*   Andrew Tuck: *The Urbanist*   Tyler Brûlé: *The Stack*

Thank you